# GREEN CATHEDRALS

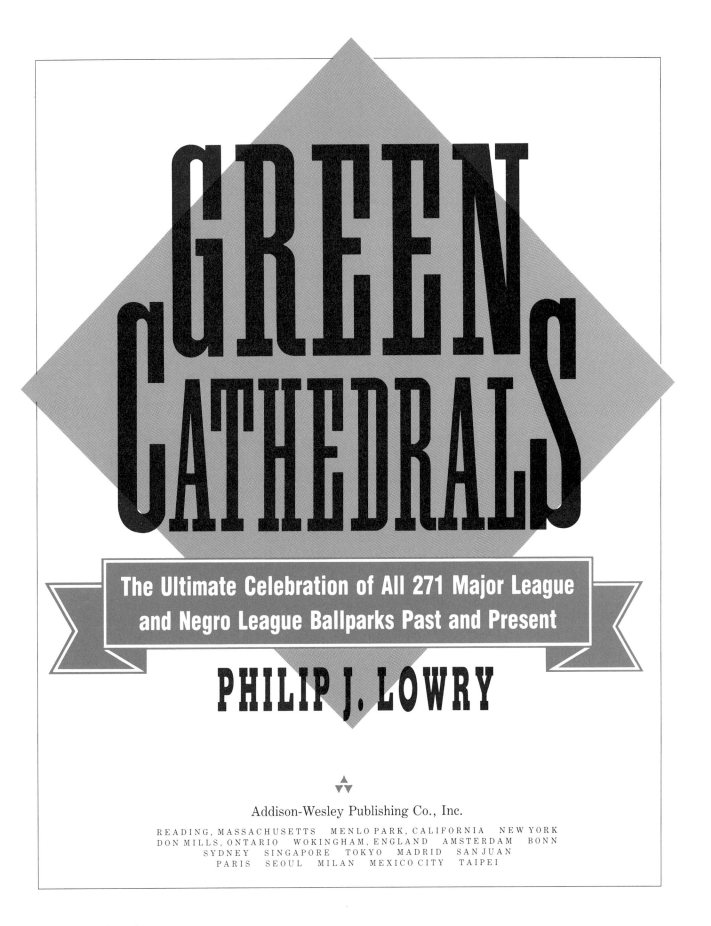

# GREEN CATHEDRALS

**The Ultimate Celebration of All 271 Major League and Negro League Ballparks Past and Present**

## PHILIP J. LOWRY

Addison-Wesley Publishing Co., Inc.

READING, MASSACHUSETTS  MENLO PARK, CALIFORNIA  NEW YORK
DON MILLS, ONTARIO  WOKINGHAM, ENGLAND  AMSTERDAM  BONN
SYDNEY  SINGAPORE  TOKYO  MADRID  SAN JUAN
PARIS  SEOUL  MILAN  MEXICO CITY  TAIPEI

**Library of Congress Cataloging-in-Publication Data**

Lowry, Philip J.
    Green cathedrals : the ultimate celebration of all 271 major league
and Negro league ballparks past and present
/ Philip J. Lowry.
      p.    cm.
    Rev. ed. of: Green cathedrals. 1986.
    Includes index.
    ISBN 0-201-56777-6
    1. Baseball fields—United States.   2. Baseball fields—United
States—History.   I. Title.
GV879.5.L68   1992
796.357′06′873—dc20             91-32016
                               CIP

Jacket design by Diana Coe
Jacket illustration by C. Michael Dudash
Text design by Joel Avirom
Set in 10-point Century Expanded by DEKR Corporation, Woburn, MA

1 2 3 4 5 6 7 8 9-DO-95949392

First printing, February 1992

This book is dedicated to Robert Bluthardt and his Ballparks Committee. Bob deserves special thanks for the hundreds of hours he has devoted to this project; without his help this book could not have been completed. It is also dedicated to the preservation of Wrigley Field in Chicago, Tiger Stadium in Detroit, and Fenway Park in Boston. May the cheers of fans, the crack of the bat, and the aroma of hot dogs never disappear from these sacred and cherished shrines of baseball.

**I**t breaks your heart. It is designed to break your heart. The game begins in the spring, when everything else begins again, and it blossoms in the summer, filling the afternoons and evenings, and then as soon as the chill rains come, it stops and leaves you to face the fall alone. You count on it, rely on it to buffer the passage of time, to keep the memory of sunshine and high skies alive, and then just when the days are all twilight, when you need it most, it stops.

—Baseball Commissioner A. Bartlett Giamatti

◆

**A**ll ballparks should look like Comiskey Park. Modern parks are too antiseptic. You come here, and it feels like baseball. It has history and character.

—Tom Seaver, talking about the old Comiskey Park, which has since been replaced by an "antiseptic" modern stadium

**W**hen there is no room for individualism in ballparks, then there will be no room for individualism in life.

—Bill Veeck, from his book, *Veeck, As in Wreck*

---

**I**t's not the critic who counts. It's not the man who points out where the grown man stumbles, or how the doer of deeds could have done them better. The credit belongs to the man who actually is in the arena, who strives violently, who errs and comes up short again and again, who knows the great enthusiasms, the great devotions, and spends himself in a worthy cause, who if he wins knows the triumph of high achievement; but who if he fails, fails while daring greatly, so his place will never be with those cold and timid souls who know neither victory nor defeat.

—President Theodore Roosevelt

---

**I**f these fellas can fight and die at Iwo Jima, why can't they play in the National Pastime?

—Baseball Commissioner Happy Chandler, on why blacks should be permitted to play baseball in the Major Leagues

# CONTENTS

"Stadium design is not hard mathematics alone, but the skill and ingenuity of the designer who applies his knowledge and experience to achieve a unique and superb result. It is progressive and adaptable. We will see new materials used, covered grandstands built, movable stands erected, better lighting installed, moving ramps to ease the climb and other new concepts tried. The people will be much the same but with new and different wants which must be satisfied."

—Homer T. Borton, then President of the Osborn
Engineering Company, the world's foremost designers of baseball parks
(from *Consulting Engineer Magazine*, August 1956.)

The "new and different wants" of the baseball fan, referred to by Homer T. Borton, can effectively be traced through three clearly defined stadium eras that follow the establishment of baseball as a popular spectator sport just prior to the turn of the century: the eras of the classic ballpark, the super stadium, and the regenerated classic ballpark.

During the first era, that of the classic ballpark, the constructions of Forbes Field (1909), Shibe Park (1909), League Park (1910), Griffith Stadium (1911), Polo Grounds (1911), Crosley Field (1912), Fenway Park (1912), Tiger Stadium (1912), Ebbets Field (1913), Wrigley Field (1914), and others were initiated by enterprising ballclub owners who saw the financial advantage of achieving larger attendances.

Prior to this era ballparks were typified by small wooden bleachers surrounded by a fence. This type of construction suffered from its combustibility and was limited in size by its structural properties. These ballparks were indeed intimate.

As baseball became more popular and ticket revenues increased, the ballpark could be increased in size and the expense justified. The classic ballpark emerged as the logical development of seating expansion from the wooden stands, with the widespread use of structural steel and, to a limited extent, reinforced concrete, allowing significant improvements to be made in seating quality and capacity. The single greatest achievement of this era was that of the upper deck. This contrivance allowed more people to sit closer to the action of the diamond than was ever before dreamed possible in the wooden-seat era. As an added advantage, the use of structural steel made the seats relatively fireproof.

Ancient Greece is often credited with developing the first significant grandstand for a sporting event. Banister Fletcher, in *A History of Architecture on the Comparative Method*, stated, "The stadium was the footrace course in cities where games were celebrated, and had a length of about 600 feet between banks of seats founded on convenient natural ground or on the spoil from excavation on flat sites." The first of these was possibly that of Olympia, constructed between 400 and 300 B.C. In essence, our use of the word *stadium* evolved from the ancient Greek name for a footrace observed by spectators.

The problems of providing a good view of the game or event faced by the ancient Greeks are very much the same we face today. A seat deck profile must be developed where the spectator looks between the heads of the spectators in the row directly in front and over the heads of those in the second lower and all succeeding rows. This is a compromise. If each spectator looks directly over the heads of those in front of him, the seat deck would become unnecessarily steep. For psychological reasons, this steepness should be limited to a maximum of 37 to 38 degrees from the horizontal. As such, the compromise seat deck takes on a concave parabolic shape that becomes increasingly steep as the seat deck is moved closer and/or higher with respect to the game or event.

The ancient Greeks, dealing with their footrace with its long, linear nature, could afford to elongate the seat deck and thereby shorten its depth. Likewise a relatively short single seat deck worked fine for the early spectators during the infancy of baseball but proved woefully inadequate when spectator crowds approached the 20,000 to 30,000 figure. In addition, the long linear seat deck of the ancient Greek footraces is not applicable to baseball, with its main attraction occurring on a diamond, 90 feet on each side.

The logical solution thus became the upper deck. With this configuration, the back half of a deep, single-seat deck could be cut off, lifted up, and pushed forward to allow a much closer and intimate view than otherwise possible. The advent of modern design methods and structural steels enabled this to be achieved.

There *are* trade-offs, however. Supports for the upper deck must extend to the lower level if one is over the other, so some seats are lost altogether in the lower level and some are unfortunately situated behind columns. If the upper deck is cantilevered, columns are elim-

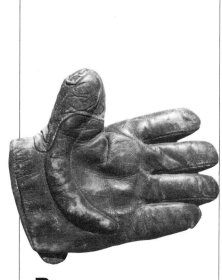

**B**aseball glove from the 1870s.

inated, but other problems arise; more about this later. Pedestrian movement also becomes a costly item. Ramps, escalators, and raised concourses with toilet and concession stands become very expensive.

Despite any problems, the era of the classic ballpark was thus ushered in. These structural steel and masonry splendors multiplied and the development of technology then seemed to be in its infancy, compared with today's high-stressed and fast-paced world. Fans came, bought tickets, and enjoyed an afternoon of baseball, watching their heroes and favorite players.

If a fan had the money or had special contacts, he or she could sit right behind home plate. A fan with less money or influence would sit along the first or third base line. The regular fan most often was content to sit in the pavilion areas along the foul lines or, for the ultimate in economy, the bleachers. If you were a kid fortunate enough to take possession of an out-of-the-park foul or homer, you could get in with the baseball as a ticket of admission. Amenities were certainly sparse by today's standards. Limited concession menus, long waits in toilet lines, stiff hard chairs or bleacher seats, and sudden downpours were expected.

But traffic jams and long delays were unheard of, since most fans could walk or trolley to their favorite pastime. The classic ballpark was totally integrated into the neighborhood. A little known but crucial benefit of this neighborhood integration was that ballparks took on an asymmetrical form as dictated by the property lines of the site. Fenway's Green Monster, bordering Lansdowne Street, literally added a new dimension to baseball, as did League Park's 40-foot high right field wall, located only 290 feet from home plate.

Sometimes the asymmetrical outfield configuration was not dictated by land constraints. When the Osborn Engineering Company worked with Jacob Ruppert, one of the New York Yankee owners in 1920, old Jacob wanted a short right field fence to accommodate his newly acquired slugger, Babe Ruth. The asymmetrical configurations of these classic era ballparks have contributed to some legendary plays.

The year 1960 arrived. Percy Faith's song "Summer Place," Francis Gary Power's ill-fated U-2 flight, and a retiring Dwight Eisenhower ushered in the so-called super stadium era. The modern stadium had truly arrived. Just as Homer Borton noted, "The people will be much the same but with new and different wants." Now, these new and different wants of the people spawned such stadiums as Candlestick Park (1960), Dodger Stadium (1962), R.F.K. (1962), The Astrodome (1965), Busch Stadium (1966), Three Rivers Stadium (1970), and its nearly identical cousin, Riverfront Stadium (1970).

A stadium had to accommodate a vast array of games and events for funding, and fans simply demanded more comfort. Stadium designers had to respond to these new criteria. They were also responding to a new order of architecture, "The Modernist Movement." Originating in Europe in the earlier part of this century, this form of architecture immigrated to this country when such notable architects as Walter Gropius and Ludwig Mies van der Rohe fled Hitler's Europe and became U.S. citizens. This form of architecture embodied simple, functional design or, in Mies's own words, "form follows function" and "less is more." In the past thirty years or so, concrete has come into its own with respect to stadium construction. Such innovations as admixtures, high-strength lightweight concrete, sophisticated reinforcing design, air entrainment and the use of computer design have allowed concrete to compete more favorably with structural steel.

With the new, lightweight, high-strength concrete, it was no longer necessary to construct massive footings to support a typical "heavy" concrete structure. Admixtures, including plasticizers, allowed easy pumping and made concrete curing relatively quick, so that prerequisite structural concrete members could readily support future pours. New developments in reinforcing steel design—in conjunction with the use of computers—enabled concrete to span greater distances and work as a more-effective cantilever. Without the advent of this technology, multi-deck stadiums of concrete could not have been built.

These recent advances played beautifully into the hands of the modernist stadium architects. Now the structure of a stadium could be vividly exposed, whereas with structural steel, a skin had to be utilized to hide its spaghetti form. Modernists delved into abstracts about symmetry and the visual presentation of a building as a freestanding entity—in full view with a park-like setting—to be aesthetically viewed by the masses. The massive relocation of the typical American city's population to the suburbs, in conjunction with a greater dependence on the automobile and its attendant parking requirements, also fostered the "stand alone" stadium concept. It no longer made sense to nestle a stadium within the confines of an urban neighborhood. Since form followed function and function was symmetry, it simply followed that the playing field configuration also became symmetrical.

Comfort was indeed the word for these second generation stadia, and that word was spelled L-O-G-E. These modern contrivances accomplished two significant things: First, they helped foster a caste system with respect to spectators and second, they wreaked havoc with upper deck seating geometries. The caste system was created in essence when loges became a necessary evil for funding purposes. Loge goers demanded optimum viewing location, exclusive parking, segregation from other fans, and catered food service. Because optimum viewing was a priority, loges were often hung from beneath the upper deck in one, two, or even as many as three tiers. A simple corollary is that the greater the amount of private funding required for a stadium, the greater the number of loges and the greater the negative impact on the upper deck geometries.

Unfortunately, with any number of loge tiers placed underneath the upper deck, the first seat of the upper deck will be higher and the whole upper deck must move back from the game or event to stay within the maximum deck angle of 37 to 38 degrees. Obviously, the further the deck moves back, the poorer the spectator's view.

The same design anomaly also applies to "column free" viewing. First incorporated in 1962 with the construction of Washington's R.F.K. Stadium, this concept has been carried over into every modern stadium since. Unfortunately, it is not the panacea it was originally thought to be. In order for columns to be eliminated, two conditions occur. One, the upper deck must be cantilevered from the back of the lower seat deck. Two, the roof over the upper deck must be limited to the amount of roof element that can be cantilevered from the back of the seat deck. Neither of these conditions thrills fans because they will be sitting further away overall, and they will not have protection from rain and sun. The cause of this can again be explained by the seating deck geometries.

Baseball is such that the seating around the infield will be in the greatest demand and, if you shorten the length of the lower deck in order to support the upper deck as reasonably close to the game or event as possible (remember, we can't place seats behind the upper deck supports), you effectively eliminate a large portion of seats from the prime infield area. As one can imagine, this condition is exaggerated when loges enter the picture. Some of the classic ballparks (Cleveland Stadium and Wrigley Field, for example) have had new loges installed under the upper deck, much to the chagrin of the fans sitting in the back of the lower deck who now suffer from "tunnel vision."

The overall failure of the super stadium era can be summed up by a conversation I had with a major southwest developer regarding the 1989 National League pennant race and subsequent World Series: "I watched the Cubs play from the upper deck of Wrigley Field and thoroughly enjoyed it, columns and all. I then watched the World Series from the upper deck of column-less Candlestick Park and couldn't see a thing without binoculars." The nineties have now arrived, and people are lamenting the demise of the classic ballpark. People wish things could be the way they used to be, and the thought of spending a lazy summer afternoon in an old ballpark watching the likes of Lou Gehrig slugging balls in his wool pinstripes seems to erase today's world of media saturation and information bombardment.

Ballparks are changing, and a third era of stadiums has emerged. A large majority of architects have abandoned the modernist school to embrace post-modernism, the incorporation of classical forms in a simplified way within the context of new building design. The era of the regenerated classic ballpark has arrived, replete with natural grass fields, asymmetrical playing fields, and old-fashioned facades. Stadia such as those in Buffalo, Baltimore, Chicago and, hopefully soon, Denver, Arlington (Texas), and Cleveland, are the vanguard of this new era. Even the word *stadium* has been replaced with *ballpark* in the new park names.

The good news is that the "fixed dome" has vanished and the sheer cost of the "operable dome" has all but guaranteed its demise. But our old friend the "loge" is still with us and seems to be multiplying at an ever-increasing rate. As cities, counties, and states suffer from ever-increasing monetary problems, private financing, at least of the magnitude of fifty percent, will ensure that the loge will be with us for years to come.

The media's role in this new era of ballparks cannot be underestimated. Along with creating player celebrities with three million dollar plus per year salaries, it also demands that the ballpark designer create a unique identity for media recognition. Many a time, Cubs station WGN panned the classic ivy-covered brick of Wrigley Field's outfield walls and, as a result, every young child in America watching knew exactly where the game was by just a glimpse. So it is with our regenerated classic ballpark. Something unique must be created with respect to the field landscaping to make it identifiable to a national television audience. The new Camden Yards ballpark in Baltimore, for example, certainly achieves this by maintaining the presence of an old restored warehouse in right field.

So where are we now? The door has been pushed partway open with the regenerated classic ballpark and its strong emphasis on comfort and its return to old-time appearances, but is it the answer? In my opinion, no. We must not be content with just green grass, asymmetrical playing fields, and decorated facades. We must push the door all the way open and achieve a more equitable balance between opulent comfort for a few at the expense of good viewing for many.

Make no mistake about it, a regenerated classic ballpark or super stadium may not ever be built without loge support, for this is political/funding policy and not an architectural design decision. It comes down to the strength of the fans, who through their attendance may influence this decision. Frankly, I can't think of a better reason to maintain and restore the remaining classic ballparks in those cities blessed to have them.

Dale Swearingen, A.I.A.
Vice President, Director of Architecture
The Osborn Engineering Company

# ACKNOWLEDGMENTS

The greatest reward in writing this manuscript has been the opportunity to work with so many generous people who have graciously shared with me their expertise. In response to my requests for detailed information on ballparks, I received 3,537 letters from authors, ballplayers, curators, fans, groundskeepers, halls of fame, historical societies, leagues, librarians, mayors, researchers, sports writers, stadium managers, teams, and umpires.

I would like to offer special appreciation to Bob Davids, Bill James, and John Thorn—generally acknowledged to be the premier baseball statisticians—for their inspiration while I was writing this book.

Those who have helped the most are: my wife, Ellen Thorvilson Lowry, our son Evan (9), and our daughter Megan (4), who have visited more dilapidated and demolished old ballpark sites in the most incredible places than they could ever have dreamed existed; our children's grandparents Horace and Gladys Thorvilson of Lake Mills, Iowa, and John and Bertha Lowry of Pittsburgh, and Nancy Miller, Executive Editor at Addison-Wesley Publishing Company.

Thanks to Bob Bluthardt, Ken Holt, Bob McConnell, Marty O'Connor, Bob Tiemann, and the late John Tattersall, the six most knowledgeable experts on ballpark history; as well as to members of the Ballparks and Negro Leagues Committees of the Society of American Baseball Research (SABR) with whom I have been privileged to work through the last decade. Messrs. Bluthardt, Holt, O'Connor, and Tiemann kindly agreed to review previous manuscripts for me. Thanks are due to them for all the errors they caught for me; the responsibility for any errors that remain is completely mine.

Thanks also to Dallas Adams, Donald Adams, Paul Adomites, Doug Alford, Luis Alvelo, Rich Arpi, Miwako Atarashi, Dinae Barts, Phil Bess, Peter Bjarkman, James Bready, Chet Brewer, Tina Brewer, Edward Brown, Dick Burtt, Jack Carlson, Robert Carr,

Bob Carroll, Reid Cherner, Dick Clark, Tiffany Cobb, Dottie Collins, Kit Crissey, Jack Croghan, Frank Cunliffe, Nancy Dickinson, Paul Doherty, Dutch Doyle, John Duxbury, Oscar Eddleton, Joe Favano, Jorge Figuerado, Peggy J. Flanagan, Bruce Foster, Michael Frank, Cappy Gagnon, Bruce Genther, Monique Giroux, Phil Goldberg, Ralph Graber, Wayne Graczyk, John Guilfoile, David Hallstrom, Tom Heitz, Francis Helminski, Bob Hoie, John Holway, Kyoko Honda, Bill Hugo, Monte Irvin, David Jenkins, Jose Jimenez, Judy Johnson, Lloyd Johnson, Tom Joswik, Cliff Kachline, Charlie Kagan, Dick Kaufman, Larry Keefe, Jim Laughlin, Buck Leonard, Larry Lester, Peter Levine, Jack Little, Bill Livingston, Norman Macht, John Maher, Steven Mau, John McCormack, Pete McMartin, Ray Medeiros, Brad Merila, Dick Miller, Bill Modoono, Carrington Montague, Charles Moore, Hugh Moore, Jr., Akiko Ogawa, John O'Malley, Buck O'Neill, Joseph Overfield, Jim Overmyer, Dan Palubniak, John Pastier, Alvin Peterjohn, David Pietrusza, Frank Rashid, Ric Roberts, Mark Rucker, Masayoshi Sawayanagi, Carl Schoen, John Schwartz, Bill Shannon, Debbie Shattuck, Melody Simmons, Janet Marie Smith, Paul Soyka, Dan Sperling, Nettie Stearnes, Turkey Stearnes, Ryuichi Suzuki, Dale Swearingen, Gordon Thomas, Antoinette Tomczyk, Stew Thornley, Angel Torrez, Christine Urban, David Voight, and Bill Wagner. Unfortunately, it is impossible to list everyone who gave so generously of their expertise, time, and energy to help make this book possible. To all those who assisted, thank you very much.

*Philip J. Lowry*
*September 14, 1991*

**T**iger Stadium.

# INTRODUCTION

This book is a celebration of the shrines of our National Pastime. It presents the humorous anecdotes, crazy stories, and vital statistics, as nearly complete as possible, for every ballpark that has ever been used for an official professional game in the Major Leagues and the Negro Leagues. From this point forward, the Negro Leagues will be defined and treated as Major Leagues.

A ballpark is a very special place. When I was a U.S. Army infantry captain two decades ago, and among other things, jumping out of perfectly good airplanes for a living, what I missed most about the United States was baseball. For many, some special ballpark houses cherished childhood memories. For my grandfather, my father, and me, that ballpark was Forbes Field. For my son, it was Tiger Stadium. For others, that special ballpark may be Yankee Stadium or Fenway Park or Wrigley Field or Dodger Stadium in the United States, or the Stade Olympique or the Sky Dome in Canada. Wherever that special ballpark is for you, I hope that you will find it within these pages.

## CATHEDRALS

I spent a very long time searching for the right title for this book. The more I have studied ballparks, the more they have begun to resemble mosques, or synagogues, or churches, or similar such places of reverent worship. There is a scene of beauty at 21st and Lehigh in Philadelphia. Where once there was the Shibe Cathedral, also called Connie Mack Stadium, there is now the Deliverance Evangelistic Church. There is a message in this.

My wife and I believe that each person travels his or her own unique religious path on their quest for that spiritual truth that will speak best to their own individual soul. I feel the same way about ballparks: that to fulfill their purpose in our National Pastime, they

1

must be allowed to have their own personalities and characteristics, or, in other words, to be unique and asymmetrical.

What I hope the title *Green Cathedrals* conveys is a quiet spiritual reverence for ballparks. For millions of baseball fans, a ballpark holds treasured memories and serves as a sanctuary for the spirit, a haven where the ghosts of Babe Ruth, Josh Gibson, Lou Gehrig, Cool Papa Bell, Cy Young, Connie Mack, Chet Brewer, Roberto Clemente, Martin DiHugo, Ty Cobb, and so many other greats from the past can continue to roam among their modern-day counterparts. *Green Cathedrals* celebrates the mystical appeal of the hundreds of ballparks, past and present, where the soul of the game of baseball resides.

# ASYMMETRY AND THE SUBTLETIES OF BASEBALL

Stereotyped symmetrical ballparks are wretchedly poor ballparks. The fact is that architects of the 1910s, constrained by urban streets already in place, made asymmetrical, unique ballparks that are better for baseball than the symmetrical concrete sterile ugly ashtrays that have been built in the last three decades.

The subtleties of the game of baseball are incredibly beautiful and balanced. A close play at the plate, a brilliantly executed double play, a diving catch over the outfield fence, an inside-the-park home run—these are every bit as wonderful as Michelangelo's *Pieta* or one of Beethoven's symphonies. However, if Royals Stadium is cloned every time a new ballpark is built in the coming decades—if every fence is 12 feet tall, if every outfield is shaped like a round half circle, if every foul line is 330 feet, if every power alley is 385 feet, if every center field fence is 410 feet, and if every playing surface is an astroturf carpet—the precious subtleties that make baseball the wonderful game it is will gradually be eroded and eventually destroyed and the beauty of the game horribly scarred.

Sloped grass terraces in the outfield, in-play scoreboards with numerous angles, high walls and low walls, short and long distances, anything that adds character to a ballpark, makes a ballpark better. When there are short 296-foot porches and second deck overhangs down the foul lines, monstrous 490-foot open spaces in center field (with monuments and bullpens and dog houses in play for long triples and inside-the-park homers to rattle around in), the pure joy and delight of the game is multiplied a millionfold. The best plays in baseball, the triples and inside-the-park home runs, have been almost eliminated and occur now only when an outfielder misses a diving catch or knocks himself out running into an outfield fence. For triples and inside-the-park home runs to occur, we again need to have some open spaces in center field, the way the parks of the 1910s and 1920s were built.

Unfortunately, ballpark asymmetry has decreased over the last three-quarters of a century, eliminating many of the peculiarities that make the ballpark a large part of the game's fascination. Specifically, asymmetry to the foul poles has declined by 92 percent compared to what it used to be. The distance to the two foul poles differed by 36 feet on average in the 16 classic North American ballparks, whereas the distance to the two poles differs by only 3 feet today in the 26 current North American ballparks. Fourteen of the 16 classic ballparks, or 88 percent, were asymmetrical, whereas today only 6 of the 26 current Major League ballparks, or 23 percent, are asymmetrical. Only 2 of the 16 classic ballparks were symmetrical, whereas today 20 of the 26 current ones are.

Outfield fences roughly three-quarters of a century ago displayed much more individual character than those in current ballparks.

**F**enway Park, Boston. A study of corners and angles after the 1933–34 renovation.

Comparing statistics for the 16 classic parks to those for the 26 current ballparks, the classic fences were 387 percent higher at their highest point than the current fences: 50 feet then vs. 13 feet today, and 59 percent lower at their lowest point than the fences today, 5 feet then vs. 9 feet now.

Nowadays, multi-tiered stands loom behind the fences. Seventy-five years ago, the fans could usually see trees and houses rather than concrete and cars. When compared to the power alley and center field dimensions for the 26 current Major League ballparks, this analysis demonstrates that the outfield fences of the 16 classic Major League ballparks approximately three-quarters of a century ago were much farther from the plate, and varied much more than those of today. Specifically, the deepest classic center field corners were 18 percent more distant than current ones. The average distance to center field was 479 feet; today, the average distance is 406 feet. In particular, classic power alley fences were 11 percent more distant than current ones. The average distance to the power alleys was 419 feet; today, the average distance is 378 feet.

Architects can learn from past design errors. Those in Denver, Washington, Orlando, St. Louis, the San Francisco Bay area, Dallas–Fort Worth, Milwaukee, Cleveland, and Japan may be designing baseball parks within the next few years. I hope that they will have the opportunity to consider these points and that they will learn from some of the mistakes made on recent stadia in Toronto and Chicago. For example, many people in the Sky Dome's top deck in Toronto cannot even see large parts of the ballfield. The first row second deck grandstand seat behind the plate that is closest to the plate in the new Comiskey Park is further from the plate than was the last row second deck grandstand seat furthest away from the plate in the old Comiskey Park. The top seat in the upper deck at the new Comiskey is almost twice as high above the field as at the old Comiskey. Think about that for a minute. Then try to remember what it is like to watch a baseball game through binoculars from a seat in the top deck at Shea Stadium, which the architects somehow managed to place in the next county.

I also hope future stadium occupants will develop the creativity to name their new ballparks something other than "Stadium." Can't we have a few "Yards," "Parks," and "Fields," or "Bowls" and "Grounds" again, please? Why can't Atlanta–Fulton County Stadium be called something like "Aaron Bowl"? Buffalo

**P**ilot Field, Buffalo, New York. The first of the "back to the classics" ballparks.

and Denver are on the right track; Buffalo has named its new ballpark Pilot Field, and Denver has named its field-to-be Coors Field.

## WHY THIS BOOK WAS WRITTEN

The idea for this project began long ago when I was growing up in Pittsburgh. My father often took me by trolley to the nearby Pirates games at Forbes Field, and I would dream of the many mysterious ballparks that I heard about on KDKA Radio and read about in the *Sun-Telegraph* newspaper.

When a Pirate would hit a homer, veteran KDKA radio announcer Rowsy Rowswell would yell "Open the window, Aunt Minnie," and then 5 seconds later, his fellow broadcaster Bob Prince would drop a piece of glass in the radio booth, creating the sensation of a tremendous crash. Everyone listening would know that Rowsy's dear old deceased Aunt Minnie up in Heaven had once again been too slow to open the window. And the next day, the *Sun-Tele* would have numerous up-close pictures of sliding runners in a cloud of dust.

Sitting in our favorite bleacher seats, down the left field line at Forbes Field on a bright sunny day at the July 7, 1959 All Star Game, I resolved one day to learn about all those faraway magical places. That idea germinated for more than three decades, but now, after what seems like a lifetime of research, I would like to share what I have learned about these magical ballparks.

KDKA Radio has sounded very different since Pirates announcers Rowsy Rowswell and Bob Prince have passed on to join their Creator and Rowsy's Aunt Minnie. The *Sun-Tele* and Forbes Field are only echoes from the past. And with photographers now banned from the field, the newspaper pictures lack the immediacy of those from days gone by.

## PREVIOUS BALLPARK BOOKS

This is the fourth book to chart the history of baseball parks in detail. The first three were Gene Mack's *Hall of Fame Cartoons of Major League Ballparks* in 1947; Bill Shannon's *The Ballparks* in 1975; and Lowell Reidenbaugh's *Take Me Out to the Ball Park* in 1983.

These three works are all outstanding and have built an excellent foundation for further research. *Green Cathedrals* builds upon that excellent foundation by presenting original research that thoroughly documents vast areas of information not covered by the other three ballpark books.

# WHAT THIS BOOK HAS THAT PREVIOUS BOOKS DID NOT

All three prior ballpark books focused almost exclusively on the period following the April 12, 1909 opening of Shibe Park, the first concrete-and-steel ballpark. This book covers the pre-1909 ballpark era in detail going all the way back to the beginning of organized Major League baseball—to Hamilton Field on the Jailhouse Flats where Fort Wayne hosted Cleveland on May 4, 1871, in the very first National Association game—and carries the story all the way to the present.

This focus on the entire period from 1871 to the present is particularly beneficial in light of the amazing diversity of Major League ballparks in the nineteenth century, from cricket grounds and polo fields to agricultural fair grounds and actual cow pastures.

Negro League ballparks are covered here in great depth for the first time. Ballpark geometry is explored in infinite detail, also for the first time. Month by month, dimensional changes have occurred amazingly frequently over the years in outfield fence distances and heights.

Such changes are crucial to an understanding of the statistical history of baseball. I believe strongly that this book will make possible future research on the relative merits of various players' individual statistics, by revealing the relative difficulties presented to hitters and pitchers in the various ballparks, which have had vastly different geometry and dimension.

For example, Sportsman's Park #3 in St. Louis had an 11.5-foot-high concrete wall in right field in 1927. On July 5, 1929, a 21.5-foot screen was added on top of the wall, making the fence 33 feet high altogether. In 1932, Jimmy Foxx of the A's hit 58 home runs; in 1927, Babe Ruth of the Yankees hit 60.

Bill Jenkinson's thorough research on home runs indicates that of Foxx's 9 singles and 1 double in St. Louis in 1932, only his June 15 double hit the screen and would have been a homer in 1927. Also, of Ruth's 4 homers in St. Louis in 1927, only his May 10 homer would have been prevented by the screen from being a homer in 1932: The May 10 homer went into the right field pavilion, whereas the May 11 homer went into the center field seats, and the August 27 and 28 homers went over the right field pavilion roof. In addition, capacity figures are given year by year. By combining new information from this original research with the verified data in secondary sources, *Green Cathedrals* presents for the first time ever a complete listing and thorough comparative analysis of every ballpark that has ever been used for an official Major League game.

## SCOPE

The purview of this book includes all sites that have ever been used for an official Major League professional game, including regular season games, playoff games, league championship series games, Dauvray Cup World Series games from 1884 to 1890, Temple Cup World Series games from 1894 to 1897, World Series games in 1903, and from 1905 to date, and All Star games from 1933 to date. Every neutral site ever used for an official game is included. Games prior to 1871 are excluded because no regular season standings for Major League professional clubs were kept until then. Exhibition, preseason, nonprofessional, and Minor League games are also excluded.

## USING THIS GUIDE TO THE BALLPARKS

No book on baseball can be complete without an asterisk controversy. After all, this is the sport that for 30 years carried *two* records for its most valued achievement of most home runs in a single season: an unasterisked record for Babe Ruth's 60 home runs in 1927, and an asterisked record for Roger Maris's 61 homers in 1961. So, for purposes of this book, the American League Chicago Black Sox of Dyersville, Iowa are considered a current Major League franchise with an asterisk, even though they only exist in the imagination and in the movie *Field of Dreams*.

**A. K. A.** (Also Known As) lists alternate names and nicknames for the park.

**OCCUPANT/S** lists team/s using the park as a home field, in chronological order.

**NEUTRAL USE/S** lists team/s using the park as a neutral site field, in chronological order.

**CAPACITY** lists the number of seats in the ballpark and how the park grew or shrank over the years. There are some inconsistencies in capacity figures. For example, they sometimes do include and sometimes do not include standing room.

**LARGEST CROWD** is the largest crowd admitted to a game at the ballpark. There are many inconsistencies when it comes to crowds. For example, the American League counts no-shows who bought a ticket as part of the attendance whereas the National League does not.

**B**usch Stadium, St. Louis. A suburban-style stadium in the center of downtown.

**SURFACE** means grass or plastic carpet. Because all older stadiums had grass "surfaces," information about carpet or grass is included for only modern ballparks.

**DIMENSIONS** lists the distance (in feet) from home plate to the outfield fences at the foul poles, power alleys, straightaway dead center field, and any unusual corners or monuments or scoreboards, and from home plate to the backstop. Dates, in parentheses, denote the first month and/or year when the boundaries stood at the stated distance. You will notice many inconsistencies related to: incorrect measurements; movement of home plate; re-measurements; continued club usage of old and incorrect information; failure to measure power alleys at exactly 45 degree angles between the foul poles and straightaway center field; and occasional incorrect usage of left field and right field measurements to mean distance to a place in straightaway left field or straightaway right field rather than to the foul poles.

**FENCES** lists the heights (in feet) of the outfield fences. Dates denote the first time the fences stood at the stated height.

**FORMER USE** describes how the site was used before the ballpark was constructed.

**CURRENT USE** chronicles the development of the site after a ballpark was demolished or abandoned.

---

**PHENOMENA** is a general category for historical data. Included here are special features of the park's physical plant, important changes over the years, and events of interest throughout the ballpark's years of operation.

# FRANCHISES

To tell the complete story of ballparks, I decided that it was necessary to include a list of all leagues that have used them to allow for easy cross-referencing. The following leagues are covered by this study:

**NA** National Association, 1871–1875

**NL** National League, 1876 to date

**AA** American Association, 1882–1891

**UA** Union Association, 1884

**PL** Players League, 1890

**AL** American League, 1901 to date

**FL** Federal League, 1914–1915

**NNL** Negro National League, 1920–1931; 1933–1948

**ECL** Eastern Colored League, 1923–1928

**NAL** Negro American League, 1929, 1937–1950

**NSL** Negro Southern League, 1932

**NEWL** Negro East-West League, 1932

All 12 of these leagues have a legitimate claim to the term "Major League." Some are defined by organized baseball as Major League, although their caliber of play is open to question: the Union Association (UA) and the Federal League (FL). Others have no official stamp of approval from organized baseball but have a legitimate historic basis for Major League status: the National Association (NA) and the Negro Leagues (NNL, ECL, NAL, NSL, and NEWL).

# HISTORIC PRESERVATION

The central theme of this book is a celebration of beautiful ballparks. I hope that the four most beautiful ballparks left will never face a wrecking ball: Tiger Stadium in Detroit, Fenway Park in Boston, Wrigley Field in Chicago, and Yankee Stadium in New York. Due to renovation efforts at all four, it is very possible that they will continue to reverberate to the crack of the batted ball well into the twenty-first century for the enjoyment of our grandchildren's generation.

We have recently witnessed the bulldozing of many perfectly good ballparks that were much better than the ugly concrete sterile ashtrays that have replaced them. Sadly, Comiskey Park has just been abandoned to the wrecking ball. We are approaching the Major League expansion decade of the 1990s with the very real possibility that the McDonald's Golden Arches of Baseball, Kansas City's Royals Stadium, will be cloned around the country.

The Detroit Tigers want to bulldoze Tiger Stadium. In 1981, I filed an application with the U.S. Department of the Interior to put Tiger Stadium on the National Register of Historic Sites. With the support of many organizations and many individuals, this application was finally approved. With a major renovation using federal funds in 1980 through 1982, Tiger Stadium was strengthened and made structurally sound for many more decades. In addition, the Tigers have an ironclad legal obligation to play at Tiger Stadium through the year 2008.

However, the future of Tiger Stadium is in grave doubt, despite the vigorous efforts of the City Council of Detroit, Wayne County, the Michigan Legislature, the Tiger Stadium Fan Club, the *Detroit Free Press* and *Detroit News*, and many fans from around the country to enforce the legal lease that binds the Tigers to play in Tiger Stadium until 2008. The Tiger Stadium Fan Club has met the Tigers' publicly voiced goals for additional revenue generation with a very professionally done architectural study called the Cochrane Plan. This plan beautifully renovates Tiger Stadium, provides the Tigers with the improvements they say they want (including 73 corporate boxes seating 1,200 people) for a fraction of the cost of a new sub-urban domed stadium.

Reasonable people may disagree about ballpark design, and about whether this or that ballpark is more beautiful or is better suited functionally to the game of baseball. But on this point there should be no doubt: The remaining four "grande dames" of ballparks (Tiger Stadium, Fenway Park, Wrigley Field, and Yankee Stadium) should be preserved for future generations.

# CONCLUSION

Because ballparks have over the years come in various sizes and shapes, they have always had distinct personalities and characters and have been like loyal friends to generations of baseball fans. No one can ever mistake Fenway Park for Yankee Stadium, as they might Busch Stadium for Riverfront.

This uniqueness of ballparks has always set baseball apart from other sports. People do not get sentimental and nostalgic about football stadia or basketball and ice hockey arenas. The recent trend toward bland sameness in ballpark design is a threat to the soul of the game. I believe very strongly that geometrical variety is essential and healthy for the game and needs to be preserved. It was 505 feet to center field at the Polo Grounds in New York, yet only 384 to center at Ebbets Field across town in Brooklyn. It is 37 feet 2 inches to the top of the wall down the left field foul line at Fenway Park in Boston but only 3 feet 10 inches in Dodger Stadium in Los Angeles.

These facts provide grist for thousands of baseball arguments and are a central factor in the allure and the popularity, the beauty and the challenge of the game. Some hopeful signs have appeared recently. The vigorous new Twins and Mariners owners have recently altered the Metrodome in Minneapolis and the Kingdome in Seattle, bringing Fenway-like asymmetry through the addition of their own mini-Blue Monsters—23-foot right field fences. The Kingdome moved the diamond so that the field itself is now very asymmetrical, whereas before it was perfectly symmetrical; the Metrodome was already asymmetrical.

Even a baseball traditionalist has to admit that some carpets and domes are acceptable if they do not completely take over—that is, if we are interested in diversity. It is true that the ball does bounce quite differently off the rug in the Humphrey Metrodome in Minneapolis than it does off the grass at Yankee Stadium in New York.

Tiger Stadium

Wrigley Field

**T**op: Tiger Stadium, Detroit. Detroit's urban jewel, but will they keep it? Middle: Wrigley Field, Chicago. The friendly confines. Bottom: Yankee Stadium, New York. Home of the New York Yankees 1923 to date.

# PART ONE

# CURRENT MAJOR LEAGUE BALLPARKS

## ANAHEIM, CALIFORNIA

# ANAHEIM STADIUM

### A.K.A.
Big A, 1966; Bigger A, 1980

### OCCUPANT
American League California Angels, April 19, 1966 to date

### CAPACITY
43,500 (1966); 44,500 (1967); 43,204 (1968); 43,202 (1969); 43,250 (1974); 43,204 (1976); 43,250 (1977); 67,335 (1981); 65,158 (1984); 64,573 (1986); 64,593 (1989)

### LARGEST CROWD
64,406 on October 5, 1982 vs. the Brewers

### SURFACE
Santa Ana Bermuda grass (1966); bluegrass (1989)

### DIMENSIONS
Foul lines: 333
Bullpens: 362
Power alleys: 375 (1966); 369 (1973); 374 (1974); 370 (1989)
Deep alleys: 386
Center field: 406 (1966); 402 (1973); 404 (1974)
Backstop: 55 (1966); 60.5 (1973)

### FENCES
Majority of the fence: 10 (wire, 1966); 7.86 (wire, 1973); 7.86 (canvas padding, 1981)

Corners between foul poles and bullpens: 4.75 (steel, 1966)
Left center between the 386 and 404 marks: 7.5 (canvas padding, 1981)
Padded posts at the left sides of both the left and right field bullpen gates: 9 (canvas padding, 1981)
Bullpen gates: 9.95 (wire, 1966)

## FORMER USE

Four farms: Camille Alec's 39 acres of orange and eucalyptus trees; Roland Reynolds's 70 acres of alfalfa; John Knutgen's 20 acres of corn; Bill Ross's and George Lenney's 19 acres of corn

## PHENOMENA

The ball carries very well in the Big A, making this a power hitters' park. ◆ The huge 230-foot-high letter "A" with a golden halo on top stood behind the fence in left field as a scoreboard support until 1980, when it was moved to its current location in the parking lot beyond right field. ◆ Two thin black television cables run in fair territory, snaking their way along the warning track from the left field corner bullpen gate to the foul pole, and then along the wall in foul territory about 50 feet toward third base, then into the stands. ◆ The outfield was enclosed and triple-decked in 1980 to accommodate the NFL Los Angeles Rams, in much the same manner as Candlestick Park in San Francisco had been enclosed nine years earlier to accommodate the NFL San Francisco 49ers. Before the park was completely enclosed, beautiful trees were visible beyond the outfield fence. Since the ballpark was enclosed, fans now see three decks of grey concrete instead. ◆ Six doors on the ivy-covered wall in deep left center behind the outfield fence are labelled as warning track, skin material, screen clay mounds, raw clay, sand, and equipment. The ballpark probably could be significantly improved by removing the inner fence from left to center, thus allowing the ivy-covered wall to be in play, and injecting at least a little of the pastoral feeling of a Wrigley Field. ◆ In a game against the Royals on September 21, 1982, Angels outfielders Freddie Lynn and Brian Dowling crashed into the left center fence while chasing a fly ball in the alley. They knocked the fence down and ended up in the grass between the inner fence and the outfield seats. Lynn made the catch. In an interesting, and hotly contested, ruling, the umpires allowed the out, reasoning that the catch was exactly the same as if Lynn had tumbled into the seats. ◆ Many outfielders have tumbled over the little 4.75-foot steel fence down the foul lines in their efforts to catch home run balls. In one Angels game against

Anaheim Stadium, Anaheim, California. The "Big A" scoreboard dominates left field. Bottom: After being fully enclosed in 1980.

the Yankees, the Yanks lost a home run when the Angels left fielder leaped into the second row of seats to make the catch, and came back out onto the field of play with the ball. The Angels, however, got a home run two innings later when the Yankee left fielder leaped into the third row of seats to make the catch, but had the ball wrestled out of his glove by the very same Angels fans who had been so cooperative with their own left fielder just two innings before. This is reminiscent of many similar scenes from baseball's hallowed past in old Yankee Stadium, Fenway, and Dodger Stadium, all of which have had or still have similarly low fences.

◆ The rule is always the same: If the fielder goes into the seats, he must come out with the ball for the out to count. This makes it perfectly legal for the fans to influence the game, and they do. Some people maintain that this is unfair, just as some say that it is unfair that all ballparks are not perfectly alike and symmetrical; it skews the statistics, they say. In so doing, I believe that they miss the very essence of baseball. If baseball ever were to become perfectly logical, it would cease to be baseball.

## ARLINGTON, TEXAS

# ARLINGTON STADIUM

**A.K.A.**
Turnpike Stadium, 1965–1971

**OCCUPANT**
American League Texas Rangers, April 21, 1972 to date

**CAPACITY**
10,500 (1965); 35,185 (April 1972); 35,739 (June 1972); 35,698 (1973); 41,097 (1979); 41,284 (1981); 43,508 (1985)

**LARGEST CROWD**
43,705 on July 23, 1983 vs. the Blue Jays

**SMALLEST CROWD**
2,513 on September 21, 1973 vs. the Angels

**SURFACE**
419 Bermuda grass

**DIMENSIONS**
Foul lines: 330
Power alleys: 380 (1972); 370 (1974); 383 (1981); 380 (1982)
Center field: 400
Backstop: 60
Foul territory: Small

**FENCES**
11 (1972); 12 (1981); 11 (1986)

**PHENOMENA**
A huge Texas-shaped scoreboard once stood behind the bleachers in the outfield. Here, the Lone Ranger rooted for the Rangers on Diamond Vision, and the Lone Star State kept track of Nolan Ryan's latest strikeout statistics. ◆ The bleachers are the largest in the Majors, spanning the entire outfield, from foul pole to foul pole. Try not to sit in section A out in left, though. Unless you twist your body around like a snake, you cannot see the field. ◆ Like Dodger Stadium and the Roman Colosseum, the field is below the surrounding parking lots. Before 1978, when the upper deck was added, fans would walk in at the very top of the stadium. ◆ Although the wind

**T**op: Turnpike Stadium, Arlington, Texas. In 1965, before being expanded into Arlington Stadium. Bottom: Arlington Stadium, Arlington, Texas. Home of the Texas Rangers.

usually blows in directly from the outfield, the ball carries well because of the heat. Because this is the hottest park in the Majors, with temperatures regularly soaring into the 100s, almost all games (even Sunday games) are scheduled at night. ◆ There are more advertising signs here than in any other Major League ballpark, which in most parks would be detrimental. Here, however, it somehow works to the park's advantage and adds to the charm and atmosphere. It may be because the signs are so numerous and varied that the effect is somewhat like that of a Minor League ballpark back in the 1930s. ◆ The seventh-inning stretch features the song "Cotton Eye Joe" for the fans to dance to instead of the traditional "Take Me Out To The Ballgame." ◆ A new facility being planned will be a classic, urban-style ballpark, with many Texas-architectural features. It will be built quite close to the current park on a section of the parking lot. Opening day is set for 1994.

# ATLANTA, GEORGIA

# ATLANTA–FULTON COUNTY STADIUM

### A. K. A.
Atlanta Stadium, 1965–1974; Launching Pad; Big Victor's Teepee; Chief Noc-A-Homa's Wigwam

### OCCUPANT
National League Atlanta Braves, April 12, 1966 to date

### CAPACITY
51,500 (1965); 50,893 (1966); 51,383 (1968); 52,870 (1974); 51,556 (1976); 52,532 (1979); 52,194 (1980); 52,785 (1982); 52,934 (1983); 52,785 (1984); 53,046 (1985); 52,006 (1986); 52,003 (1987); 52,007 (1990)

### LARGEST CROWD
53,775 on April 8, 1974 for Opening Night vs. the Dodgers

### SMALLEST CROWD
737 on September 8, 1975 vs. the Astros

### SURFACE
Grass: Prescription Athletic Turf (PAT)

### DIMENSIONS
Foul lines: 325 (1966); 330 (1967)
Left center: 385 (1966); 375 (1969); 385 (1974)
Center field: 402 (1966); 400 (1969); 402 (1973)
Right center: 385 (1966); 375 (1969); 385 (1973)
Backstop: 59.92
Foul territory: Huge

### FENCES
6 (wire, 1966); 10 (4 plexiglass above 6 wire, 1983); 10 (plexiglass, 1985)

### PHENOMENA
Hank Aaron hit his 715th homer to left field here on April 8, 1974, off Al Downing of the Dodgers at 9:07 P.M. before a sellout crowd that had waited all winter for the event. Atlanta's Dion James hit a fly ball to Mets center fielder Kevin McReynolds that killed a dove and fell for a double on April 12, 1987. That dove is the only bird

**F**ulton County Stadium, Atlanta. One of the many circular parks of the 1960s and 1970s.

ever known to have been killed by a fair batted ball during a Major League game. ◆ If you buy a ticket in Section 105, Row A, Seat 1, you may think you have bought yourself a good seat. But unless you enjoy being right behind Ted Turner's private box, with the security guards, Jane Fonda's golden retriever, and a flock of autograph hounds swarming between you and the game, you may want to move. ◆ Three large statues outside the stadium honor Ty Cobb, Hank Aaron, and Phil Niekro. ◆ An 80-year-old historic calliope organ was installed here in 1971. ◆ With an altitude of more than 1,000 feet above sea level, this is the highest park in the Majors, which results in numerous home runs, and the nickname "The Launching Pad." ◆ Big Victor, a large Native American totem pole-like figure, stood behind the left field fence in 1966. His huge head tilted, and his eyes rolled when a Brave hit a home run. He was a huge success with the fans, but experienced mechanical problems with his neck and eyes and was retired by the Braves management. His parting request was that the Braves knock in more homers. Chief Noc-A-Homa and his Wigwam replaced Big Victor in 1967. From 1967 to 1971, the Wigwam stood on a 20-foot square platform behind the left field fence. In 1972 the Chief moved to right field, but returned to left field the next year. In 1978 the intrepid Chief moved again, this time to left center, occupying 235 seats between aisles 128 and 130, in rows 18 through 30. With the Braves favored to win their first National League pennant since arriving in Atlanta, and smelling additional playoff revenue, Braves management removed the Chief and his Wigwam in early August

1982 to make room for 235 more seats. This may or may not have upset the Great Spirit, but it definitely did something to upset the first-place Braves, who promptly went into a tailspin that threw them out of first place. Amazingly, the Chief's dramatic return in the first week of September sparked the team's comeback to win the 1982 National League West crown. In 1983, history repeated itself, with drastic consequences for the Braves. This time, the Chief's removal on August 11 marked the start of another long losing streak, which could not be overcome by his return on September 16th.

# BALTIMORE, MARYLAND

# ORIOLE PARK AT CAMDEN YARDS

## OCCUPANT
American League Baltimore Orioles, April 6, 1992 to date

## CAPACITY
46,500

## SURFACE
Grass

## DIMENSIONS
Left field: 333
Left center: 373
Deepest left center: 410
Center field: 399
Right center: 386
Right field: 318
Backstop: 57.5

## FENCES
Left field to center field: 7
Right field: 25

## PHENOMENA
The Major League's newest ballpark continues the encouraging trend of a return to the classic, urban-style parks of several generations ago. The facility was planned by the Maryland Stadium Authority, which was created by the state legislature on July 1,

**O**riole Park at Camden Yards, Baltimore. Perhaps the new standard of the classic park.

1986. ◆ The 85-acre site in downtown Baltimore, just a short walk from the waterfront, covers 71 city blocks that have been occupied since the city's earliest days in the 1700s. Site archaeology revealed the diverse history of the area: open fields and farms in the 1700s, rowhouses and light industry in the mid-1800s, a railroad (hence the name of Camden Yards) and heavy commerce at the turn-of-the-century. Archaeologists unearthed the remains of the George Ruth, Sr. saloon, the enterprise of Babe Ruth's father. ◆ The park features a grass field with asymmetrical dimensions and a slightly misshapen outfield, giving the park its own personality. Anchoring the right field side of the park is the old Baltimore & Ohio warehouse, 1016 feet long and only 51 feet wide, spared from demolition. It offers a tempting set of windows for any batter who cares to hit over 432 feet. The building houses team offices with other areas leased to private firms. ◆ The park's up-to-date facilities mix well with its classic style: 72 sky boxes and 3 party suites for the well-financed fans, special seating for the disabled, highly efficient and modern rest rooms and concession stands, and not a bad seat in the house! ◆ At a total construction cost of $105 million (not including the $99 million for property acquisition and demolition), the park will be financed by lotteries and a bond issue. Baltimore's downtown renaissance continues with this facility, a classic addition to a game and a city that have a century-old relationship.

## BOSTON, MASSACHUSETTS

# FENWAY PARK

**A.K.A.**
Fenway Park Grounds, 1910s and 1920s

**OCCUPANTS**
American League Boston Red Sox, April 20, 1912 to date
National League Boston Braves, September 7–29, 1914; 1914 World Series; April 14–July 26, 1915

**CAPACITY**
35,000 (1912); 35,500 (1947); 35,200 (1949); 34,824 (1953); 34,819 (1958); 33,368 (1960); 33,357 (1961); 33,524 (1965); 33,375 (1968); 33,379 (1971); 33,437 (1976); 33,513 (1977); 33,538 (1979); 33,536 (1981); 33,465 (1983); 33,583 (1985); 34,182 (1989); 34,171 (1991)

**LARGEST CROWD**
Total: 49,000, with 40,627 paid, on September 22, 1935 vs. the Yankees. Paid: 41,766 on August 12, 1934 vs. the Yankees

**SMALLEST CROWD**
409 on September 29, 1965 vs. the Angels

**SURFACE**
Bluegrass

**DIMENSIONS**
Left field: 324 (1921); 320.5 (1926); 320 (1930); 318 (1931); 320 (1933); 312 (1934); 315 (1936)
Left center: 379 (1934)
Deep left center at flagpole: 388 (1934)
Center field: 488 (1922); 468 (1930); 388.67 (1934); 389.67 (1954)
Deepest corner, just right of dead center: 550 (1922); 593 (1931); 420 (1934)
Right center, just right of deepest corner where the bullpen begins: 380 (1938); 383 (1955)
Right of right center: 405 (1939); 382 (1940); 381 (1942); 380 (1943)
Right field: 313.5 (1921); 358.5 (1926); 358 (1930); 325 (1931); 358 (1933); 334 (1934); 332 (1936); 322 (1938); 332 (1939); 304 (1940); 302 (1942)
Backstop: 68 (1912); 60 (1934)
Foul territory: Smallest in the Major Leagues

## FENCES

Left field: 25 (wood, 1912); 37.17 (tin over wooden railroad ties framework, upper section; over concrete, lower section 1934); 37.17 (hard plastic, 1976)
Left field wall to center field bleacher wall behind flagpole: 18 sloping down to 17 (concrete, 1934); (canvas padding on lower section, 1976)
Center field to bullpen fence: 8.75 (wood, 1940)
Right center bullpen fence: 5.25 (wood, 1940)
Right field wall and railing: 3.42 at bullpen sloping up to 5.37 at foul pole (steel, 1940)

## PHENOMENA

The 37-foot-high Green Monster in left completely dominates the field of play. Now all green, before 1947 it used to be covered with picture advertisements, most prominently a Gem razor blades sign. The only "in-play" ladder in the Major Leagues starts near the upper left corner of the scoreboard, 13.4 feet above the ground, and rises to the top of the Green Monster. This allows the groundskeepers to remove batting practice home run balls from the netting above the Wall before the game begins. Red Sox left fielder Ted Williams had to watch in amazement as Jim Lemon's fly ball ricocheted off the ladder into center field for an inside-the-park home run. Before 1976, the Wall consisted of a framework of wooden railroad ties (2 by 4's) covered by tin. When the ball hit the railroad ties, it would thud and bounce back toward the infield. But when the ball hit between the 2 by 4's, it would plunk and drop straight down because the tin would give way a little. In 1976, the railroad ties and tin gave way to a hard plastic surface. ◆ The only two American League playoff games ever held have been played here. The Red Sox lost both: in 1948 to the Indians and in 1978 to the Yankees. ◆ The huge Citgo sign built in 1965 is on a building at 660 Beacon Street in nearby Kenmore Square. It looms over the Wall in left center. The Jimmy Fund sign is in right. Over the decades, it has assisted in raising millions of dollars for children who have cancer. ◆ The flagpole was removed from the field of play in 1970. The pole had been in play, about 5 feet in front of the Wall in deep left center, for six decades. ◆ All of the original seats were made of oak. ◆ The 593-foot measurement, for the deepest center field corner, is cited in the official Major League Baseball Blue Books for 1931, 1932, and 1933. Some argue that this

**F**enway Park, Boston. Looking along the Green Monster toward the center field bleachers.

could be a misprint whereas others claim that this measurement was to the deepest corner of the distant wall behind the right center bleachers, which was in play. This would correspond to the outer wall of the ballpark, still visible by looking away from the plate from the top row of the current bleachers. ◆ The electronic scoreboard installed in 1976, and the luxury boxes behind the plate installed over the course of several years beginning in 1982, have significantly altered the wind currents. Whereas before the wind would tend to either be blowing in or out, it now swirls around, held captive by the looming scoreboard and luxury boxes. This turns a high Fenway pop fly in foul territory into an interesting adventure. Often, what starts out as a foul ball above the seats ends up drifting out into the infield and ends up as a fair ball. ◆ There have been six balls hit out of the park to the right of the flagpole: Hank Greenberg, May 22, 1937; Jimmy Foxx, August 12, 1937; Bill Skowron, April 20, 1957; Carl Yastrzemski, May 16, 1970; Bobby Mitchell, September 29, 1973; and Jim Rice, August 15, 1973. ◆ Duffy's Cliff was a 10-foot high mound that formed an incline in front of the left field wall from 1912 to 1933, extending from the left field foul pole to the flagpole in center. It was named after Red Sox left fielder Duffy Lewis, who, from 1912 through 1917, was the acknowl-

**F**enway Park, Boston. Citgo sign looms over the Green Monster.

edged master of defensive play on the cliff. It was greatly reduced but not completely eliminated in 1934. ◆ The Right Field Belly is the name for the low railing and wall that curve out sharply from the 302-foot marker at the right field foul pole into deep right field. Many a right fielder has run toward the foul line and watched helplessly as a 302-foot pop fly sails over the railing for a home run. ◆ The scoreboard numbers showing runs and hits are 16 × 16 inches and weigh 3 pounds each. The numbers showing errors, innings, and pitcher's numbers are 12 × 16 inches and weigh 2 pounds each. ◆ The wooden bleachers in foul territory down the left field line burned down on May 8, 1926. The charred remains were removed, drastically increasing the size of foul territory there for the rest of the season. ◆ No ball has ever been hit over the right field roof. Given the distance, that could conceivably change someday. Several balls have hit the uprights above the Wall and should have been homers, but have been declared in play by the umpires. These were hit by Jackie Jensen, Brooks Robinson, Frank Malzone, Gene Conley, Tony Conigliaro, Mickey Mantle, and Mike Easler. Mike Higgins once hit a homer off the huge loudspeaker horn that used to stand on the top of the wall in left center. ◆ Life at Fenway can be rough for left fielders and pitchers, but it can be even tougher on pigeons. Willie Horton's foul ball once killed a

pigeon. In 1945, A's right fielder Hal Peck's throw to the plate deflected off a pigeon to the second baseman, who tagged Skeeter Newsome out trying to slide into second with a double. That pigeon was fortunate enough to survive. ◆ The infield grass was transplanted from Huntington Avenue Baseball Grounds to Fenway in 1912. ◆ The 1912 central grandstand was made of concrete and steel, with wooden wings parallelling the foul lines beyond the infield. During the winter of 1933–1934, all of the wooden grandstands were replaced with concrete and steel. A fire on January 5, 1934 destroyed much of what had already been built, but all was finished for the season opener on April 17, 1934. ◆ In 1936 a 23.33-foot net was placed atop the Wall in left to protect the windows on Lansdowne Street. In 1978, Yankee shortstop Bucky Dent made the net infamous with a playoff homer that brought gloom to all of New England. Fred Snodgrass of the Giants made an error in center field in the bottom of the 10th inning on October 16, 1912 in the 8th game of the World Series, giving the series to the Red Sox, 4 games to 3, with 1 tie. ◆ In 1940, in an effort to help Ted Williams hit home runs, the Red Sox added the right field bullpens. Called Williamsburg, the new bullpens reduced the distance to the fence by 23 feet. Before 1934, balls to deep center field could bounce behind the right center field bleachers and remain in play, causing the umpires to lose sight of the center fielder while he was attempting to retrieve the ball. ◆ On May 17, 1947, a deadeye seagull bombardier dropped a 3-pound smelt on the mound, leaving Browns pitcher Ellis Kinder dumbfounded and fishy-smelling in the middle of his windup. ◆ The initials of former owner Thomas A. Yawkey and his wife Jean R. Yawkey (TAY and JRY) appear in Morse code in two vertical stripes on the scoreboard in left field. ◆ The screen behind home plate, designed to protect fans and allow foul balls to roll back down onto the field of play, was the first of its kind in the Majors. ◆ The right field flagpole was called Pesky's Pole because Johnny Pesky hit it numerous times for home runs. The roped-off section of seats in the center field bleachers was called Conig's Corner in the late 1960s, after Tony Conigliaro. The left field bluegrass removed in the post-1967 resodding is now the lawn for Carl Yastrzemski's suburban Lynnfield home. ◆ The left field scoreboard installed on the Wall in 1934 was reduced in size by dropping the National League scores and moved 20 feet to the right in 1976. The low concrete base of the left and center field walls was padded after the 1975 World Series, after Fred Lynn crashed into the concrete wall in center field. Seven years later, Lynn actually crashed through the fence in Anaheim Stadium. ◆ The left field foul line was measured by Art Keefe and George Sullivan in October 1975 as 309 feet 5 inches. On October 19, 1975, the *Boston Globe* used aerial photography and measured it at 304.779 feet. Osborn Engineering Company blueprints document the distance as 308 feet. The sign on the wall says 315 feet. All requests to measure the distance, including mine, have been rejected by the Red Sox. They seem to enjoy the mystery. ◆ After a black plastic cat, which had been unsuccessful in the role as a lucky rabbit's foot, was buried below a headstone in the Red Sox bullpen in 1955, Herb Score of the Indians proceeded to blank the Sox 19–0, making his own comment on the influence of rabbit's feet. ◆ Carlton Fisk's homer, possibly influenced by his nationally televised body English from between the plate and first base, bounced off the left field foul pole on October 22, 1975 at 12:33 A.M. to win the sixth game of the World Series over the Reds. ◆ It has been said that Fenway is a place "where you can sit for hours and feel a serenity that does not exist anywhere else in the world."

# CHICAGO, ILLINOIS

# WRIGLEY FIELD

## A.K.A.
North Side Ball Park, 1914; Weeghman Park, 1914–1918; Whales Park, 1915; Cubs Park, 1916–1925; Wrigley Seminary; Bobby Dorr's House

## OCCUPANTS
Federal League Chicago Whales, April 23, 1914 to October 3, 1915; National League Chicago Cubs, April 20, 1916 to date

## CAPACITY
14,000 (1914); 18,000 (1915); 20,000 (1923); 38,396 (1927); 40,000 (1928); 38,396 (1938); 38,000 (1939); 38,396 (1941); 38,690 (1949); 36,755 (1951); 36,644 (1965); 37,702 (1972); 37,741 (1973); 37,272 (1982); 38,040 (1986); 38,143 (1987); 39,600 (1989); 38,710 (1990)

## LARGEST CROWD
Total: 51,556, with 19,748 paid, on June 27, 1930 vs. the Dodgers. Paid: 46,965 on May 31, 1948 vs. the Pirates.

## SMALLEST CROWD
440 on September 21, 1966 vs. the Reds

## SURFACE
Grass, mixture of Merion bluegrass and clover

## DIMENSIONS
Left field: 345 (April 1914); 310 (May 1914); 327 (June 1914); 343 (1921); 325 (1923); 348 (1926); 364 (1928); 355 (1938)
Left center deepest corner in the well: 357 (1938)
Power alleys: 368 (1938)
Center field: 440 (1914); 447 (1923); 436 (1928); 400 (1938)
Right center deepest corner in the well: 363 (1938)
Right field: 356 (April 1914); 345 (June 1914); 321 (1915); 298 (1921); 299 (1922); 318 (1923); 321 (1928); 353 (1938)
Backstop: 62.42 (1930); 60.5 (1957); 62.42 (1982)
Foul territory: Very small

## FENCES
Left field corner: 15.92 (11.33 brick, with Boston and Bittersweet Ivy, below 4.59 plywood)

Transition between left field corner and bleachers: 12.5 (screen and yellow railing on top of brick wall)
Left center to right center: 8 (screen, 1914); 11.33 (brick with ivy, 1938); 11.33 (brick with ivy and a chicken wire basket in front, 1970)
Left field scoreboard: 40 (wood July 9 to September 3, 1937)
Center field screen: 19.33 (8 wire above 11.33 brick, June 18, 1963 to October 1964)
Right center triangle: 17.5 in front of catwalk steps sloping down to 15.5 (screen, 1938; plywood, 1979, removed in 1985)
Right field corner: 15.5 (11.33 brick with ivy below 4.17 plywood)

### FORMER USE
A seminary

### PHENOMENA
As well as being the most beautiful 4 acres of bluegrass in the world, Wrigley Field is the only remaining Federal League ballpark. Wind influences Wrigley more than any other Major League park. On a warm day, with the wind blowing out to Lake Michigan from the southwest, home runs fly out all over the place, and the score can easily be 26–23. On the other hand, on a cold day, with the wind blowing in off the lake from the northeast, the place is a pitcher's delight, and the score can easily be 1–0. More home runs than normal are caused by the high altitude of over 600 feet above sea level, by the heat involved in mostly daylight games, by windy conditions blowing out toward the outfield, an extremely small amount of foul territory, and excellent visibility. ◆ The beautiful ivy vines on the outfield wall have provoked plays such as Cub left fielder Andy Pafko losing Tiger Roy Cullenbine's hit in the 1945 World Series, and Roberto Clemente's attempt to uncork one of his great throws to the plate with an empty white Coke cup. ◆ Wrigley is the only park where it is more difficult to hit a home run down the foul line than to hit one 50 or so feet out in fair territory because the bleachers protrude into the outfield. ◆ The places where the bleachers curve out into the field of play in both power alleys are called the Wells. The 368 sign in left center is somewhat over toward straightaway center from the true power alley, reached by going from the plate through a point exactly halfway between 3rd base and 2nd base. So the actual power alley distance at Wrigley Field in left center is probably around 350 or 355 feet. ◆ Lights were inside the park in the early 1940s ready to be installed, but Mr. Wrigley donated them to the war effort instead on December 8, 1941, thus allowing Wrigley Field to remain dark for five addi-

**W**rigley Field, Chicago. The outfield shape before 1937.

tional decades. The
first Cubs night games here were played in
1988, 40 years after the Tigers had become the next-to-last of the
original 16 National and American League franchises to install
lights. (The first night game in baseball history was played between
two amateur teams. The game began literally out in the Atlantic
Ocean, at 8 P.M. on September 2, 1880, in Hull, Massachusetts, at
Nantasket Beach, out on the Sea Foam House Lawn. With the
score tied at 16 between Jordan Marsh and Company and R. H.
White and Company after nine innings, the game was called by
curfew at 9:30 P.M. to allow the 300 fans and the players to catch
the last ferry boat back to the mainland.) Most baseball fans, including myself, wanted to see the tradition of day baseball preserved at Wrigley. But Dallas Green determined that the issue was
not lights vs. no lights, but rather Wrigley or move out of town.
Seen in this new way, with the issue changed to Wrigley vs. an
unneeded new plastic suburban ashtray luxury toilet-bowl type
dome in suburban Schaumberg, most baseball fans saw the need for
lights. Frustrated by neighborhood activists from getting the lights
he needed, Green even considered shutting down Wrigley and playing at Comiskey as a tenant of the White Sox for a year, hoping

that the neighborhood would feel the loss of income and go along with the installation of the lights. The first scheduled Cubs night game at Wrigley on August 8, 1988, was postponed after three innings by rain, so the first official Cubs night game here was August 9, 1988. (The first actual night game here was the All American Girls Professional Baseball League [AAGPBL] All Star Game, played here in July 1943 before 7,000 fans with temporary lights installed just for that one game.) The introduction of lights has thankfully preserved Wrigley Field for generations to come. If the Cubs had made it into the playoffs in either 1986 or 1987, they would have had to play all League Championship Series and World Series home games at Busch Stadium in St. Louis because of the lack of lights here. Despite the addition of lights in 1988, the majority of games are still played during the day. The agreement reached between the Cubs and the city concerning lights limits the team to 18 night games per year. Because of this, night games at Wrigley are an "event" and are always sold out. ◆ As in several other parks, an IBM Home Run Distance calculation appears on the center field scoreboard after a home run. After the game, a blue flag with a white "W" flying from the center field flagpole signifies a Cub win; a white flag with a blue "L" a Cub loss. Ernie Banks's number 14 is on the left field foul pole flag; Billy Williams's number 26 is on the right field foul pole flag. The foul pole screens have the distances marked vertically on plywood signs as "355" in left and "353" in right. ◆ There are arched dormers on the roof. The most distant current outfield measurement sign is at Wrigley Field. On the roof of a house across Sheffield Avenue in right center, the sign says "495." The center field 400 sign is slightly to the right of straightaway center field. That means that, given the curvature of the wall, the exact distance to dead center is probably somewhere between 401 and 404 feet. ◆ The Chi-Feds, who played in the Federal League here during 1914 and 1915, built the world's first permanent concession stand here in 1914. ◆ On April 20, 1916, the team mascot, Joa the Cubbie Bear, was present for the Cubs first National League game. During July 1916, Joa lived in a cage outside the park on Addison Street. ◆ On May 2, 1917, Native American Olympian Jim Thorpe of the Reds homered off Jim Hippo Vaughn of the Cubs in the top of the 10th inning with the only hit of the game in the famous "Double No-Hitter." Reds pitcher Fred Toney pitched 10 innings of no-hit ball for the win. Vaughn took the loss, having given up only one hit in 10 innings. ◆ A vestige of the 1920s stands one block southeast of the park on Clark Street, the Cubs Park Storage Company. Cubs Park was the name of the field from

**W**rigley Field, Chicago. Opened in 1914 as Weeghman Park.

Dear fan,          1-7-87

Say NO to TV-ball, support Wrigley Field and day baseball. Time is running out for our classic ballyards. Only 5 remain in the major leagues. Rumors of domes persist for Cleveland and the Chicago White Sox, leaving only Tiger Stadium, Fenway Park, and Wrigley Field as the last outposts of baseball.

*"deflate-a-dome"*
Vote NO in your city

*"Great American Ballparks"*
by Gordon Tindall, Decorah, Iowa

**W**rigley Field, Chicago. Many fans believe that the old ballparks are better than the new ones.

1916 to 1926. ◆ In 1923, the foul lines were shifted slightly. In the winter of 1926–1927, the left field bleachers were removed, the grandstand was double-decked, and the field was lowered several feet. In 1929, 1932, and 1935, extra outfield bleachers were built over the streets in left and right on Waveland and Sheffield for World Series games. ◆ The ballpark was located so fans could get here on the Milwaukee Road train. ◆ Babe Ruth's debated "called shot" homer off Cubs pitcher Charley Root in the 5th inning of the third game in the 1932 World Series occurred here on October 1, 1932. Did he call his homer and point to where he was going to hit it, or didn't he? Recently discovered film footage of the incident indicates that he definitely gestured, but whether the gesture was aimed at pointing out an intended home run or at the Cubs bench remains unclear. Perhaps that is as it should be, since mysteries are part of the enduring wonder of baseball lore. ◆ Bobby Dorr, the Cubs groundskeeper, lived in a six-room apartment in the 1930s at the ballpark, adjacent to the left field corner gate. The apartment is still there. ◆ The 27-foot-high, 75-foot-wide scoreboard was built in 1937 by Bill Veeck. Its top is 85 feet above the field. The 10-foot-diameter clock was added in 1941. In 1937, the bleacher stairsteps were built with potted plants and eight huge Chinese elm trees, to complement the ivy. The trees died, but the stairsteps are still there. The ivy on the outfield walls in 1937, planted by Bill Veeck, included 350 Japanese bittersweet plants and 200 Boston ivy plants. ◆ During the 1937 season, new outfield bleachers and the six red gates in the outfield wall were built. The gates were repainted blue in 1981. ◆ The hitter's background section was opened to fans from mid-1937 through 1940; 1948 through April 19, 1952; and during the 1962 All Star Game. ◆ The William Wrigley Jr. Water Fountain is in the lobby under the first base stands, near the Frank Chance Plaque, by the Friendly Confines Cafe and the Cubs Hall of Fame. It was dedicated in 1938 by a handshake between the previously quarreling Messrs. Tinker and Evers, two of the three legendary "Tinker to Evers to Chance" trio of Chicago infielders of the early 1900s. ◆ Cubs catcher Gabby Hartnett's "Homer in the Gloamin'" here on September 28, 1938, off Pirates pitcher Mace Brown, just moments before the critical game would have had to have been called a tie, won the 1938 pennant for the Cubs. ◆ The bleachers were expanded to their present capacity in the 1940s. The right field wall was remodeled in 1950–1951. ◆ On April 14, 1951, Sam Snead hit the only ball to ever reach the scoreboard. It was a golf ball, teed off from the plate. Only two batters have come close to hitting the scoreboard. Roberto Clemente's homer sailed just left of the scoreboard; Bill Nicholson's went just right of the scoreboard. ◆ On June 9, 1962, right field bleacher fans showered Dodgers right fielder Frank Howard with peanuts and made him miss Bob Lillis's fly ball. It was ruled a single. ◆ A batters' background wire fence (8 feet high and 64 feet wide) stood on the top of the center field wall from June 18, 1963 through the end of the 1964 season. It was called the Whitlow Fence because Cub Athletic Director Robert Whitlow put it up there to provide his woeful batters with a good hitting background. The screen prevented 10 homers: 4 for the Cubs and 6 for the visitors and one each by 500+ homer hitters Ernie Banks and Willie McCovey. It resulted in 6 triples and 4 doubles. The famous Bleacher Bums were formed in 1966 by 10 bleacher fans. ◆ The green astroturf cover on the center field seats used for batters' background debuted on May 18, 1967. ◆ The entire upper deck was rebuilt in 1968–1971. On April 14, 1976, Mets slugger Dave "King Kong" Kingman hit a home run 550 feet over Waveland, and against a frame house three doors down on the east side of Kenmore Avenue. If the ball had carried 3 feet higher, it would have crashed through a window, smashed a television screen on which Naomi Martinez was watching Kingman round the bases, and been the first ever home run in true living color stereo. ◆ Before 1981, the outfield wall distances were marked on plywood markers screwed into the brick. Since then, they have been painted directly on the brick. Bill Buckner's hit was lost in the ivy for a homer in 1982 vs. the Mets. An entire rebuilding and renovation program was carried out in the 1980s. In 1981–1982, all of the Cubs offices were rebuilt under the seats behind home plate. In 1983, a brand new ticket office was built. In 1984–1985, the clubhouse was renovated. Seats were added in July 1985 to the catwalks near each foul pole in fair territory. As previously mentioned, lights were added in 1988. In 1989, sixty-seven private luxury boxes were built, as well as new press boxes and broadcasting booths. ◆ Pete Rose tied Ty Cobb's all-time hits record here with his 4,191st hit on September 8, 1985 off Cubs pitcher Reggie Patterson. ◆ When the Bears played football here, they used a shoehorn to fit the gridiron into the available space. They added bleacher seats on the left field grass in front of the brick wall, and the north endzone ended 18 inches in front of these bleachers. The southeast corner of the south endzone was actually suspended in midair over the top step of the first base dugout! Over the years, receivers actually caught touchdown passes and disappeared into the dugout, only to reappear and be mobbed by teammates in the traditional touchdown celebration.

# COMISKEY PARK II

**OCCUPANT**
American League Chicago White Sox, April 18, 1991 to date

**CAPACITY**
44,702 (1991)

**LARGEST CROWD**
42,976 on July 25, 1991 vs. the Blue Jays

**SURFACE**
Play-All system grass turf, consisting of sand, pea gravel, peat, calcined clay, and bluegrass

**DIMENSIONS**
Foul lines: 347
Power alleys: 383
Center field: 400
Backstop: 60

**A**rmour Field, Chicago. An attempt to integrate the ballpark with the neighborhood.

### FENCES

8 (canvas padding)

### FORMER USE

Houses and a baseball tavern, where Babe Ruth went between games of doubleheaders against the Sox

### PHENOMENA

Since this stadium is so much like Kansas City's Royals Stadium, let's remember the old Comiskey Park. The longest Major League game ever, in terms of actual playing time, occurred there on the successive evenings of May 8–9, 1984, when the White Sox defeated the Brewers 7–6 in a 25-inning game that lasted 8 hours and 6 minutes. Suspended at 1:05 A.M. after 17 innings on the first evening, the game was decided the next evening by Harold Baines's home run, which just cleared the center field bullpen fence. The White Sox had scored twice in the bottom of the 9th, and three times in the bottom of the 21st to keep the game tied. They would have won in the bottom of the 23rd, except that Murphy's Law struck again: When something can go wrong, it will. White Sox base runner Dave Stegman was ruled first safe, then out at the plate. Third base coach Jim Leyland, now the Pirates manager, helped Stegman to his feet after Stegman tripped rounding third base to score the winning run. Had he not tripped, Stegman would have scored easily. As it was, even after tripping, he reached the plate before the throw from the outfield and was ruled safe, but then he was ruled out for coach's interference. This game is rich in "might-have-beens." Had it been a game in the National League, where there is no curfew, it would have ended at 3:42 A.M., and broken by 19 minutes the then-current Major League record of 3:23

**A**rmour Field, Chicago. **What the White Sox** *could* **have built.**

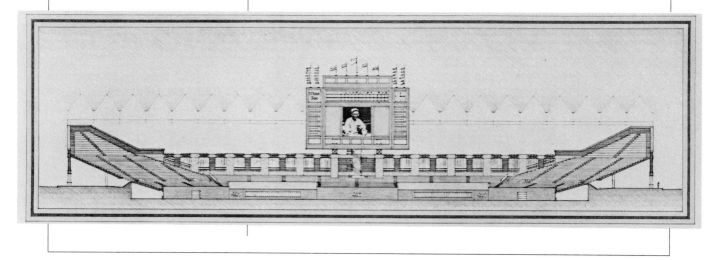

A.M., set by the Expos and Phillies at the Vet on August 10, 1977. If this had been the case, then Tom Seaver would not have had the chance to come on in relief the next night and be the winning pitcher. Had it been played during either of the two periods between 1910–1948 or 1976–1980, when Comiskey Park had no inner fence in center, Baines's drive would have been caught easily and the two teams might still be playing, or at the very least, have broken the Major League record for innings played in one game. That record still stands at 26 innings, set seven decades ago, back on May 1, 1920 at Braves Field in Boston, when the Dodgers and Braves battled to a 1–1 tie finally called due to darkness. But best of all, had the game been the second game of that foggy September 24, 1971 Houston at San Diego twi-night doubleheader, whose start was delayed until 12:01 A.M., it would have finished at 8:07 A.M. CST, which is 9:07 A.M. EST, and the last few innings could have been covered live by Jane Pauley, Bryant Gumbel, and Willard Scott on the "Today" Show. ♦ On August 12, 1990, the Rangers and White Sox sat through a 7-hour 23-minute rain delay at the start of their scheduled Sunday afternoon game at Comiskey Park, before it was finally postponed. Hometeam owners, rather than the umpires, have the responsibility for calling off a game until it begins, and the White Sox made the decision to wait so long. It was the Rangers' last trip to Chicago, the Sox were in a tight pennant race with the A's at the time, and they didn't want to give away their home advantage and have to play the game in Texas if the game could not be played that day in Chicago. ♦ The former ballpark was hallowed ground upon which the legends of the game had played: Babe Ruth, Josh Gibson, Lou Gehrig, Luis Aparicio, Satchel Paige, Minnie Minoso, Walter Johnson, and so many others. This unneeded new stadium is not hallowed ground.

**A**rmour Field, Chicago. A classic facade for a modern park.

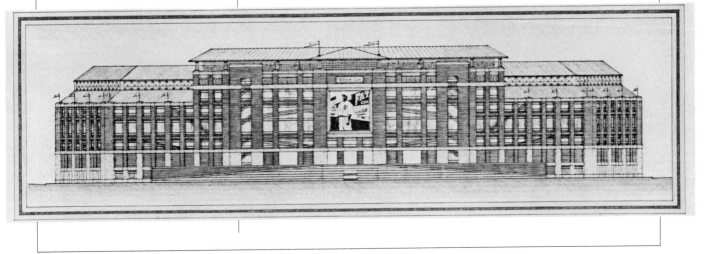

# CINCINNATI, OHIO

# RIVERFRONT STADIUM

**R**iverfront Stadium, Cincinnati. Where the Big Red Machine rolled.

**OCCUPANT**
National League Cincinnati Reds, June 30, 1970 to date

**CAPACITY**
51,050 (1970); 51,744 (1971); 51,726 (1972); 51,786 (1975); 51,963 (1977); 52,392 (1979); 51,786 (1980); 52,392 (1981)

**LARGEST CROWD**
56,393 on October 16, 1975 vs. the Red Sox

**SURFACE**
AstroTurf-8

**DIMENSIONS**
Foul lines: 330
Power alleys: 375
Center field: 404
Backstop: 51
Foul territory: Small

**FENCES**
12 (1970); 8 (1984)

**PHENOMENA**
On April 17, 1976, just as the Saturday afternoon NBC "Game of the Week" between the Giants and Reds was to begin, a swarm of bees attacked the field between third and home, causing a 35-minute delay. ◆ If you stand in the upper rows of the upper deck in right field, you have a wonderful view of the Cincinnati skyline. ◆ Riverfront was the first ballpark to paint metric distances on the outfield walls: 100.58 down the lines, 114.30 to the alleys, and 123.13 to center. To get the distance in fathoms, one has to go to Seattle's Kingdome. Riverfront was the first carpeted field to put Astroturf in the entire infield, leaving dirt only in sliding pits around the bases. The rest of the carpeted stadia soon followed their lead. ◆ There have been only 14 home runs into the upper deck red seats. ◆ This is the only ballpark in the Major Leagues where the fans travel upstairs to watch the game, and then back downstairs to drive home. There is a parking garage beneath the stadium.

# CLEVELAND, OHIO

# CLEVELAND STADIUM

**A.K.A.**
Lakefront Stadium, 1930s; Cleveland Public Municipal Stadium, 1930s; Municipal Stadium, 1940s and 1950s

**OCCUPANT**
American League Cleveland Indians, July 31, 1932 to September 24, 1933; April 15, 1947 to date

**NEUTRAL USES**
American League Cleveland Indians, August 2, 1936 vs. New York Yankees; May 30 to September 24, 1937, all Sunday and all holiday games between Memorial Day and Labor Day; April 1938 to June 1939 all Sunday, all holiday, but only selected other important games; June 27, 1939 to September 1946 all night, all Sunday, and all holiday, but only selected other important games

**CAPACITY**
78,000 (1931); 78,189 (1947); 78,192 (1948); 77,700 (1949); 78,811 (1953); 73,811 (1954); 74,056 (1967); 76,977 (1968); 76,713 (1976); 76,685 (1981); 74,208 (1982); 74,483 (1989)

**LARGEST CROWD**
86,563 total, with 84,587 paid on September 12, 1954 vs. the Yankees

**SMALLEST CROWD**
365 on September 19, 1956 vs. the Senators

**SURFACE**
Bluegrass

**DIMENSIONS**
Foul lines: 322 (1932); 320 (1933); 319 (April 27, 1947); 320 (June 6, 1947); 321 (1948); 320 (1953)
Corners where inner fence meets stadium walls: 362 (June 6, 1947); 360 (1980); 370 (1991)
Power alleys: 435 (1932); 365 (1947); 362 (1948); 385 (1949); 380 (1954); 400 (1965); 390 (1967); 395 (1968); 385 (1970); 395 (1991)
Short left center: 377 (1980); 390 (1991)
Deep left center: 387 (1980); 400 (1991)

**C**leveland Stadium, Cleveland. The largest seating capacity in both leagues.

Grandstand corners: 435 (1932)
Bleacher corners: 463 (1932)
Corners where inner 8-foot fence meets tall 16-foot straightaway center fence: 417 (1991)
Center field: 470 (1932); 467 (1938); 450 (1939); 468 (April 1947); 410 (April 27, 1947); 408 (1966); 407 (1967); 410 (1968); 400 (1970); 415 (1991)
Deep right center: 395 (1980); 400 (1991)
Short right center: 385 (1980); 390 (1991)
Backstop: 60 (1991)
Foul territory: Large

## FENCES

Left and right field: 5.25 (concrete, 1932); 5.5 (wire, April 27, 1947); 5.25 (concrete, June 6, 1947); 6 (concrete, 1955); 9 (wire, 1976); 7 (wire, 1977); 8 (canvas padding, 1984)
Center field: 12 (concrete, 1932); 5.5 (wire, April 27, 1947); 8 (wire, 1975); 9 (wire, 1976); 8 (wire, 1977); 8 (canvas padding, 1984); 16 (for a 36-foot-wide area in dead center, angling down to the lower fences in the alleys, canvas padding, 1991)

## PHENOMENA

The park opened formally on July 1, 1931, a year before the first Indians home game here on July 31, 1932. The Indians enlarged the field of play significantly in 1991, believing that this would help their team, which lacked power hitters but had plenty of fleet-footed outfielders. The fences were moved back 13 feet in deep left center from 387 to 400, 15 feet in center from 400 to 415, and 5 feet in deep right center from 395 to 400. The Indians also added a 36-foot-long higher fence in straightaway center, raising that portion of the fence from 8 feet to 16 feet. It is still a lot smaller than when it opened in 1932. Then center field was 470 feet from home plate. Built in the hope that the 1932 Olympics would be held here, the event was awarded to Los Angeles instead. ◆ Unhappily for Cleveland, the Indians have not appeared in post-season play since 1954. ◆ The groundskeepers' tools were in play in foul territory in the 1930s and 1940s. ◆ For 15 years, from 1932 to 1947, before the inner fences were installed on April 27 after the first two weeks of the 1947 season, there was a steep incline in front of the center field bleacher wall. The incline is still visible during Browns football games when a pass receiver scores and goes out of the endzone and up the steep incline in front of the Dog Pound, as the baseball bleachers are called during the Cleveland football season. ◆ There was also a strange shape in the power alleys caused by the end of the double-decked grandstand, where the fence jumped abruptly deeper to the bleacher wall in center. The April 27, 1947 inner fence curved all the way to the foul poles. On June 6, 1947 it was changed so the inner fence just stretched across center field, hitting the permanent wall at the 362 mark, 42 feet out from the foul poles. Teepees were erected in 1946 in the center field bleachers. The foul poles are 32 feet 8 inches high, 5 inches wide, and the attached screen on the fair territory side is 22 inches wide. No one has ever hit a ball into the center field bleachers. ◆ On September 23, 1949, Bill Veeck and the Indians buried their 1948 pennant in center field before a game, the day after they were mathematically eliminated from the race. ◆ There was a bandstand in center field between the fence and the bleachers in 1953. Today there is a picnic area in the same place. Center field standing room area was made into a garden in 1957. ◆ On September 16, 1964, Senator batter Don Zimmer's 3rd inning hit bounced off the right field fence and was then kicked inadvertently by Indian right fielder Chico Salmon through a small hole in the wall. Although Washington manager Gil Hodges argued for a homer, the umpires gave Zimmer only a double. ◆ On Beer Night, the Indians forfeited their June 4, 1974 game when unruly fans took over the field and would not leave. ◆

Cleveland Stadium was featured in two movies: *The Kid from Cleveland* in 1949, and *Fortune Cookie* in 1966. Amazingly, it was not featured in the great movie about the Indians, *Major League*: That one was mysteriously filmed at Milwaukee's County Stadium, although several short scenes of Cleveland Stadium did make it into the movie.

Cleveland Stadium, Cleveland. Home of the Indians.

# DETROIT, MICHIGAN

# TIGER STADIUM

### A.K.A.
The only ballpark that has been hugged by its fans; Bennett Park 1896–1911; Navin Field, 1912–1937; Briggs Stadium, 1938–1960

### OCCUPANTS
American League Detroit Tigers, April 20, 1912 to date; Negro National League Detroit Stars, 1920–1931; Negro East-West League Detroit Wolves, 1932; Negro National League Detroit Stars, 1933; Negro American League Detroit Stars, 1937

### CAPACITY
23,000 (1912); 29,000 (1923); 36,000 (1936); 58,000 (1938); 54,000 (1953); 52,904 (1961); 52,687 (1962); 52,850 (1963); 53,089 (1967); 54,220 (1969); 54,226 (1976); 53,676 (1979); 52,687 (1981); 52,806 (1984); 52,416 (1989)

### LARGEST CROWD
Total: 58,480, with 57,130 paid, on May 19, 1946 vs. the Red Sox; Paid: 58,369 on July 20, 1947 vs. the Yankees

### SMALLEST CROWD
404 on September 24, 1928 vs. the Red Sox

### SURFACE
Grass

### DIMENSIONS
Left field: 345 (1921); 340.58 (1926); 339 (1930); 367 (1931); 339 (1934); 340 (1938); 342 (1939); 340 (1942)
Left center: 365 (1942)
Center field: 467 (1927); 455 (1930); 464 (1931); 459 (1936); 450 (1937); 440 (1938); 450 (1939); 420 (1942); 440 (1944)
Right center: 370 (1942); 375 (1982)
Right field: 370 (1921); 370.91 (1926); 372 (1930); 367 (1931); 325 (1936); 315 (1939); 325 (1942); 302 (1954); 325 (1955)
Backstop: 54.25 (1954); 66 (1955)
Foul territory: Small

### FENCES
All fences: 5 concrete topped by screen

Left field: 20 (1933); 5 (1934); 20 (World Series, 1934); 5 (1936); 30 (1937); 10 (1938); 12 (1940); 15 (1946); 12 (1953); 14 (1954); 12 (1955); 11 (1958); 9 (1962)
Center field: 9 (1940); 15 (1946); 11 (1950); 9 (1953); 14 (1954); 9 (1955)
Right of flagpole: 7 (1946)
Right field: 8 (1940); 30 (1944); 10 (1945); 20 (1950); 8 (1953); 9 (1958); 30 (1961); 9 (1962)

### FORMER USE

Used as a haymarket in the 1890s

### PHENOMENA

On April 28, 1896, with home plate out where right field is now, Bennett Park was opened for a Minor League Western League game, and the Detroit Wolverines defeated the Columbus Senators 17–2. Bennett Park was used by the American League Tigers from April 25, 1901 to September 10, 1911 for Major League games. The field was named for Charlie Bennett, a catcher who played for the National League Detroit Wolverines in the 1880s at Recreation Park, where Harper–Grace Hospitals are now. Bennett lost both legs in an 1894 train accident, but he lived until 1927 and was a great Tigers fan. The infielders had a ready-made excuse for errors, since the infield at Bennett Park had been made by just laying 2 inches of topsoil over cobblestones: "One of the cobblestones just worked its way up through the loam." The sun would shine directly into the batters' eyes in the late afternoon, when the games were played in those days. ◆ To prevent fans from seeing the games free from "wildcat" bleachers on National (now Cochrane) and Cherry (now Kaline) Streets, the Tigers management hung dozens of canvas strips (3 feet wide and 40 feet high) behind the outfield bleachers. When you sit in the dugouts, you are sunk down well into the ground. ◆ Should we tear down the White House or the Statue of Liberty just because they are old? Should the Tigers be allowed to tear down Tiger Stadium just because it is old? The Tigers' answer is yes. The Tigers' answer is wrong. Not everything in this world needs to be modernized, refurbished, renovated, updated, and then bulldozed to make way for progress. The fight to preserve Tiger Stadium is rooted in the demonstrable proof that when it comes to baseball parks, we used to make them better in the 1910s than we do now. New is usually better than old. But in the case of ballparks, old is clearly better than new. Tiger Stadium was saved from demolition in 1974 when owner John Fetzer told the Pontiac Silverdome committee, "This franchise belongs to the inner city of Detroit; I'm just the caretaker." Tiger Stadium is the first and only ballpark to be hugged by its fans, on April 20, 1988. Hugged again on June 10, 1990, it is the only stadium with its own buttons, shirts, and sweatshirts that thousands of fans wear to encourage its preservation. A determined fight is being waged by the Tiger Stadium Fan Club, the Michigan Legislature, the Detroit City Council, the *Detroit News* and *Free Press* newspapers, the people of Michigan, Wayne County, and Detroit, and many ballpark fans from all around the country to preserve this beautiful park. Speaking about the preservation of historic ballparks, Roger Angell, America's premier chronicler of baseball, states, "We are entirely in earnest . . . We are trying to conserve something that seems as intricate and lovely to us as any river valley. A thousand small relationships, patterns, histories, attachments, pleasures, and moments are what we draw from this game, and that is why we truly worry about it, grieve for it now, and are filled with apprehension . . . at the thought of its transformation into another bland and death-like pause on the evening ribbon of dog-food and gun-fights and deodorants and crashing cars. Not everyone feels this way of course, but who among us feels none of this?" ◆ The right field second deck overhangs the lower deck by 10 feet. In 1944, and again in 1961, a screen in right field extended from the foul pole out 100 feet toward right center

**N**avin Field, Detroit. Outfield bleachers in the 1930s.

and required balls hit down the right field foul line to be hit into the second deck to be home runs. ◆ The only homers ever hit over the left field roof have been hit by Harmon Killebrew, Frank Howard, and Cecil Fielder. Home plate and the batters' boxes are oriented toward right center field rather than straight out to the mound. This gives right-handed pitchers more outside corner strike calls and can disorient visiting batters. ◆ Patsy O'Toole, a famous fan in the 1930s, would often scream, "Keep cool with O'Toole." ◆ The first homer at Navin Field, on May 5, 1912, came on a fluke bounce that hopped through the side door of the left center field scoreboard. ◆ This stadium has the only double-decked bleachers in the Majors. The upper deck runs from left center to center, the lower deck from center to right center. ◆ The 125-foot-high flagpole used to be in play in deep center, just to the left of the 440 mark. This made it the highest outfield obstacle in play ever in baseball history. Some of its closest rivals include the 90-foot-high flagpole at Savannah, Georgia's Grayson Stadium, the 82-foot-high flagpole at Cincinnati's Crosley Field, the 70-foot-high screen in left field at Johnstown, Pennsylvania's Point Stadium, the 68-foot-high scoreboard in left center field at Boston's Braves Field, the 60-foot-high Lifebuoy Soap sign in right field at Philadelphia's Baker Bowl, the 60-foot-high clubhouse in center field at New York's Polo Grounds, the 60-foot-high Ballantine Beer sign in right center field at Philadelphia's Shibe Park, the 60-foot-high scoreboard in center field at Buffalo's Offermann Stadium, and the 60-foot-high screen in right field at Milwaukee's Borchert Field. ◆ The scoreboard now on the left field fence was originally placed at the 440-foot mark in dead center in 1961, but was moved when Norm Cash, Al Kaline, and Charlie Maxwell complained that it hindered the batters' view of the pitch. ◆ There is a string of spotlights mounted under the 10-foot overhang to illuminate the right field warning track, which is shadowed from the normal light standards. ◆ An area in front of the plate, known as Cobb's Lake, was always inclined and soaked with water by the groundskeepers to slow down Ty Cobb's bunts, keep them fair, and make infielders slip as they tried to field them. When slugging teams came to visit, manager Ty Cobb had the groundskeepers put in temporary bleachers in the outfield, so that long drives would be just ground rule doubles. When weak-hitting teams came to town, the temporary seats

**T**iger Stadium, Detroit. Known as Briggs Stadium from 1938–1960.

disappeared. ◆ A sign above the entrance to the visitors' clubhouse says "Visitors' Clubhouse—No Visitors Allowed." ◆ The stadium was double-decked from first to third base during the winter of 1923 to 1924. The Tigers built a huge left field bleacher section which completely covered Cherry Street, now Kaline Drive, during 1934, and left it up for the 1935 season. It was dismantled during the winter of 1935 to 1936. Ducky Medwick, the Cardinals left fielder, was pelted with fruits and vegetables from the left field bleachers in the seventh game of the 1934 World Series, causing Commissioner Kenesaw Landis to order him off the field for his own safety. ◆ The Tigers had put up a 20-foot screen in left in 1933, but had taken it down for the 1934 season. They put the screen back up for the World Series, left it up for the 1935 season, but took it down for the 1936 season. In 1937, they raised the screen to 30 feet. Capacity was increased in the winter of 1935 to 1936 by double-decking the right field stands, and in the winter of 1937 to 1938 by double-decking both the left field stands and the center field bleachers. In 1936, a 315-foot marker was placed on the second deck in right field. It remained there through the 1940s. In 1942 and 1943, the center field distance was only 420 feet.

## DYERSVILLE, IOWA*

# FIELD OF DREAMS

**OCCUPANT**
American League Chicago Black Sox, 1988 to date

**CAPACITY**
84

**SURFACE**
Grass and Iowa's best farm soil

**DIMENSIONS**
Left field: 281 (1988); 102 (1989); 281 (1990)
Center field: 314
Right field: 262

**FENCES**
None (April corn just planted); 1 (May corn); 2 (June corn); 3 (July corn); 4 (August corn); 6 (September corn); 8 (October corn)

*In the movie *Field of Dreams*

## FORMER USE

Cornfield

## PHENOMENA

This is the only current Major League ballpark without dugouts. It also has the most beautiful surroundings of any park in the Majors. There is a constant humming from the corn dryer behind the farmhouse down the first base line in the autumn, and there are always a bat and some baseballs sitting on the first base players' bench for visitors to use, rain or shine, summer or winter, scorching summer heat, or chilling winter blizzard. ◆ Sports editor Herb Trapp is busy in September and October because he has to try to cover both the Dyersville Beckman High School Blazers Big Bend Conference football games vs. their traditional rivals the Maquoketa High School Wildcats and the Comanche High School Indians, as well as the Black Sox home games. ◆ The small bleachers behind first base are moved regularly to mow the grass underneath. They consist of seven rows of 12 seats each. The top row seat closest to home plate still has the heart carved into it, where the movie's star farmer declared his love for his wife Annie. ◆ Visiting teams stay at the Colonial Inn and visit the Jack Becker Woodcarving Museum, the National Farm Toy Museum, and the 212-foot-high Basilica of St. Francis Xavier. Thousands of visiting fans from all over the world have considered their trip here to be a memorable pilgrimage. Rumors abound that Roy Hobbs and his teenage son sneak onto the field and play catch. Al Ameskamp, a nonbaseball fan and owner of the property in left and left center, replanted his property with corn in 1989, but he received so many polite requests to restore the grass that he did so in 1990. On behalf of every person who has ever visited this ballfield, heartfelt thanks Al! "It just doesn't get any better than this." "Hey, is this heaven? No, it's Iowa." (Scene from the 1988 film *Field of Dreams* with Kevin Costner, Amy Madigan, Burt Lancaster, and James Earl Jones. Players, including Shoeless Joe Jackson but not Shoeless Bo Jackson, appear out of and disappear into the cornfield in left center.) A magical place, this ball field is nestled in Iowa cornfields between the Maquoketa and the Turkey Rivers. Once anyone has visited this field, he or she will understand why this book is reverently named *Green Cathedrals*. ◆ The following letter received by Don Lansing, the co-owner of the field, summarizes how many people feel about the site: "Dear Don, You don't know me. My name is Jim Bohn. My son Matt, age 12, died in the crash of United Airlines Flight 232 in Sioux City on July 19, 1989. This past spring I had taken my son to see the movie

*Field of Dreams.* We loved the movie. Matt loved baseball. So do I, as did my father before me. I have always coached Matt's team. For the past six years we have had a great time enjoying each other and baseball. As you may know, the plane crashed in an Iowa cornfield. I found the whole idea very ironic: The story of an Iowa corn farmer who plows up his cornfield to make a baseball field where dreams come true; and my son who loved baseball dying in an Iowa cornfield where my dreams came to an end. I hope to visit our field. I hope I will have the chance to walk with my son one more time." ◆ Jerry Ryan and Lynn Burke survived the totalling of their car by a semi-trailer truck on Interstate-80 and continued their travel from Rochester, New York to the Field of Dreams to get married on September 1, 1989 at dusk. After the wedding, they disappeared into the cornfield in left center.

## HOUSTON, TEXAS

# ASTRODOME

**A**strodome, Houston. Never a rainy day at the park, but no sunny days either.

### A.K.A.
Harris County Domed Stadium, 1965; Eighth Wonder of the World

### OCCUPANT
National League Houston Astros, April 12, 1965 to date

### CAPACITY
46,217 (1965); 46,000 (1966); 44,500 (1968); 45,000 (1975); 47,690 (1982); 54,816 (1990)

### LARGEST CROWD
50,908 on July 22, 1966 vs. the Dodgers

### SMALLEST CROWD
2,600 on October 2, 1985 vs. the Bruins

### SURFACE
Infield: Grass in 1965 (a Tifway 419 Bermuda grass specially selected for indoor use, which unfortunately died during the 1965–1966 off-season); AstroTurf-8 on all but the normally dirt part of the infield, 1966–1970; entirely AstroTurf-8, with dirt only in the sliding pits around the bases, 1971 to date

Outfield: Grass from April 12, 1965 to July 19, 1966, when it completely died out; AstroTurf-8, July 19, 1966 to date

## DIMENSIONS

Foul lines: 340 (1965); 330 (1972); 340 (1977); 330 (1985)
Power alleys: 375 (1965); 390 (1966); 378 (1972); 390 (1977); 378 (1985); 380 (1990)
Center field: 406 (1965); 400 (1972); 406 (1977); 400 (1985)
Backstop: 60.5 (1965); 67 (1990)

## FENCES

Left and right fields: 16 (9 concrete below 3 wire, 2 concrete, and 2 wire plus railing, 1965); 12 (concrete, 1969); 10 (canvas padding, 1977)
Center field: 12 (concrete, 1965); 10 (canvas padding, 1977)
Apex of dome: 208

## PHENOMENA

The Astrodome is the second Major League covered stadium, the first being the field under the Queensboro 59th Street Bridge in New York City used by the Negro National League New York Cubans in the 1930s. The blame for the plague of domed stadia rests with Judge Roy Hofheinz. Working in the mid-1950s with designer Buckminster Fuller on a plan for a covered shopping center based on Fuller's geodesic dome (which never got further than the drawing boards), Hofheinz happened to visit Rome and discovered that in 80 A.D. the Roman Colosseum had been covered for a time with a velarium, or awning, which was pulled by slaves to keep the intense sunlight away from the spectators. Unfortunately, while thinking of shoppers inside a covered geodesic dome, and gladiators fighting under an awning, he somehow hatched the idea of a domed baseball stadium. The plague that would later infest not only Houston but also New Orleans, Seattle, Pontiac, Vancouver, Indianapolis, Minneapolis, St. Petersburg, Tokyo, Montreal, and Toronto was born. Football and baseball mix like oil and water when forced into the same stadium, with sickening results. ◆ The first indoor baseball game was on Christmas Day in 1888 in Philadelphia. The Downtowners defeated the Uptowners 6–1 inside the State Fairgrounds Building. ◆ The maximum height of the dome is 208 feet, just beyond second base. The roof had 4,796 clear panes of glass originally, but they caused a glare that prevented fielders from seeing the ball, thus causing two of the eight roof sections to be painted white. Unfortunately, this killed the grass, and, more unfortunately, introduced the world to Astroturf. ◆ This has always been a pitcher's park. Like Dodger Stadium, there are very few high scoring games here. At 390 feet, it used to have the most distant power

**A**strodome, Houston. World's first domed baseball park.

alleys in the Majors, excepting Yankee Stadium's Death Valley in left center, until the power alley fences were shortened to 378 feet in 1985. Since then, it is difficult to understand why there are not more home runs hit here. For example, it is actually smaller now, and has lower fences, than the Homerdome in Minneapolis. Black rubber cushions are attached to the outfield walls in the power alleys, about 1 foot off the ground and about 1 foot high. Only three balls have ever been hit into the fifth and highest level, all in left field, by Jimmy Wynn, Doug Rader, and Andre Dawson. The first two seats are marked by a Cannon and a Rooster, nicknames for Wynn and Rader. ◆ It is hard to see through the screen from behind the plate. ◆ In its inaugural season of 1965, the Astrodome was the scene of a unique groundskeeping argument. The New York Mets claimed that the groundskeepers were roof keeping as well by manipulating the air conditioning system so that air currents helped Astro long balls and hindered visitors' long balls. The Mets buttressed their argument by pointing out that the huge Message Board had actually boasted that the air currents were shifted every half inning, by 1 mile per hour blowing in in the top of every inning, and by 1 mile per hour blowing out in the bottom of every inning. The argument raged long and furiously, but ended inconclusively. ◆ There are shoe shine stands behind home plate. ◆ On April 28, 1965, Mets announcer Lindsey Nelson broadcast a game from inside a gondola suspended above second base from the apex of the dome. On June 10, 1974, Phillie Mike Schmidt hit the public address speaker 117 feet up and 329 feet from home. It would have been a 500+ foot homer, way up in the center field pavillion seats, but it ended up as a single as the ball dropped in center field. ◆ Capacity went up in 1990 when Judge Roy Hofheinz's luxury apartment in right field was torn down to make way for more seats. ◆ On June 15, 1976, a game was rained out because of flooding in the streets. ◆ This is the only place in the Majors or Minors where fielders can jump a fence in front of the dugouts to catch foul balls. The fence is 4.50 feet high, which is high enough to be an obstacle when you're trying to keep your eyes on a baseball high over your head. So on the occasions when a foul ball is hit high enough to give an infielder time to attempt to jump the fence, it is interesting to watch what happens. When an infielder does everything correctly, vaulting the fence and then catching the ball, it's an amazing sight.

## KANSAS CITY, MISSOURI

# ROYALS STADIUM

### A.K.A.
Harry S Truman Sports Complex; Baseball's Golden Arches

### OCCUPANT
American League Kansas City Royals April 10, 1973 to date

### CAPACITY
40,613 (1973); 40,762 (1974); 40,760 (1979); 40,628 (1981); 40,635 (1982); 40,625 (1985)

### LARGEST CROWD
42,633 on October 9, 1980 vs. the Yankees

### SURFACE
AstroTurf-8

### DIMENSIONS
Foul lines: 330
Power alleys: 375 (1973); 385 (1980)
Center field: 405 (1973); 410 (1980)
Backstop: 60
Foul territory: Small

### FENCES
12 (canvas padding); 12 (10 canvas padding under 2 wire down the foul lines); 12 (completely wire sections in left center field and right center field in front of the bullpens)

### PHENOMENA
This is actually not such a bad ballpark. The problem with it is that ever since it was built in 1973, it has become the Golden Arches of Baseball. Considered perfect by architects and teams, it has been cloned and packaged like fast food, for quick delivery to any city desiring a new franchise. Baseball needs diversity. If every new ballpark ends up being a clone of Royals Stadium, the National Pastime will become the National Bore. ◆ Waterfalls and fountains run for 322 feet on the embankment overlooking center field and right center field. A huge 30 by 40-foot Sony JumboTron color video display board, installed in 1991, towers over the left field embankment. ◆ Royals Stadium has the best visibility for hitters in the Majors. Homers are few here because the power alleys are

deep and the fence cuts away sharply from the 330-foot foul poles. ◆ Kenny Pippin is the brain behind the 9-minute, 58-second water-show performed after every game. He gets into his frogman suit to clean the huge pond periodically. ◆ After the 5th inning, 14 tarp crew members race from the right field bullpens, and one runs in from the visitors' left field bullpen to tidy up the base areas. Fan-A-Gram records the results; the Terrific Toma Turf Treaders have finished in as few as 26 seconds. ◆ The Fellowship of Christian Athletes Building overlooks the ballpark in left field. The huge Royals scoreboard is topped by a crown. ◆ When it rains, thousands of sawed webworm moths fly around the park. This is a problem because when it rains at a Royals home game, one is in for a long wait. Because so many Royals fans travel great distances from throughout the Midwest to see the game, and because the carpet drains so well, there have been many long rain delays. The Royals' ownership does not want to force fans to return home without having seen the game concluded. In fact, this was the rationale behind the decision made in the late 1980s to not replace the rug with real grass, despite the wishes of the vast majority of Kansas City fans, players, and groundskeepers. ◆ Millions of crickets make lots of noise during night games. The park has a very pleasant picnic-type atmosphere. Unfortunately, along with Busch Stadium in St. Louis, this is the only place in the Major Leagues where the security guards won't let you into the outfield bleachers without a bleacher ticket, even if you have a box seat ticket. ◆ The Royals' trophies and uniforms and the 1985 World Series cup are on display through the 6th inning in the aisleway at section 107. ◆ The lights atop the stadium curve out over the stands down the foul lines, leaving the upper deck fans near the foul poles in relative darkness. ◆ The best groundskeeper in baseball, George Toma, has the ironic job of maintaining a carpet. But he keeps busy: The entire complex is beautifully sodded and maintained, including the left center field grass bank, and beyond it, the Runway and the Baja. The Runway is a 30-foot-wide, 150-foot-long plush grass track used by the Royals for running behind the left field fence. The Baja is the entire area beyond the outfield fence, planted with 125 pine trees in the Jimmy Palmarine Forest.

**R**oyals Stadium, Kansas City, Missouri. It broke the string of the circular parks.

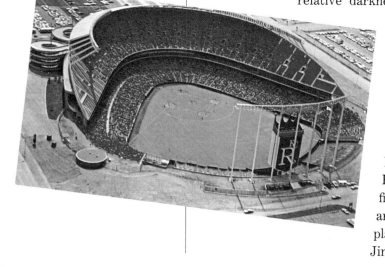

# LOS ANGELES, CALIFORNIA

# DODGER STADIUM

## A.K.A.
Chavez Ravine: during American League use 1962–1965 by the Angels; Taj O'Malley; Taj O'Malley's Golden Gulch

## OCCUPANTS
National League Los Angeles Dodgers April 10, 1962 to date; American League Los Angeles Angels April 17, 1962 to September 2, 1965; American League California Angels September 2 to September 22, 1965

## CAPACITY
56,000 (1962). Some numbers just never seem to change!

## LARGEST CROWD
Dodgers: 56,242 on October 24, 1981 vs. the Yankees

## SMALLEST CROWD
Angels: 476 on September 19, 1963 vs. the Orioles

## SURFACE
Santa Ana Bermuda grass

## DIMENSIONS
Foul lines: 330
Power alleys: 380 (1962); 370 (1969); 385 (1983)

**D**odger Stadium, Los Angeles. More comfortable than Ebbets Field, but not as quirky.

Center field: 410 (1962); 400 (1969); 395 (Marked, 1983); 400 (Actual, 1983)
Backstop: 65 (1962); 68.19 (1963); 75 (1969)
Foul territory: Large

### FENCES

Left center to right center: 10 (wood, 1962); 8 (canvas padding, 1973)
Foul poles to bullpens in the left field and right field corners: 3.75 (steel, 1962); 3.83 (steel, 1969)
The Dip: Where the low corner steel walls and the screen bullpen fences meet, 3.42 (steel, 1962); 3.5 (steel, 1969)

### FORMER USE

The area was home to numerous squatters and grazing goats. On August 21, 1957, Manuel Arechiga, his wife, and four granddaughters were evicted from their house, but not before inflicting bites and bruises on sheriff's deputies assigned the task of evicting them.

### PHENOMENA

This is a classic pitcher's park. The park is spacious and the ball does not carry well. The number of high scoring games here is amazingly low. ◆ By far this is the cleanest park in the Majors; Dodger Stadium is the only Major League ballpark that is completely repainted every off-season. ◆ Amazingly, there have been just five playoffs because teams were tied after the regular season in the National League, and the Dodgers have been involved in all five: four league playoffs and one division playoff. The Dodgers have won only one of these playoffs, in 1959 against Milwaukee, while losing in 1946 to the Cardinals, in 1951 and 1962 to the Giants, and in 1980 to the Astros. In 1962, in an exact repeat of the circumstances 11 years earlier and a continent away in the Polo Grounds, the Dodgers went into the 9th inning of the third National League playoff game here leading 4–2 and ended up losing the pennant to the Giants. ◆ Dodger Stadium was designed by architect Emil Praeger to be easily expandable to 85,000 seats, simply by filling in the outfield with the decks that wrap around from foul pole to foul pole. That the Dodger management has never succumbed to greed and expanded the stadium, which is regularly filled, and that they have maintained it as a baseball-only park, is to their great credit. This is the only current ballpark to have never changed its capacity. It has held 56,000 seats each and every year since it opened in 1962. Along with the modernized Yankee Stadium, Dodger Stadium is a modern stadium that has somehow managed to retain the classical character of the old ballparks and thereby avoid the "concrete sterile ashtray" appearance of most modern-era stadia. The infield dirt and the outfield warning track are made up of 70 percent crushed red building brick and 30 percent mountain clay and calcium chlorate. There are beautiful palm trees beyond the fence down the foul lines. The see-through windows in the bullpen fence were installed in 1974. ♦ According to the groundskeeper here, although the center field 400 sign came down in 1980, it is still 400 feet to center: The two 395 signs are left and right of dead center. This causes most baseball publications to make the mistake of saying that it is only 395 feet to center here. There were no drinking fountains when the stadium was first built. The original design had a huge fountain in center field, like that now found in right center field at Royals Stadium. It was discovered that the foul poles installed in 1962 were completely in foul territory, instead of right along the foul lines in fair territory, where they are supposed to be. The Dodgers received special dispensation from the National League to make them fair, but only for the 1962 season. During the off-season, home plate was moved slightly so that the poles are now fair. ♦ Willie Stargell of the Pirates is the only man ever to hit a homer completely out of Dodger Stadium. He did this twice to right field, first on August 5, 1969 off Alan Foster for 506 feet 6 inches over the pavilion roof, and then again on May 8, 1973 off Andy Messersmith for 470 feet. That one landed on the pavilion roof and bounced over it and out of the park.

# MILWAUKEE, WISCONSIN

# COUNTY STADIUM

**OCCUPANTS**

National League Milwaukee Braves, April 14, 1953 to September 22, 1965; American League Milwaukee Brewers, April 7, 1970 to date

**NEUTRAL USES**

American League Chicago White Sox for nine 1968 games and eleven 1969 games May 15, 1968 to September 26, 1969

**CAPACITY**

35,911 (1953); 43,091 (1954); 43,110 (1955); 43,768 (1958); 43,827

(1959); 43,826 (1961); 47,611 (1970); 54,187 (1973); 53,192 (1975); 52,293 (1976); 53,192 (1979); 54,187 (1980); 53,192 (1981)

### LARGEST CROWD
56,562 on October 17, 1982 vs. the Cardinals

### SMALLEST CROWD
913 on May 4, 1965 vs. the Astros

### SURFACE
Bluegrass

### DIMENSIONS
Left field: 320 (1953); 315 (1975)
Short alleys: 355 (1953); 362 (1962)
Power alleys: 376 (1953); 374 (1955); 377 (1962)
Deep alleys: 397 (1953); 392 (1955)
Center field: 404 (1953); 410 (1954); 402 (1955)
Right field: 320 (1953); 315.37 (1954)
Backstop: 60

### FENCES
Left and center fields: 4 (wood, 1953); 8 (wood, 1955); 8.33 (wood, 1959); 10 (canvas padding, 1985)
Right field: 4 (wood, 1953); 10 (wood, 1955); 10 (canvas padding, 1985

### FORMER USE
The Story Stone Quarry

### PHENOMENA
For 20 years before the park was expanded in 1973, patients at the National Soldiers Home Veterans Administration Hospital sat outside their rooms on Mockingbird Hill overlooking right field and watched the games for free. Spruce and fir trees formed Perini's Woods behind the center field fence. Planted in 1954, the trees were replaced by bleacher seats in 1961. The Braves Reservation, a picnic area down the left field line, was inaugurated in 1961. It disappeared in the 1973 expansion. ◆ Whenever a Brewer hit a homer, Bernie Brewer used to slide into a huge beer stein in right center. Bernie was removed from the premises in 1985 by the security guards for having one too many. ◆ The only homer ever hit over the left field roof was by Jose Canseco. ◆ If you get section 21, row 35, seat 1,

ask for a different ticket. You're stuck right next to a brick chimney, and all that you can see is right field. (Except for section 21, row 35, seat 1, there is not a better place to see a ball game in America.) They have the best bratwurst and the best tailgate parties in all of baseball here.

## MINNEAPOLIS, MINNESOTA

# HUBERT H. HUMPHREY METRODOME

**A.K.A.**
Thunderdome, Sweat Box

**OCCUPANT**
American League Minnesota Twins, April 6, 1982 to date

**CAPACITY**
54,711 (1982); 55,122 (1983); 55,244 (1986); 55,883 (1989)

**LARGEST CROWD**
55,376 on October 25, 1987 vs. the Cardinals

**SURFACE**
SporTurf (1982–1986): Liveliest bounce by far in the Majors; Astro-Turf (1987 to date): Still pretty bouncy, but not quite as much so

**DIMENSIONS**
Left field: 344 (1982); 343 (1983)
Left center: 385
Center field: 407 (1982); 408 (1983)
Right center: 367
Right field: 326 (1982); 327 (1983)
Backstop: 60
Foul territory: Small

**FENCES**
Left field: 7 (canvas padding, 1982); 13 (6 plexiglass above 7 canvas padding, 1983)
Center field: 7 (thin canvas sheet, 1982)
Right field: 7 (canvas padding, 1982); 13 (6 thin canvas sheet over 7 canvas padding, 1983); 23 (16 thin canvas sheet over 7 canvas padding, 1985)
Apex of dome: 186

**M**etrodome, Minneapolis. Air pressure keeps up the roof and blows fans out the doors.

### PHENOMENA

This is a fascinating ballpark, even though it is a dome. There are five different areas where balls can bounce off the outfield walls in drastically different ways. In addition, the ball can bounce off all the speakers suspended from the air-supported roof and remain in play. The 7-foot center field fence is made of a thin sheet of canvas, with considerable give. A ball hitting the wall doesn't bounce very far, and sometimes it just dies. A center fielder jumping against it at the 408-foot mark can actually catch a ball hit 410 or 411 feet because the canvas gives a few feet as the center fielder crashes into it. The 23-foot right field fence, called the Hefty Bag, is a 16-foot thin sheet of canvas atop a 7-foot wall made of extremely hard canvas padding. The ball drops straight down off the top of the wall but bounces quickly off the lower portion of the wall. The 13-foot wall in left is formed of a 6-foot section of plexiglass atop a 7-foot wall made of much softer canvas padding. The ball rockets off the plexiglass, but bounces much more slowly off the soft canvas padding below. ◆ This is a power hitter's park, although its dimensions do not indicate this. In fact, the only dimensions that are smaller than normal are right center at 367 and right field at 327, both only 3 feet less than the normal 370 and 330 feet, respectively. ◆ A comparison of the Metrodome with the Astrodome in Houston is interesting. The Astrodome, with its reputation for being a pitcher's park with few home runs, is actually smaller than the Metrodome. The Astrodome is 13 feet shallower in left, 8 feet shallower in center, and 5 feet shallower in left center, while it is 13 feet deeper in right center and 3 feet deeper in right. In addition, the Metrodome's outfield walls are higher by 13 feet in right and right center and higher by 3 feet in left and left center, while lower only in center, by 3 feet. All one can say is that the ball evidently carries better in the Metrodome than in the Astrodome. ◆ The curvature of the wall behind the plate causes wild pitches and passed balls to bounce directly off the backstop directly toward first base. Evidently this is because the stadium is centered on the 50-yard line rather than on the baseball diamond. It is the only current Major League baseball park where a wild pitch or passed ball won't bounce straight back toward the plate. It was nicknamed the "Sweat Box" because it lacked air conditioning prior to June 28, 1983. Attendance soon increased significantly after the air conditioning was added. The white air-supported fabric Teflon roof makes it very difficult to see the ball when it is hit high in the air. Sections 107 to 113 are football seats, which in baseball season are tilted up and back to create a 40-foot wall behind the 23-foot right field fence. The roof collapsed

**M**etrodome, Minneapolis. A 23-foot wall was in right field.

in the fall of 1982 but was repaired quickly. Twins batter Randy Bush hit a ball off the roof in 1983. The ball was caught foul for an out by Blue Jays catcher Buck Martinez. On May 4, 1984, in the top of the 4th inning, A's batter Dave "King Kong" Kingman hit a ball that went through a hole in the two-layered Teflon-coated fiberglass roof. Twins third sacker John Castino and shortstop Houston Jiminez waited and waited, but the ball never came down. Kingman hit it out of the park but got only a double. The A's argued but never got their deserved home run ruling. ◆ Balls bounced very high off the carpet from 1982 to 1986 because of the SporTurf carpet. Yankee manager Billy Martin once protested a game here because he said the carpet turned pop fly singles into doubles. Mariners batter Jim Presley bounced a ball off the speaker behind the plate that was caught by Twins catcher Tom Nieto. There are more home runs when the air conditioning is turned off, which lends some credence to the possibility that the Mets were correct when they protested a 1965 game at the Astrodome. Then, they accused the Astros grounds crew of manipulating the air conditioning to help Astro long balls, and to slow down Mets long balls, as mentioned earlier. ◆ The American League playoffs and the World Series of 1987 set new decibel records for noise here in what came to be called the Thunderdome. A game on April 27, 1986 vs. the Angels was delayed in the 8th inning for 9 minutes as a violent rainstorm knocked out the lights and had the scoreboards and the roof swaying. Those present who were interviewed stated that it actually felt like the stadium was going to fall down.

# MONTREAL, QUEBEC

# STADE OLYMPIQUE

## A.K.A.
Olympic Stadium; Big Owe

## OCCUPANT
National League Expos de Montréal, April 15, 1977, to date

## CAPACITY
60,000 (1976); 58,838 (1977); 60,476 (1979); 59,511 (1980); 59,984 (1981); 58,838 (1982); 59,149 (1985); 59,123 (1987); 59,226 (1988); 59,149 (1989); 60,011 (1990); 60,111 (1991)

## LARGEST CROWD
59,282 on September 16, 1979 vs. the Cardinals

## SURFACE
Astroturf

## DIMENSIONS
Foul lines: 325 (1977); 330 (1981); 325 (1983)
Power alleys: 375
Center field: 404 (1977); 405 (1979); 404 (1980); 400 (1981); 404 (1983)
Backstop: 62 (1977); 65 (1983); 53 (1989)
Foul territory: Large

## FENCES
12 (wood, 1977); 12 (canvas padding, 1989)
Apex of dome, when the umbrella is down: 171

## PHENOMENA
Labatt's noise-meter high above right field is baseball's answer to the NBA Sacramento Kings' Arco Arena Noise-Meter. Unfortunately, the Expos fans don't usually approach the sound levels achieved in places like the Metrodome, Fenway, and Wrigley. ◆ One throwback to earlier days here is that fans can ride the subway to the ballpark. The only difference is that since this is a French-speaking city, the subway is called the metro. In order to go to the ballpark on the metro, you just get off at either the Pie IX or the Viau metro station. ◆ The tower, at 556 feet, is 1 foot taller than the Washington Monument. It is angled at 45 degrees vs. the 5 degrees for the Leaning Tower of Pisa in Italy; it is 50

stories tall vs. the 7 stories for the Leaning Tower of Pisa. Since the tower was finished, the roof has increased the offense by removing the extreme cold conditions in April, September, and October. ◆ The stadium was built for the 1976 Olympics. There is a plaque and statue at the main entrance dedicated to Jackie Robinson, who starred at the Delorimier Downs for the Montreal Royals in 1946. ◆ The 556-foot-high inclined tower in center field from section 766 in left center to section 767 in right center is the world's tallest inclined structure ever built. From the top, reached by a 2-minute funicular ride in a 90-passenger cable car, one can see for 50 miles. The tower holds an umbrella roof which is hoisted up on 26 cables to retract the roof or lowered on the cables to put on the roof in case of inclement weather. It takes 25 minutes to retract the roof or to lower it into place. The tower stood half-finished from 1976 to 1987 and finally became a retractable covered dome stadium in 1989. The retractable dome is silver on top, and orange on the bottom, with 26 white cones that link the roof to the tower. It consists of 60,696 square feet of Kevlar, weighing 50 tons. (Kevlar is the material used in army helmets used by airborne troops.) The roof was not retractable from 1987 until 1989 due to generator problems. ◆ Youppi has been the team mascot here since 1979. ◆ There were two rain delays here in 1989, despite the retractable roof. The roof cannot be deployed when the wind is greater than

**O**lympic Stadium, Montreal. Orange roof took 15 years to complete.

*Stade.Olympique, Montréal, Québec*

**O**lympic Stadium, Montreal, Quebec. An engineering marvel, but is it a ballpark?

25 miles per hour. So when unexpected rain comes, accompanied by winds higher than 25 miles per hour, the unique situation of a rain delay at a domed stadium results. Some unique game delays have occurred here. For example, in 1987, an 18-wheeler truck was in a pre-game parade and somehow managed to run right through the outfield fence. In the same year, there was an explosion followed by a fire in the huge Umbrella Roof Tower above center field. In 1985, some seals from a pre-game circus act refused to leave the outfield, and the grounds crew could not catch the slippery critters. The same thing happened later that year with a squirrel. In 1988, some of the 500 high school bands in a pre-game ceremony lost their music and had to go get extra scores. ◆ Dave Kingman and Darryl Strawberry have hit the technical ring, which surrounds the stadium on the inside of the roof. Kingman's was ruled foul but it could not be known for sure because there was no foul pole on the roof. As a result, an orange line was painted on the technical ring. Strawberry's drive to right field, similarly close to the foul line, hit the ring and was ruled fair only because of the orange line.

## NEW YORK, NEW YORK

# YANKEE STADIUM

### A.K.A.
American League Baseball Grounds, 1923; The House That Ruth Built

### OCCUPANTS
American League New York Yankees, April 18, 1923 to September 30, 1973; Negro National League New York Black Yankees, 1946–1948; American League New York Yankees April 15, 1976 to date

### CAPACITY
58,000 (1923); 62,000 (1926); 82,000 (1927); 67,113 (1928); 62,000 (1929); 71,699 (1937); 70,000 (1942); 67,000 (1948); 67,205 (1958); 67,337 (1961); 67,000 (1965); 65,010 (1971); 54,028 (1976); 57,145 (1977); 57,545 (1980)

### LARGEST CROWD
Total: 85,265, with 81,622 paid, on September 9, 1928 vs. the Athletics; Paid: 81,841, with 83,533 total, on May 30, 1938 vs. the Red

Sox; Current smaller configuration: 56,821 on October 14, 1976 vs. the Royals

## SMALLEST CROWD
413 on September 22, 1966 vs. the White Sox

## SURFACE
Merion bluegrass

## DIMENSIONS
Left field: 280.58 (1923); 301 (1928); 312 (1976); 318 (1988)
Left side of bullpen gate in short left center: 395 (1923); 402 (1928); 387 (1976); 379 (1985)
Right side of bullpen gate: 415 (1928)
Deep left center: 460 (1923); 457 (1937); 430 (1976); 411 (1985); 399 (1988)
Left side of center field screen: 466 (1937)
Center field: 490 (1923); 461 (1937); 463 (1967); 417 (1976); 410 (1985); 408 (1988)
Deep right center: 429 (1923); 407 (1937); 385 (1976)
Right side of bullpen gate: 344 (1937)
Right field: 294.75 (1923); 295 (1930); 296 (1939); 310 (1976); 314 (1988)
Backstop: 82 (1942); 80 (1953); 84 (1976)
Foul territory: Large backstop for the catcher, but small for fielders down the foul lines

## FENCES
Left field: 3.92 (3 wire above 0.92 concrete, 1923); 8 (canvas padding, 1976)
Left center: Left of visitors' bullpen—3.58 (3 wire above 0.58 concrete); Right of visitors' bullpen—7.83 (3 wire above 4.83 concrete); all of left center—7 (canvas padding, 1976)
Center field: Left of screen—13.83 (3 wire above 10.83 concrete, 1923); screen when up for hitters' background—20 (1953); 22.25 (1959); 22.42 (1954); screen when down—13.83; Right of screen—14.5 (3 wire above 11.5 concrete, 1923); all of center field—7 (canvas padding, 1976)
Right center: Left of home bullpen—7.83 (3 wire above 4.83 concrete, 1923); Right of home bullpen—3.58 (3 wire above 0.58 concrete, 1923); 8 (canvas padding, 1976); 9 (canvas padding, 1979)
Right field: 3.75 (3 wire above 0.75 concrete, 1923); 10 (canvas padding, 1976)

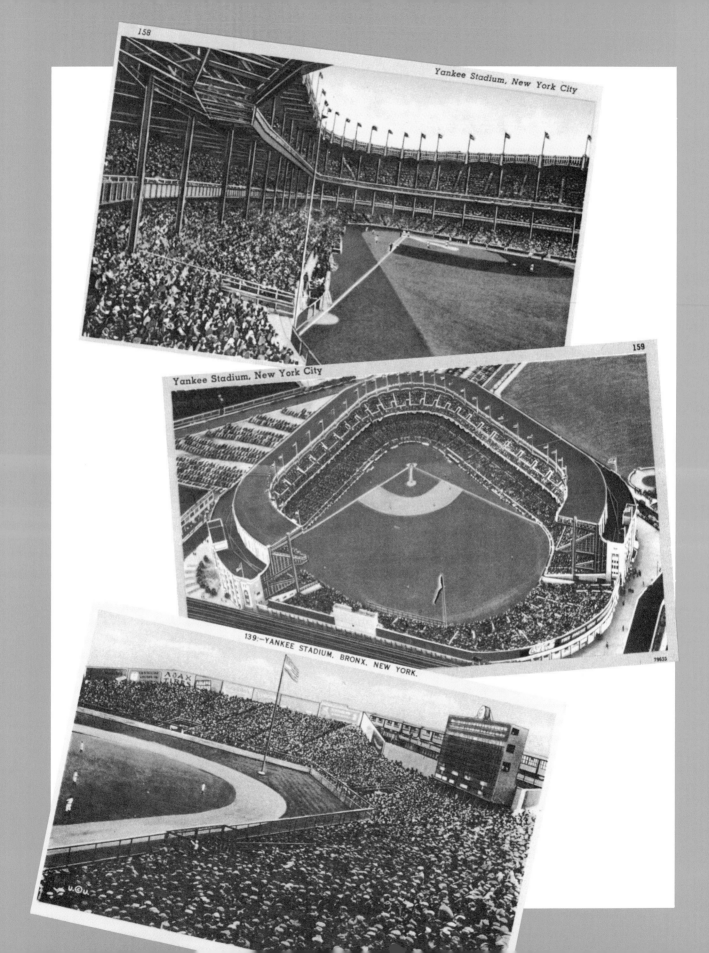

158      Yankee Stadium, New York City

Yankee Stadium, New York City      159

139.—YANKEE STADIUM, BRONX, NEW YORK.

## FORMER USE

City plot 2106, lot 100, a farm originally granted by the British before the Revolutionary War to Mr. John Lion Gardiner

## PHENOMENA

Casey Stengel once watched a long drive to center go past his center fielder and rattle around behind the monuments while his outfielder had trouble picking it up. Finally Casey yelled, "Ruth, Gehrig, Huggins, someone throw that darned ball in here NOW!" ◆ The current fence here is asymmetrical, but not because it was built that way. It is 8 feet high in left, 7 feet high in left center and in center, 9 feet high in right center, and 10 feet high in right. According to the Yankees, the fence itself is uniformly one height; the field itself slopes, which is the reason for the various heights in the outfield. This is surprising, since the field was completely reshaped during the 1974 to 1975 restorations, and one would have thought that the landscapers would have levelled off the field. That they did not adds to the mystique of this beautiful ballpark. ◆ The restoration of Yankee Stadium in 1974 and 1975 was one of baseball's finest moments. Baseball purists may argue that it was more beautiful before its renovation and that the restorers should have kept the dimensions the same as they had been, with the monuments in play, the 3-foot fences down the lines, the hugest and best bleachers ever built, the Death Valley in left center. Taxpayers may argue that it cost too much. But the alternative was the New Jersey Meadowlands Yankees. ◆ The pre-renovation Yankee Stadium lives on in Shelter Island, New York, home to a 500,000-piece, 2.5- by 3-foot model of the Stadium as it was in 1973, made by Brad Merila. The model took 8,000 hours and 16.5 years to construct. The tarpaulins are made out of drinking straws, the foul poles out of music wire, and the stadium itself out of balsa strips from $\frac{1}{16}$ to $\frac{1}{32}$ of an inch thick. ◆ No discussion of Yankee Stadium can be complete without a discussion of the 1983 Pine Tar Game, or perhaps we should say, games. With the Yanks leading Kansas City with two outs in the top of the 9th, the Royals, down to their last out, had a rally going when George Brett hit a dramatic home run to put Kansas City ahead. After Brett had circled the bases and retreated to the dugout, Yankee manager Billy Martin strolled out to the plate and politely asked the umpires to inspect Brett's bat to see whether the pine tar on it was illegally applied too far away from the handle. The umpires gathered around, inspected the bat, found that it was indeed illegal, and called Brett out and the game over. Brett and the entire Kansas City team came unglued, and the

Yankee Stadium, New York. Top: 296 feet to right field. Middle: The house that Babe Ruth built. Bottom: 490 feet to center field.

police had to escort the umpires to their dressing room. The Royals manager calmed down just enough to officially protest the game. In one of those decisions that keeps the national pastime so interesting, American League President Lee MacPhail overruled the umpires, upheld the Royals' protest, stated that the punishment for an illegal bat should not be to take away the home run but to disallow the illegal bat's further use, and ordered the game to be continued on the Royals' next trip to New York. Then it was discovered that the Royals didn't have any more trips to New York that year, and they were ordered to travel to New York to finish the last four outs of the game, and any possible extra innings, on August 18, 1983. Brett, having been thrown out of the game after it was over way back when, was not even present for the game's conclusion. As the Yankees took the field, Billy Martin went out and appealed to the home plate umpire that Brett had never touched the plate. The umpire said that he had touched the plate. There were so few fans that everyone could hear Martin's loud reply, "How do you know, you weren't even here at that game?" Unfortunately for Martin, the umpire pulled out of his back pocket an officially notarized legal document, in which the home plate umpire who had been present 2

**Y**ankee Stadium, New York. After the renovation, the famed facade moved to the outfield.

**Y**ankee Stadium, New York. A short home run to right, but what about Death Valley in center?

months before, swore that Brett had indeed touched home plate.

Finally realizing that he had lost the argument, Martin retreated to the dugout. Hal McRae promptly made the third out of the top of the 9th, and Dan Quisenberry promptly retired the Yankees 1-2-3 in the bottom of the 9th. The longest and most controversial game in baseball history was finally over. ♦ Center field monuments and plaques were in fair territory before the 1974 to 1975 renovation: Lou Gehrig on the left, Miller Huggins in the middle, and Babe Ruth on the right. The monuments were just left of straightaway center and were in the deepest part of the park. However, the fence was not marked there, so we do not know exactly what the measurement was to dead center from 1937 to 1973. The 1937 to 1966 mark of 461 and the 1967 to 1973 mark of 463 are cited as the center field measurements for that time period, but these marks were actually 20 or 30 feet to the right of dead center. Straightaway center, to the wall behind the monuments and the flagpole, was probably around 475 to 480 feet from 1937 to 1973. Since 1976, the same monuments and plaques unfortunately have been hidden behind a succession of shorter and shorter fences as Yankee Stadium's distinctive left center field Death Valley has been destroyed. Hopefully the Yankees will someday remove the ugly inner fences and return the light of day and proper visibility to these monuments and plaques, which provide so much of the legendary mystique to this historic ballfield. There are also plaques beyond the fence dedicated to Ed Barrow, Jacob Ruppert, Joe DiMaggio, Mickey Mantle, Casey Stengel, Joe McCarthy, Pope Paul VI, Thurman Munson, Pope John Paul II, and Billy Martin. ◆ At the opening ceremonies on April 18, 1923, the Yanks defeated the Red Sox 4–1 before a crowd of 74,217. An additional 20,000 fans were turned away at the gates. ◆ Yankee Stadium has witnessed some of baseball's most emotional good-byes: Babe Ruth on June 13, 1948, and Lou Gehrig on July 4, 1939. Their legends live on in this hallowed stadium. ◆ In 1937, Joe DiMaggio caught a Hank Greenberg drive behind the flagpole in center. The flagpole was located approximately 10 feet in front of the 461 mark on the center field fence; before the 1937 renovation, the flagpole had been about 25 feet in front of the 490 mark in center. The Bloody Angle was a unique area down the right field foul line that existed only during the 1923 inaugural season. Because of the layout of the diamond during 1923, the right field foul line and the right field wall met at such a crazy angle that right fielders could never tell where the ball would bounce. During the winter of 1923 to 1924, home plate was moved 13 feet to eliminate the problem, and the dimensions of the outfield remained the same. ◆ Yankee Stadium has witnessed the most famous 60th and 61st homers ever hit. On September 30, 1927, Babe Ruth hit his 60th off Senators pitcher Tom Zachary; the ball landed 2 feet fair in the first row near the right field foul pole. On October 1, 1961, Roger Maris hit his 61st off Red Sox pitcher Tracy Stallard; it landed in box 163D of section 33 in right field. And, yes, there are asterisks involved. The Yankees played 154 games in 1927; Ruth played in 150. The Yankees played 163 games in 1961 (one tie game and 162 that were won or lost); Maris played in 161. A ball hitting the foul pole in the 1930s was in play, not a homer. ◆ Huge twin patriotic eagle emblems used to hang at the main gate. ◆ During the 1930s and 1940s, a green curtain screen in center field was sometimes raised and lowered like a window shade to give Yankee batters much better visibility than the visiting batters. The shade forced visiting batters to face a background of white-shirted bleacher fans but allowed Yankee hitters to face a dark green background. If a Yankee slugger ever hit one toward the screen, it was quickly lowered so as not to prevent a home run, but these occasions were rare because the screen was so distant from the plate: 466 feet. It was removed during the World Series to sell more seats.

*Mickey Mantle Day–Yankee Stadium*

**Y**ankee Stadium, New York. Mickey Mantle's #7 is retired on June 8, 1969.

◆ The bleachers in right center were often called Ruthville and Gehrigville. There are huge outer cathedral windows, making this beautiful ballpark seem all the more like a church. The warning track in 1923 consisted of red cinders and was used for important track events. Later on, red brick dust replaced the cinders. Before the 1974–75 renovation, extra grass was kept near the monuments, in play in center field. Underneath second base there was a 15-foot-deep brick-lined vault with electrical, telephonic, and telegraph connections for boxing and religious events. The vault was removed in the renovation. ◆ As originally constructed, from May 5, 1922 to April 18, 1923, three concrete decks extended from behind home plate to each corner, with a single deck in left center, and wooden bleachers around the rest of the outfield. In the winter of 1927–28, second and third decks were added to left center, and several rows of box seats were removed in left, extending the foul line from 281 to 301. In the winter of 1936–37, the wooden bleachers were replaced with concrete ones. During the 1937 season, second and third decks were added in right. The bleacher changes shortened straight-away center from 490 to 461. Auxiliary scoreboards were built in the late 1940s, which covered up the 367 right center sign and the 415 left center sign. Minor modifications were made in the winter

**Y**ankee Stadium, New York. This is a 2 × 3-foot balsa wood model made by Brad Merila.

of 1966–1967. During this work, new 463 and 433 signs appeared in the power alleys, and the exterior was painted blue and white. ◆ According to eyewitnesses, Josh Gibson hit the only fair ball out of Yankee Stadium, near the left field foul pole in a 1934 Negro National League doubleheader. Some people consider this just a story. Three participants in the 1982 Ashland Oil Company–sponsored reunion of Negro League veterans in Ashland, Kentucky, independently confirmed that they had seen this event. ◆ There is another interesting story concerning the possibility of another fair ball hit out of the park, in approximately the same spot. Mickey Mantle remembers being on the Yankee bench sometime in the mid-1960s during a rainy late-season game against Washington. Senators slugger Frank Howard hit a ball that Mantle says went out of the park fair, near the left field foul pole. Yankee left fielder Frank White agrees, remembering well the mammoth smash. Playing left at the time, White says he didn't even move his feet; he just turned around to see how far it would go. He and Mantle both remember that hundreds of kids looked all over the third deck for about 25 minutes and never found the ball. The umpire, having lost the ball in the rain and fog and the glare of the lights, waited for a moment to see if he could see where the ball was found. When the ball was not recovered, he ruled it a foul ball. There was no argument; everyone just seemed to want to finish the game. ◆ Mantle himself hit a ball off Kansas City pitcher Bill Fischer that missed clearing the 108-foot 1-inch-high roof in right center by only 6 inches on May 22, 1963. Because this ball was out in the power alley (around two-thirds of the way from the 296 mark at the right field foul pole to the 394 mark or around 360 feet from home plate) it might have been more powerful than either Gibson's or Howard's hits, since they apparently cleared the roof right down the left field foul line, where the distance from the plate was then only 301 feet. It has been calculated that if Mantle's hit, still rising when it hit the third deck facade, had cleared the roof and left Yankee Stadium, it would have traveled approximately 620 feet. ◆ During the 1974–1975 renovation, the beautiful copper art deco frieze facade that encircled the entire roof was removed. A portion was placed atop the bleachers in center. It might be best to be thankful that at least a portion of this distinctive piece of the historic ballpark was saved. It can also be argued that it was a sacrilege to have tampered with it at all. ◆ Dodgers left fielder Al Gionfriddo made his great World Series catch here, which caused the normally unemotional Joe DiMaggio to kick the dirt as he was running between first and second base and saw what he thought was a home run turn into just a long out.

# SHEA STADIUM

**A. K. A.**

Flushing Meadow Stadium, 1964; William A. Shea Municipal Stadium

**OCCUPANTS**

National League New York Mets, April 17, 1964 to date; American League New York Yankees, April 6, 1974 to September 28, 1975

**CAPACITY**

55,000 (1964); 55,300 (1965); 56,000 (1968); 55,300 (1969); 55,601 (1986); 55,300 (1988); 55,601 (1990)

**LARGEST CROWD**

59,083 on July 9, 1969 vs. the Cubs

**SURFACE**

Bluegrass

**DIMENSIONS**

Foul lines: 330 (marked, 1964); 341 (actual, 1964); 341 (marked, 1965); 338 (1979)
Power alleys: 371
Center field: 410
Backstop: 80
Foul territory: Very large

**FENCES**

Foul lines: 16.33 (4 wire and railing above 12.33 brick, 1964); 12.33 (brick, 1965); 8 (wood, 1979)
Power alleys: 8 (wood)
Center field: A small section 8.83 (wood), mostly 8 (wood)

**PHENOMENA**

This stadium was designed to be expandable to 90,000 seats, by simply completing the three decks all the way around the outfield. After its successful initial season in 1964, plans were made to add a dome and 15,000 seats, but engineering studies showed that the foundation would not support the proposed dome. ◆ Shea is the noisiest outdoor stadium, because airplanes landing and taking off from La Guardia Airport fly right over the ballfield. The noise is often so deafening that radio and television broadcasts of games cannot be heard when the planes are overhead. ◆ A good seat is loge section 31, box 483A, seat 1, right on top of the right field foul

**S**hea Stadium, New York. Left: Home of the 1969 Miracle Mets. Middle: The largest scoreboard in the Majors. Right: Take the IRT No. 7 for NL baseball in New York.

pole. Throughout the game, you can wonder why the pole is called the foul pole if it is in fair territory. ◆ The park is named for attorney William A. Shea, who obtained the Mets franchise for New York. ◆ The right center field scoreboard is the largest in the Majors: 86 feet high with a Bulova clock on top, about 25 feet behind the outfield fence, and 175 feet long. ◆ There are practice facilities under the right field stands. ◆ Behind the fence in center, just to the right of the 410 mark, is a Mets Magic Top Hat. When a Met hits a homer, a red Big Apple rises out of the black top hat, which actually looks more like a big kettle. ◆ In Shea's inaugural season, there were two ways for a ball hit down the foul lines to get embroiled in controversy. The first was for it to bounce fair and then roll into foul territory. If the ball bounced off the outfield fence in foul territory, it could roll around a corner where the extra football seats were stored and still be in play. The left fielder or right fielder would have to go around the corner and chase down the ball in among the football seats, then race back around the corner and fire the ball back to the infield. All the while, he would be out of view of the umpires, all of the players except the center fielder, most of the fans, and most importantly, the base runners. Many would-be doubles became triples and inside-the-park home runs. Unfortunately, this interesting situation was eliminated by the creation of a screen fence, which kept such balls from bouncing around the corner. When baseball has controversy, it is alive. The

fans are arguing, booing, or cheering; the managers and umpires
are having a good, old-fashioned rhubarb; and all is well with the
national pastime. When all controversy is eliminated, as with the
construction of this little screen fence, the fans and the game of
baseball suffer. The second way for controversy to erupt in 1964
was for a ball to be hit down the foul line for a home run. The fences
down the foul lines were 16.33 feet high, with a 4-foot wire screen
atop a 12.33-foot brick wall, with a railing above the wire. Many
balls would go through the railing and be home runs; others would
bounce off the railing and be ruled in play. To eliminate this problem,
the foul lines from 1965 to 1978 had an orange home run line painted
at the top of the 12.33-foot brick wall. Any ball hitting the 4-foot
wire screen and railing above the orange line was a homer. Like a
similar ground rule at Crosley Field in Cincinnati in center field,
this caused many controversies, so in 1979 an inner 8-foot wooden
fence was installed. ◆ There is a church-like spire beyond the center field fence with a "Serval Zippers" sign. ◆ Shea has by far the
worst visibility for batters in the Majors. ◆ The outfield fences are
also marked as 358 and 396. From 1973 to 1979, there were also
distance markers, outside the field of play: 428 on the rear bullpen
walls, 442 at the base of the left center light tower, 420 at the
bottom edge of the right center field scoreboard on the center field
side, and 405 on the right field side.

## OAKLAND, CALIFORNIA

# OAKLAND-ALAMEDA COUNTY COLISEUM

**O**akland Coliseum, Oakland. Better teams and ownership have made this a great place to see a game.

### A.K.A.
Oakland Coliseum Complex; Oakland Mausoleum, 1970s

### OCCUPANT
American League Oakland Athletics, April 17, 1968 to date

### CAPACITY
50,000 (1968); 49,649 (1977); 50,255 (1981); 50,219 (1983); 50,255 (1985); 50,219 (1986); 49,219 (1987); 50,219 (1988); 49,219 (1989); 48,219 (1990); 47,450 (1991)

### LARGEST CROWD
Total: 50,164 on April 17, 1968 vs. the Orioles; Paid: 49,671 for the All Star Game on July 14, 1987

### SMALLEST CROWD
653 on April 17, 1979 vs. the Mariners

### SURFACE
Bluegrass

### DIMENSIONS
Foul lines: 330
Power alleys: 378 (1968); 375 (1969); 372 (1981)
Center field: 410 (1968); 400 (1969); 396 (1981); 397 (1982); 400 (1990)
Backstop: 90 (1968); 60 (1969)
Foul territory: Huge, largest in the Majors

### FENCES
8 (plywood, 1968); 10 (plywood and plexiglass, 1981); 8 (canvas padding, 1986)

### PHENOMENA
The Athletics ownership, the same people who run Levi Straus, have managed to create a fun picnic atmosphere which is the best among the new concrete circular stadia. For those who remember the days (just a short decade ago) when the A's almost always lost and the crowds could often be counted in the hundreds, the transformation is incredible. The stadium was known as the Oakland Mausoleum during the sad days in the late 1970s when the A's

stunk, the fans were few, the scoreboard and the toilets and the public address system and most everything else didn't work, and every part of the stadium was ugly grey concrete and deathly quiet, even when the A's had a rally going. ◆ In 1986, an old-fashioned hand operated scoreboard was installed that shows all the Major League line scores. The A's management understands the soul of baseball. The ballpark is surrounded by beautiful green ivy slopes. The backstop is in a notch cut in the stands. Charlie O. the mule was here in the late 1960s. The A's serve by far the best food in organized baseball. The steel shell of the pitcher's mound was exposed on opening day April 17, 1968 and had to keep being covered between innings. The right field scoreboard was installed in June 1968. ◆ Fly balls do not carry well here at night. This, coupled with a huge amount of foul territory, reduces batting averages by roughly 5 to 7 points, making this the best pitchers' park in the American League. ◆ Upcoming home stands shown on the new Diamond Vision scoreboard show the A's destroying visiting teams. ◆ Fans sitting at the foul poles can catch home run fair balls by reaching in front of the foul pole screens.

**O**akland Coliseum, Oakland. A pitcher's park with plenty of foul ground to snag errant pop flies.

# PHILADELPHIA, PENNSYLVANIA

# VETERANS STADIUM

**A. K. A.**
Vet

**OCCUPANT**
National League Philadelphia Phillies, April 10, 1971 to date

**CAPACITY**
56,371 (1971); 55,730 (1973); 56,581 (1974); 58,651 (1977); 65,454 (1981); 66,507 (1983); 66,744 (1985); 66,271 (1986); 64,538 (1987); 62,382 (1988); 64,538 (1989); 62,382 (1990)

**LARGEST CROWD**
67,064 on October 16, 1983 vs. the Orioles

**SURFACE**
AstroTurf-8: Fast, but slower since a new rug was installed in 1977

**DIMENSIONS**
Foul lines: 330
Power alleys: 371
Center field: 408
Backstop: 60
Foul territory: Large

**V**eterans Stadium, Philadelphia. Where the Phillies finally captured the World Series title in 1980.

**V**eterans Stadium, Philadelphia. The largest NL park, with an arena and football stadium just a few parking lots over.

### FENCES

6 (wood, April 1971 except for plastic tarp over the right field wall); 6 (wood all the way around the outfield, May 1971); 8 (wood, June 1971); 12 (6 plexiglass above 6 wood, 1972)

### PHENOMENA

"I stand at the plate in the Vet in Philadelphia, and I don't honestly know whether I'm in Pittsburgh, Cincinnati, St. Louis, or Philly. They all look alike."—Richie Hebner's comment on new stereotypical ashtray stadia is the most eloquent argument for a return from symmetric plastic multipurpose stadia to asymmetric, real baseball parks. The rounded rectangular shape is called an octorad by the architectural profession. ◆ Don't sit in the lower deck in left field, section 350, row 14, seat 3 because every time the ball is hit up in the air, the second deck will come between you and the ball. ◆ The Vet serves the smallest hot dogs in baseball. ◆ A plastic tarp covered the unfinished right field wall in April 1971. Fly balls hitting the plastic would just drop down and lie still at the base of the wall. ◆ Outside the park, you can find a statue of Connie Mack, and another of a sliding base runner. ◆ A Liberty Bell used to hang from the center field roof level. It was hit only once: by Greg Luzinski on May 16, 1972. ◆ During Opening Day festivities, a baseball was dropped from a helicopter to the Phillies catcher on April 10, 1971.

# PITTSBURGH, PENNSYLVANIA

# THREE RIVERS STADIUM

## A.K.A.

The House that Clemente Built; Delaware Indian Burial Ground; Kilbuck Island; Where the Cheese Dip Runneth Over; Skunk Heaven

## OCCUPANT

National League Pittsburgh Pirates, July 16, 1970 to date

## CAPACITY

50,500 (1970); 50,235 (1971); 50,364 (1979); 50,230 (1980); 54,499 (1981); 54,598 (1983); 54,490 (1984); 54,429 (1985); 54,438 (1986); 58,727 (1988); 58,729 (1990)

## LARGEST CROWD

57,533 on October 10, 1991 vs. the Braves

## SURFACE

TartanTurf, 1970–1982; AstroTurf, 1983 to date

## DIMENSIONS

Foul lines: 340 (1970); 335 (1975)
Power alleys: 385 (1970); 375 (1975)
Center field: 410 (1970); 400 (1975)
Backstop: 60
Foul territory: Large

## FENCES

10 (wood)

## PHENOMENA

On December 3, 1987, a fan drove his car into the stadium and overturned a 70-gallon jug of cheese dip. ◆ The stadium is built on a site that was an island during the French and Indian Wars. It was an Indian burial ground, a fact discovered when the Big Flood of 1763 uncovered many graves. General George Washington fought here during one of the many battles over the nearby fort, which was first called Fort Duquesne by the French and then renamed Fort Pitt by the British. The area was named Kilbuck Island after a friendly Delaware Indian chief. The back channels of the Allegheny River filled up with silt, and the site was no longer an island by 1852. ◆ The Phillies-Pirates game here on May 3, 1986 was delayed in the top of the 7th inning when a skunk wandered out onto the playing field and successfully evaded his human pursuers for 7 minutes. There are rumored to be a group of skunks that live permanently under the stands, perhaps feeding on dropped peanuts and other food. ◆ The Honus Wagner statue, which used to stand beyond the left field bleachers, between old Forbes Field and the Carnegie Museum, now stands outside of Three Rivers Stadium. Babe Ruth's 714th home run and Billy Mazeroski's World Series–winning home run in 1960 are commemorated in the stadium's Allegheny Club, an 8-by 12-foot area of the 406-foot marker section of the Forbes Field brick wall where Mazeroski's ball left the park. ◆ Erik Sirdo created an original design for this stadium called "Stadium over the Monongahela." The stadium would have been a bridge, standing above two parking lot levels, all sitting above the Monongahela River, with plenty of room for boats to pass beneath. ◆ There are numbers painted on the four seats in the right field upper deck where Willie Stargell's longest homers have landed. Only seven home runs have ever been hit into the 70-foot-high upper deck at Three Rivers. Stargell's four came off Mets pitcher Ron Taylor on August 9, 1970; off Cubs pitcher Ken Holtzman on May 30, 1971; off Expos pitcher Howie Reed on June 30, 1971; and off Braves pitcher Gary Gentry on May 31, 1973. The three others were hit by Bob Robertson off Padres pitcher Steve Arlin to left field on July 16, 1971; by the Phillies Greg Luzinski off Pirates pitcher Don Robinson to left field on April 18, 1979; and by Bobby Bonilla off Padres pitcher Eric Show to right field on July 12, 1987. ◆ Without the inner fence, the outfield would be 342 down the lines and 434 to center.

**T**hree Rivers Stadium, Pittsburgh. Built near the site of a nineteenth-century park.

Eliminating the inner fence would make this a much better and more interesting ballpark. The first World Series night game was played here vs. the Orioles on October 13, 1971. Pittsburgh had also hosted the first All Star night game, at Forbes Field, in 1944, and would later host the first night League Championship Series game on October 7, 1975.

## ST. LOUIS, MISSOURI

# BUSCH STADIUM II

**A. K. A.**
Civic Center Stadium 1966; Busch Memorial Stadium 1966–1983

**OCCUPANT**
National League St. Louis Cardinals, May 12, 1966 to date

**CAPACITY**
49,275 (1966); 49,450 (1967); 50,126 (1971); 50,100 (1974); 50,126 (1975); 50,222 (1980); 53,138 (1987); 54,224 (1988); 54,727 plus 1,500 standing room for a total of 56,227 (1990). This is the only current Major League ballpark that counts standing room in its official capacity figure.

**LARGEST CROWD**
55,347 on October 20, 21, and 22, 1987 vs. the Minnesota Twins

**SMALLEST CROWD**
1,519 on September 14, 1989 vs. the Pirates

**SURFACE**
Grass, 1966–1969; AstroTurf on all but the normally dirt part of the infield, 1970–1976; entirely AstroTurf with dirt only in the sliding pits around the bases, 1977–1983; new AstroTurf-8 carpet, 1984 to date

**DIMENSIONS**
Foul lines: 330
Power alleys: 386 (1966); 376 (1973); 386 (1977); 383 (chicken wire basket extends out 3 feet from a height of 8.50 feet to 10.50 feet since July 1983); 378 (1992)

Center field: 414 (1966); 410 (1971); 414 (1972); 404 (1973); 414 (1977); 402 (1992)

Backstop: 64. Vin Scully's unofficial measurements during the 1985 World Series showed this to be 50 feet rather than 64 feet.

Foul territory: Large

## FENCES

Left and right fields: 10.5 (padded canvas, 1966); 8 (padded canvas, 1992)

Center field: 10.5 (padded canvas, 1966); 8 (wood, 1973); 10.5 (padded canvas, 1977); 8 (padded canvas, 1992)

## PHENOMENA

From 1970 to 1976, the entire field was carpeted except for the part of the infield normally dirt on a grass field. In 1977, this was carpeted except for the sliding pits. This is one of two instances where there was a full dirt infield, with an otherwise fully carpeted field; the other was Candlestick Park in 1971. Since a new AstroTurf-8 carpet was installed in 1984, the pitcher's mound drops into the ground with a push of a button. Open arches surround the field at the roof line, 130 feet above the playing field, allowing fans in the upper deck behind first base and the right field foul line to see the beautiful Gateway Arch towering over left field. ◆ The right field scoreboard light showed a cardinal in flight from 1966 to 1982 when a Cardinal hit a home run. The same show was put on each time Lou Brock set a new base-stealing record. ◆ The St. Louis Sports Hall of Fame is on level 3 near gate 6. The statue of Stan Musial was unveiled in 1968 and stands outside the stadium. The chicken wire basket, like that at Wrigley Field, was installed in front of the left center field and right center field bleacher sections in July 1983. It is 2 feet high and protrudes 3 feet into the outfield, reducing the home run distance by 3 feet, from 386 to 383 in the power alleys. It does not raise the height of the 10.50-foot wall, however, because it starts 8.50 feet above the ground. There is no basket in front of the center field bleacher section since this section is used only for football. ◆ "Take Me Out to the Ball Game" is not sung during the 7th inning stretch. Instead, the Clydesdale horses gallop on the scoreboard, and the organ plays the King of Beers theme song. "Take Me Out to the Ball Game" is sung in the middle of the 8th inning.

# SAN DIEGO, CALIFORNIA

# SAN DIEGO JACK MURPHY STADIUM

### A.K.A.
San Diego Stadium, 1969–1980; Jack Murphy Stadium; The Murph

### OCCUPANT
National League San Diego Padres, April 8, 1969 to date

### CAPACITY
50,000 (1967); 44,790 (1973); 47,634 (1974); 47,491 (1976); 48,460 (1977); 51,362 (1979); 48,443 (1980); 51,362 (1981); 51,319 (1983); 58,671 (1984); 58,433 (1986); 59,022 (1990); 59,254 (1991)

### LARGEST CROWD
58,359 on October 7, 1984 vs. the Cubs

### SMALLEST CROWD
1,413 on September 11, 1973 vs. the Astros

### SURFACE
Santa Ana Bermuda grass

### DIMENSIONS
Foul lines: 330 (1969); 327 (fence, 1982); 329 (foul poles, 1982)
Power alleys: 375 (1969); 370 (1982)
Center field: 420 (1969); 410 (1973); 420 (1978); 405 (1982)
Backstop: 80 (1969); 75 (1982)

### FENCES
Left and right fields: 17.5 (concrete, 1969); 9 (line painted on concrete, 1973); 18 (concrete, 1974); 8.2 (canvas padding, 1982)
Center field: 17.5 (concrete, 1969); 10 (wood, 1973); 18 (concrete, 1978); 8.2 (canvas padding, 1982); 8.7 (one small section in right center, canvas padding, 1982)

### FORMER USE
The wide and shallow San Diego River used to run through the whole area, which was then a marshy swampland. The river is now diverted through the area south of the stadium, behind first base.

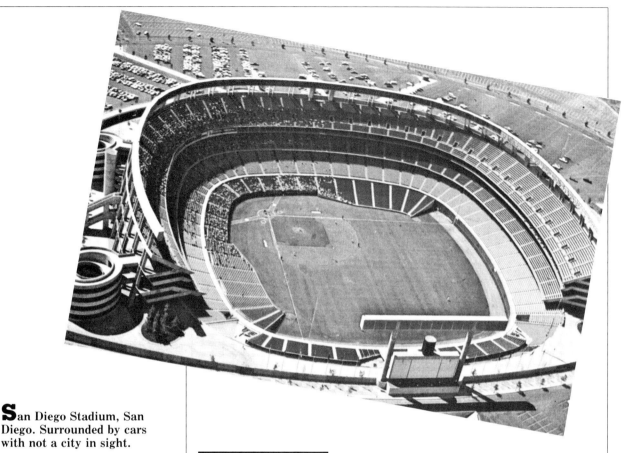

**S**an Diego Stadium, San Diego. Surrounded by cars with not a city in sight.

## PHENOMENA

Jack Murphy Stadium is the only Major League ballpark, and the Padres are the only Major League franchise, to have hosted a night for a former Negro League ball player. In tribute to one of the greatest pitchers of all time, Chet Brewer Night was held in July 1989 for a game vs. the Chicago Cubs, shortly before Mr. Brewer passed away at the age of 85. Chet, who but for the lack of Negro League statistics, would probably be recognized for having chalked up over 600 victories in his long career with the Kansas City Monarchs (more than Cy Young's 511), was wheeled to home plate by his wife Tina. ◆ Jack Murphy Stadium is named for the sports editor who successfully campaigned to bring Major League baseball to San Diego. ◆ The Padres' most famous fan is Ted Giannoulas, also known as the San Diego Chicken. The foul poles sit 2 feet behind the fence and 1 foot in front of the wall. This means that it is possible for a curving fly ball to leave the park fair as a home run, but pass to the foul side of the foul pole. Many Padres fans will tell you that this has happened on several occasions. ◆ The right center scoreboard sits directly behind the right center seats. Before the 1983 expansion, the scoreboard was so hot that fans there could easily feel the heat on their backs. ◆ This is the only Major League park where the bullpen dirt area touches the foul lines. On Thursday afternoon games, a man usually sits in the first row of the left field seats with The Claw. The Claw is a homemade invention which he lowers down the left field concrete wall over the top of home run balls that have cleared the inner fence but not the wall. He pushes a button, and The Claw collapses on the ball, enabling the man to reel in his catch. ◆ This is the only place in the universe where a foul ball can be caught out of sight of all umpires and all players except the center fielder and those sitting in the bullpen. This location is in either bullpen near the foul poles. Second base umpires have to run fast to be able to see such catches. ◆ The stadium was expanded during the 1983 and 1984 seasons by extending the three decks across from left center to center field and further down the right field foul line, and adding a permanent section of bleachers in right and right center, which replaced the two temporary sections of bleachers that had perched since 1967 on a grassy bank out in right center. Amazingly, the expansion was ready just in time to witness the Padres rally from a two-game deficit to win three straight here from the Cubs to capture the 1984 pennant. ◆ Ivy was planted on the center field fence in 1980. Why it was taken down afterward is not known, but the ivy should be put back. ◆ From July to October 1978, there was a 20-foot-wide black batters' eye section on both the center field wall and the inner center field fence. When the playoffs and the World Series came here in 1984, huge parts of left field and left center were horribly ugly because the grass had died underneath where the third base seats swivel around for San Diego State and Charger football games. These areas were actually painted green for the playoffs against the Cubs and for the World Series against the Tigers. The next year, an outstanding groundskeeper was hired, and the grass at The Murph has been beautiful and healthy year round ever since. ◆ In the 1960s, this was the first grass multipurpose stadium to sod the infield with grass after the last baseball game of the season and then remove it after the last football game of the season. In the winter of 1989 to 1990, a beautiful mural was built behind the right center field scoreboard, showing thousands of fans cheering in a stadium. ◆ Only seven batters have homered into the second deck in left field: Kevin Mitchell, Chris James, Kevin McReynolds, Dick Allen, Ivan Murrell, Nate Colbert, and Dave Kingman.

# SAN FRANCISCO, CALIFORNIA

# CANDLESTICK PARK

### A.K.A.
The 'Stick; Maury's Lake; Cave of the Winds; Windtunnel; Croix de Candlestick; North Pole

### OCCUPANT
National League San Francisco Giants, April 12, 1960 to date

### CAPACITY
43,765 (1960); 42,553 (1961); 42,500 (1965); 58,000 (1972); 59,080 (1975); 58,000 (1976); 62,000 (1989)

### LARGEST CROWD
62,084 on October 9, 1989 vs. the Cubs

### SMALLEST CROWD
748 on September 16, 1974 vs. the Braves

### SURFACE
Bluegrass (1960); Astroturf except for dirt in the infield (1971); Astroturf with no dirt in the infield except for the sliding pits at first, second, and third bases (1972); bluegrass (1979)

### DIMENSIONS
Left field: 330 (1960); 335 (1968)
Left center: 397 (1960); 365 (1961)
Center field: 420 (1960); 410 (1961); 400 (1982)
Right center: 397 (1960); 375 (1961); 365 (1982)
Right field: 330 (1960); 335 (1968)
Backstop: 73 (1960); 70 (1961); 66 (1975); 65 (1982); 66 (1985)
Foul territory: Large

### FENCES
10 (wire, 1960); 8 (wire, 1972); 12 (6 canvas padding below 6 plexiglass, 1975); 9 (6 canvas padding below 3 plexiglass, 1982); 9 (wire, 1984); 9.5 (the 59 fence posts in fair territory, 1984)

### FORMER USE
Candlestick Point, with its rock outcroppings, was leveled to fill in the water to create parking lots.

**C**andlestick Park, San Francisco. The windiest ballpark ever after expansion.

### PHENOMENA

The park is named for the jagged rocks and trees that rose from the surrounding tidelands like giant candlesticks. ◆ In 1957, San Francisco Mayor Christopher showed New York Giants owner Horace Stoneham around the projected site for this ballpark in the morning on purpose (it's not very windy here in the morning). The wind, cold, and fog here are well known, but too much has been made of it. The Giants have the windiest, coldest, and foggiest ballpark in the Major Leagues. So what? Somebody has to. ◆ The most intelligent thing anybody has ever done about the wind here is to turn it into a strategic advantage. In 1989, Giants manager Roger Craig, knowing that the wind and cold had been used as an excuse for the Giants incompetence for long enough, banned his players from making any negative comments about the weather at

the 'Stick. He said Vince Lombardi used the cold and the snow to his advantage in Green Bay, and that he could do the same with the cold and the wind at Candlestick. To the tune of "Hum Baby," Craig's all-purpose phrase for optimism, the Giants proceeded to win the 1989 National League pennant. ◆ Bay View Hill overlooks the park from behind third base. If you sit in section 1, row 10, seat 22, be prepared to crane your neck. Even though you are sitting right behind the plate, the pole holding up the screen behind the plate obstructs your view. ◆ Many fans arrived by boat in the 1960s. Before the park was completely enclosed, so many fans would stream out of the bleachers in right center when Mays and McCovey batted and crowd up against the flimsy cyclone fence, that a white line was painted on the asphalt 20 feet behind the fence. Fans had to stand behind this line. ◆ Kids still tumble out of their seats to chase homers that land between the fence and the seats, but since the park was enclosed this now happens in left center. ◆ It was to have been the only hot-water-heated open air stadium in history, but the natural gas–fired boiler system with 35,000 feet of 0.75-inch pipe failed to work in 1960. When told how much it would cost to fix the system and make it operational, the city and the Giants decided to make do with the only nonoperational hot-water-heated open air stadium in history. ◆ Fifty-nine posts every 20 feet or so on the outfield fence can cause strange bounces. The post tips extend 6 inches above the 9-foot wire fence. ◆ Before the stadium was enclosed, wind blew in from left center and out toward right center. This fact cost Willie Mays any chances he would have had to challenge the Ruth 714/Aaron 755 record for total home runs in a career. ◆ Now that the stadium is enclosed, the wind is a swirling monster, just as strong and cold as before. ◆ Back in the 1960s, when every Dodgers-Giants game was like a holy war, the base path between first and second was completely drenched, complete with numerous puddles, before the game to make it more difficult for Dodgers base stealer Maury Wills to steal second. The base path came to be called Maury's Lake. The umpires protested to the Giants that the location of the foul poles was several inches out into fair territory, rather than being right on the foul line, in the third inning of opening day on April 12, 1960. The Giants agreed to move the poles during the off-season. This is just the opposite of the Dodgers' experience, when the umpires discovered that their foul poles were completely in foul territory at the opening of Dodger Stadium 2 years later. ◆ Giants pitcher Stu Miller was blown off the mound by the wind in the 1961 All Star game. ◆ The stadium was enlarged and fully enclosed in the spring and summer of 1971 to house the NFL 49ers. Architect John Bolles's boomerang-shaped concrete shell baffle behind the upper tier's last row of seats, intended to protect the park from the wind, failed to work. ◆ Candlestick was the scene of the Beatles' last public concert on August 29, 1966. ◆ In the winter of 1978 to 1979, the Giants showed their good judgment, ripped up man's carpet, and replaced it with God's grass. ◆ The cold here limits the number of home runs. ◆ Croix de Candlestick pins have been awarded to fans since 1983 at the conclusion of night extra inning games. The pins are now treasured collectors' items. ◆ Just as the third game of the 1989 Battle of the Bay Area World Series was to begin here, an earthquake put a 6-inch crack in section 53 of the upper deck in right field, and several chunks of concrete fell to the lower deck. Miraculously, not one person in the sold-out stadium was injured.

**C**andlestick Park, San Francisco. It survived the great earthquake in the 1989 World Series.

HOME OF THE GIANTS

# SEATTLE, WASHINGTON

# KINGDOME

### A.K.A.
King County Domed Stadium, 1976–1977; The Tomb in the 1980s

### OCCUPANT
American League Seattle Mariners, April 6, 1977 to date

### CAPACITY
59,059 (1976); 59,438 (1979); 59,059 (1980); 59,438 (1981); 59,850 (1988); 58,150 (1989); 57,748 (1991)

### LARGEST CROWD
58,905 for the All Star Game on July 17, 1979

### SURFACE
AstroTurf

### DIMENSIONS
Left field: 315 (1977); 316 (marked, 1978); 314 (actual, 1978); 324 (1990); 331 (1991)
Left center: 375 (1977); 365 (1978); 357 (1981); 362 (1990); 376 (1991)
Deep left center: 385 (1990)
Center field: 405 (1977); 410 (1978); 405 (1981); 410 (1986); 405 (1991)
Deep right center: 375 (1990)
Right center: 375 (1977); 365 (1978); 357 (1981); 352 (1990)
Right field: 315 (1977); 316 (marked, 1978); 314 (actual, 1978); 314 (marked, 1990)
Backstop: 63
Foul territory: Large

### FENCES
Left field: 11.5 (wood, 1977); 17.5 (6 plexiglass over 11.5 wood, 1988)
Center field: 11.5 (wood, 1977)
Right field: 11.5 (wood, 1977); 23.25 (wood, 1982)
Apex of dome: 250
Speakers in left (3), left center (1), and center (1): 102 (1977); raised to 133.5 (1981); the 11 other speakers, 132

### PHENOMENA
The Kingdome was rescued from the dead by new ownership in 1990. Now it has much better food, it is newly painted, and some

**K**ingdome, Seattle. Host park for the 50th All-Star Game.

asymmetrical dimensions have been added to make it a much more fun place to be. But try to sit closer than 617 feet from home plate, which is how far away you'll be if you sit in section 332, row 18. It had been called The Tomb by visiting sportswriters and players because of its sickeningly gray concrete and quietness. ◆ A large American flag flies above the concrete dome. There are numerous "in-play" objects that are suspended, including 14 loudspeakers, 59 wires, and 75 streamers. The long red, white, and blue streamers are suspended from the ceiling: 19 red, 37 white, and 19 blue. These streamers can tangle up an infield fly and deflect it from the pitcher's mound to behind second base, or vice versa. The streamers were originally put up to help fielders track infield popups, and some fielders say that they help. The area in short right field is still so notorious for lost pop flies that it is known as The Bermuda Triangle. Two foul balls have gone up but have never come down; both were ruled strikes. ◆ On August 4, 1979, Ruppert Jones of the Mariners hit a foul ball that stuck in the speaker above the first base dugout, thus disproving the old adage of physics that what goes up must come down. On May 20, 1983, Brewer Ricky Nelson did the same thing. Four foul balls have bounced off speakers and been caught for outs: August 3, 1979, caught by the A's pitcher; September 3, 1979, caught by the Mariners' first baseman; May 19, 1980, caught by the Mariners' first baseman; April 25, 1985, caught by the Mariners' pitcher. ◆ Other foul balls have bounced off the no-longer-used NBA Seattle Supersonics basketball speakers above first base and also the old basketball scoreboard above and behind home plate, which have not been caught. For example, on July 26, 1982 John Castino of the Twins hit a ball off the basketball speaker above first that landed in the photographers' bay. One fair ball bounced off a roof support wire and remained in play. On April 11, 1985 Dave

Kingman of the A's hit a ball off a speaker that was caught for an out in deep left, which otherwise would have been a monstrous home run. One fair ball has struck the right field speaker but bounced foul. Ken Phelps of the Mariners was robbed of a tape-measure homer on August 13, 1987 when the ball struck the right field loudspeaker in fair territory, but bounced off crooked and landed foul. Seven fair balls have bounced off speakers and remained in play: On April 25, 1979, Butch Hobson of the Red Sox tripled off the left center speaker; on June 5, 1979, Willie Horton of the Mariners singled off the left field speaker; on April 9, 1980, Ted Cox of the Mariners tripled off the left center speaker; on May 19, 1980, Jim Anderson of the Mariners doubled off the left field speaker; on June 14, 1980, Ken Singleton of the Orioles doubled off the left center speaker; and on August 19 and 20, 1980, Bob Watson of the Yankees hit a double off the left center speaker and a triple off the center field speaker. ◆ An entire continent away from Boston's 37-foot Green Monster and facing the Pacific rather than the Atlantic, Seattle's 23-foot Mini-Green Monster in right and right center is called the Walla Walla and is painted blue. Its appearance in 1982 made Mariners home games much more interesting. ◆ The Astroturf carpet is rolled out by the Rhinoceros machine and smoothed by the Grasshopper machine after it has been zipped together. The USS *Mariner* is a huge yellow sailing ship behind the center field fence that fires a cannon after every Mariner homer. ◆ There are baby changing areas in aisles 111, 113, 201, and 203. From below, the domed roof looks like it is made up of thousands of bricks. There are 42 air conditioning units: 16 in fair territory and 26 in foul territory, with 8 ducts in each unit. These 336 ducts blow air in toward the field, which means fewer home runs in what would normally be a "Homer Dome" because of the short power alleys, at 357 feet throughout the 1980s. ◆ The outfield distances were marked on fences in both feet and fathoms during 1977 to 1980: 1 fathom equals 6 feet. ◆ The third deck is highest at third base and in right field. American League East and American League West standings are posted on the right field third deck facade. ◆ Sick's Stadium's home plate is on display in the Royal Brougham trophy case, in the Mariners Hall of Fame, behind the first base seats on plaza level. ◆ In the winter of 1980 to 1981, five loudspeakers (three above left field and one each above left center field and center field) were raised from 102 to 133.5 feet to reduce the chances of their being hit again. When the Mariners marked their power alleys as 375, the measurement was not to the actual 357-foot power alley: It was somewhat deeper, about halfway between the actual location of the power alley and dead center. Why the Mariners did this is not known, and they won't say. It may be that they did not want it publicly known that the stadium was primarily designed with football in mind and that they considered their 357-foot power alleys too short.

## TORONTO, ONTARIO

# SKYDOME

**OCCUPANT**
American League Toronto Blue Jays, June 5, 1989 to date

**CAPACITY**
50,516 (1989)

**LARGEST CROWD**
50,326 on July 26, 1991 vs. Kansas City

**SURFACE**
AstroTurf

**DIMENSIONS**
Foul lines: 330 (1989); 328 (1990)
Power alleys: 375
Center field: 400
Backstop: 60

**FENCES**
10 (canvas padding, 1989); Apex of dome (roof closed): 310

**FORMER USE**
Water supply pumping station at the site of second base

**PHENOMENA**
On August 27, 1990, the Jays had the roof open because it was a beautiful night for baseball. In the bottom of the 5th inning, however, home plate umpire Don Denkinger had to delay the game because millions of gnats were making the field unplayable. Finally, the retractable roof was closed to keep out further gnats. ◆ Try not to sit in aisle 504, row 9, seat 101 or 102. Seat 101 is so bad they won't even sell it to you. But they do sell seat 102, and you

can only see one-third of the outfield because you are next to the huge 33-foot by 115-foot Jumbotron scoreboard in right center, triple the size of any other. ◆ The Skydome is everything a new ballpark should not be. There are no bleachers. There is no grass. This park should be carefully compared to the new Oriole Park at Camden Yards, which is everything a new ballpark should be. ◆ This is the only park where the attendance both fluctuates constantly and is uncountable. There is a luxury hotel in center field with 348 rooms, 70 of which have a view of the game. There are five levels. The Sky level would be level 600 except that there is no sky, so there is no level 600. The retractable 310-foot-high, four-paneled roof could cover a 31-story building, making it by far the tallest dome in Major League baseball: The apexes of the Major League domes are 310 in Toronto, 250 in Seattle, 208 in Houston, 186 in Minneapolis, and 171 in Montreal. ◆ The roof can be closed in 20 minutes. Only three of the four panels move. The panels are made out of a single polyvinylchloride membrane over an insulated acoustic steel sheet metal. When the roof is open, the closed end of the stadium serves as a wind scoop which causes a downdraft in the outfield that tends to prevent home runs. ◆ During the first home stand with the Brewers in June 1989, the roof was open when it started to rain, so the crew shut the roof. Unfortunately, the roof jammed just short of full closure, leaving a waterfall to shower down directly on the batter, catcher, and umpire. The game was finally postponed, because the grounds crew could not stop the waterfall.

Ebbets Field, Brooklyn, N. Y.

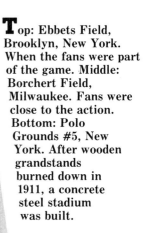

**T**op: Ebbets Field, Brooklyn, New York. When the fans were part of the game. Middle: Borchert Field, Milwaukee. Fans were close to the action. Bottom: Polo Grounds #5, New York. After wooden grandstands burned down in 1911, a concrete steel stadium was built.

Sunday at Borchert Field

Polo Grounds, New York City

157

7A-H2098

# PART TWO

# FORMER MAJOR LEAGUE BALLPARKS

## AKRON, OHIO

### LEAGUE PARK

**OCCUPANT**
Negro National League Akron Black Tyrites, 1933

**CAPACITY**
4,500

**DIMENSIONS**
Left field: 315
Center field: 385
Right field: 345

**PHENOMENA**
The Negro East-West League Pittsburgh Crawfords vs. New York Black Yankees game here on August 8, 1932, was the first game of a doubleheader, with the second game played later in nearby Canton.

## ALBANY, NEW YORK

### RIVERSIDE PARK

**NEUTRAL USES**
National League Troy Trojans September 11, 1880; June 15, September 10, 1881; May 16–18, 30, 1882

94 ◆ GREEN CATHEDRALS

## ALTOONA, PENNSYLVANIA

# COLUMBIA PARK

**A.K.A.**
Fourth Avenue Grounds; Waverly Field; Fourth Street Park

**OCCUPANT**
Union Association Altoona Pride, April 30–May 31, 1884

## ASHEVILLE, NORTH CAROLINA

# MCCORMICK FIELD

**NEUTRAL USES**
Some Negro American League Birmingham Black Barons games in the 1930s and 1940s

**CAPACITY**
3,500 (1924); 3,000 (1940); 3,500 (1985)

**DIMENSIONS**
Left field: 328 (1924); 365 (1940); 325 (1985); 328 (1988)
Left center: 360 (1988)
Center field: 397 (1924); 410 (1940); 414 (1985); 404 (1988)

McCormick Field, Asheville, North Carolina. Baseball mural outside the ballpark.

Right center: 325 (1988)

Right field: 301 (1924); 325 (1940); 301 (1985)

## PHENOMENA

This park was built in 1924 and is still used. It is a most beautiful park thanks to the surrounding trees and foliage. Upon the demise of Ebbets Field, its old clock was moved from Brooklyn to Asheville and now resides on the top of the outfield fence scoreboard. The vines on the outfield wall are thicker than those at Chicago's Wrigley Field. The park was totally rebuilt for the 1992 season.

McCormick Field, Asheville, North Carolina. Top: Baseball in the Smoky Mountains since 1924. Bottom: The most beautiful outfield in the world.

## ATLANTA, GEORGIA

# PONCE DE LEON PARK

### OCCUPANTS
Negro Southern League Atlanta Black Crackers, 1932; Negro American League Atlanta Black Crackers, 1938

### CAPACITY
11,000 (1903); 15,000 (1924); 12,500 (1949)

### DIMENSIONS
Left field: 365 (1932); 330 (1938); 315 (1949)
Left center: 525
Center field: 462 (1932); 448 (1938); 410 (1949)
Right field: 321 (1932); 324 (1938); 330 (1949)

### FENCES
Left field: 2 (hedge, April 1949); 4 (cyclone fence, May 1949)
Left center: 25
Center field: 6
Right center: 35 (magnolia tree halfway up a very steep embankment with no fence)
Right field: 15

**P**once de Leon Park, Atlanta, Georgia. Huge magnolia tree in play in right center.

140—Ponce De Leon Park, Atlanta, Ga.

## ATLANTIC CITY, NEW JERSEY

# BACHARACH PARK

### OCCUPANT
Eastern Colored League Atlantic City Bacharach Giants, 1923–1928

### PHENOMENA
Negro League World Series second game 1926; Negro National League Baltimore Black Sox vs. Homestead Grays August 26, 1933.

## AUSTIN, TEXAS

# CLARK FIELD

### NEUTRAL USES
Some Negro American League Houston Eagles games in 1949 and 1950

### CAPACITY
5,000 (1928)

### DIMENSIONS
Left field: 350 to the Cliff—313 at ground level
Left center: At the scoreboard—375 to the Cliff—357 at ground level
Center field: 401 to the Cliff—341 at ground level
Right center: 363 to the Cliff—303 at ground level
Right field: 300

### FENCES
10. Complicated measurements courtesy of the March 16, 1967 Breazeale-Sims geological survey. Cliff height: Mostly 12, but sloping from 0 to 30 (limestone cliff in right center to left field, tapering off to ground level at the left field foul pole, rising sharply amidst a rocky hill to around 30 feet in height at the fence in dead center)

### PHENOMENA
This is perhaps the most unique baseball park in history: In fact, it is the only two-tiered field ever. With a 12-foot-high cliff separating the upper outfield in left around to right center from the infield and

**C**lark Field, Austin, Texas.
A cliff divided the outfield into
lower and upper plateaus.

401' to here

top of cliff

Texas Homerun

120

lower outfield, there
were two levels of play, the upper tier and the
lower tier. ◆ A typical play occurred in 1973 when the University
of Texas Longhorns got an inside-the-park home run to third base.
The ball was hit way over the center fielder's head, so the left
fielder scrambled up the Cliff to retrieve the ball on the Plateau
and hold the batter to a triple, the center fielder went back to the
Cliff to leap for the attempted catch, the shortstop went into short
center for a relay throw, and the third baseman covered third
awaiting a throw. The ball fooled the entire defense by bouncing
crooked off the top of the Cliff into deep left field, and, as the batter
rounded second, he was closer than anyone to the ball. The third
baseman ended up fielding the ball in deep left, and his throw was
nowhere close to getting the batter out at home. ◆ The park
opened on March 24, 1928, with the Detroit Tigers defeating the
Longhorns 12–8. ◆ According to local legend, Lou Gehrig hit the
longest home run ever, travelling 611 feet, high over the 40-foot-
high fence in dead center, in a New York Yankees-Texas Longhorns
exhibition game in the spring of 1929.

# BALTIMORE, MARYLAND

# MADISON AVENUE GROUNDS

**NEUTRAL USE**

National Association Washington Olympics, July 8, 1871

**PHENOMENA**

The park opened in the 1860s.

# NEWINGTON PARK

**OCCUPANTS**

National Association Lord Baltimores, April 22, 1872–October 14, 1874; National Association Marylands, April 14–July 11, 1873; American Association Baltimore Orioles, May 9–September 30, 1882

**PHENOMENA**

The Baltimore Orioles played all their 1882 American Association home games here.

# ORIOLE PARK I

**OCCUPANT**

American Association Baltimore Orioles, May 1, 1883–October 10, 1889

**PHENOMENA**

The Orioles rigged up a screen over center field in 1888 to prevent fans from watching for free from nearby rooftops.

# BELAIR LOT

**OCCUPANT**

Union Association Baltimore Unions, April 17–August 24, August 26–September 24, 1884

**PHENOMENA**

On July 4, 1884, with a sellout crowd inside, and about a thousand fans outside perched on surrounding housetops, telephone poles, and steeples of the Number 6 Fire Engine House, a shed beyond the left field fence collapsed, dropping many people over the fence into the park. St. Louis Unions left fielder Lew Dickerson caught one fan on the fly, perhaps saving his life. ◆ On August 25, 1884, the Unions officially abandoned Belair Lot because it was so small but returned a day later because the park they had moved to, Monumental Park, was too lumpy.

# MONUMENTAL PARK

# ORIOLE PARK II

# ORIOLE PARK III

**OCCUPANT**

Union Association Baltimore Unions, August 25, 1884

**PHENOMENA**

The Unions decided to move all the rest of their home games here, beginning August 25, 1884, because Monumental Park was so much bigger than Belair Lot. But after only one game, they moved back to Belair Lot because the Monumental Park field surface was so uneven and bumpy.

**OCCUPANT**

American Association Baltimore Orioles, August 27, 1890–May 9, 1891

**PHENOMENA**

Preston Orem incorrectly states in his classic 19th century book on baseball that the American Association Orioles opened their 1891 American Association season at the refurbished old Union Association grounds, which would have been Belair Lot. Local newspapers conclusively prove that the team played here at Greenmount and 29th before May 11, 1891.

**OCCUPANTS**

American Association Baltimore Orioles, May 11–October 3, 1891; National League Baltimore Orioles, April 12, 1892–October 10, 1899

**CAPACITY**

30,000 (1891); 11,000 (1897)

**DIMENSIONS**

Left field: 300
Right field: 350

**FENCES**

16

**PHENOMENA**

There were separate bicycle racks on Barclay Street for gentlemen and for ladies. Fly balls to right were quite an adventure. The field sloped downhill to the fence in right. In addition, the water from Brady's Run, just beyond the right field fence, created a perpetual swamp in right field by oozing underneath the fence. Some of the seats were chairs from Forepaugh's Theatre.

# ORIOLE PARK IV

**OCCUPANT**
American League Baltimore Orioles, April 26, 1901–September 29, 1902

**PHENOMENA**
There was a flagpole in play in right center. Beyond the right field fence stood a huge tree partially extended over the fence. The outfield fence was angled like that in Ebbets Field. The lower two-thirds of the fence were angled away from the plate whereas the top one-third was vertical.

# ORIOLE PARK V

**OCCUPANTS**
Federal League Baltimore Terrapins, April 13, 1914–October 2, 1915; Negro American League Baltimore Elite Giants, 1938–July 3, 1944

**CAPACITY**
16,000 (1914); 14,000 (1944)

**DIMENSIONS**
Left field: 300 (1914); 305 (1944)
Center field: 450 (1914); 412 (1944)
Right field: 335 (1914); 310 (1944)
Backstop: 76

**FENCES**
25

# MARYLAND BASEBALL PARK

**NEUTRAL USES**
Negro League World Series 3rd and 4th games, 1924; 3rd game 1926

**OCCUPANTS**
Eastern Colored League Baltimore Black Sox, 1923–1928; Negro American League Baltimore Black Sox, 1929

# BUGLE FIELD

## OCCUPANTS
Negro East-West League Baltimore Black Sox, 1932; Negro National League Baltimore Black Sox, 1933–1934

## PHENOMENA
The park was named after the Bugle Coat and Apron Supply Company, Maryland's largest laundry in the 1920s and 1930s. Joe Cambria, the Washington Senators' top scout, and Matty Reinholdt owned the laundry, the ballpark, and the Black Sox in the 1930s.

# VENABLE STADIUM

## OCCUPANT
Negro American League Baltimore Elite Giants, July 5, 1944–1950

## CAPACITY
78,000 (1923); 60,000 (1940); 80,000 (1941); 80,000 (1942); 30,000 (1944); 76,658 (1947); 58,917 (1948); 31,000 (1950)

## DIMENSIONS
Left field: 270 (1944); 291 (1949)
Right field: 406 (1944); 291 (1949)

## PHENOMENA
The minor league attendance record of 52,833 was set here during the September 1944 Little World Series vs. Louisville.

# WESTPORT STADIUM

## OCCUPANT
Negro American League Baltimore Elite Giants, 1950

## PHENOMENA
Location: 3000 Annapolis Road and Westport Boulevard. Its concrete foundations can still be seen in a field behind a new shopping center.

# MEMORIAL STADIUM

**A. K. A.**
Babe Ruth Stadium, 1953

**OCCUPANT**
American League Baltimore Orioles, April 15, 1954–September 30, 1991

**CAPACITY**
31,000 (1950); 47,855 (1953); 47,778 (1958); 49,375 (1961); 49,373 (1964); 52,184 (1965); 52,185 (1968); 52,137 (1969); 53,208 (1970); 52,862 (1979); 53,208 (1982); 52,860 (1983); 53,198 (1985); 54,076 (1986); 54,002 (1987); 54,017 (1988); 53,371 (1991)

**LARGEST CROWD**
54,458 on October 9, 1966 vs. the Dodgers

**SMALLEST CROWD**
655 on August 17, 1972 vs. the White Sox

**SURFACE**
Bluegrass

**DIMENSIONS**
Foul lines: 291 (1950); 309 (1954)
Where the 7-foot fence met the 14-foot wall: 360
Power alleys: 446 (1954); 447 (1955); 405 (1956); 380 (1958); 370 (1962); 385 (1970); 375 (1976); 378 (1977); 376 (1980)

**M**emorial Stadium, Baltimore, Maryland. Center field was a hedge in 1954.

Center field: 410 (1950); 445 (1954); 450 (1955); 425 (1956); 410 (1958); 400 (1976); 405 (1977); 410 (1978); 405 (1980)
Backstop: 78 (1954); 58 (1961); 54 (1980); 58 (1991)
Foul territory: Large

## FENCES

Foul line corners: 11.33 (concrete, 1954); 14 (11.33 concrete below 2.67 plywood, 1959)
Left center to right center: 10 (hedges, April and May 1954); 8 (wire, June 1954); 7 (wire, 1955); 6 (wire, 1958); 14 (wire, 1961); 6 (wire, 1963); 7 (canvas padding, 1977)

## FORMER USE

A football stadium, known variously as Venable Stadium, Municipal Stadium, Metropolitan Stadium, and Babe Ruth Stadium, built in 1922. Major renovations began on the football stadium in 1949, which eventually resulted in the creation of Memorial Stadium. A second deck was constructed from the fall of 1953 through the spring of 1954.

## PHENOMENA

The Orioles have class. Memorial Stadium was replaced in 1992 by a beautiful new baseball park in Camden Yards, near the Inner Harbor, where the Ramcor Building and Maryland Cup Facility used to be. This ballpark incorporates B & O Railroad Long Building Warehouse to be used as the Orioles offices, overlooking right field along with the old Bromo Seltzer Tower. The field is asymmetrical and was designed to bring back the classical look of Fenway and Wrigley, while at the same time providing the modern amenities for fans. The contrast of this new ballpark with the Skydome in Toronto and other newly built antiseptic stadia could not be greater. ◆ The old ballpark's outfield wall here curved sharply away from the plate at the 309-foot foul poles, causing difficult bounces for visiting players because the ball bounced out toward center field, rather than back toward the infield. Beautiful trees on the center field embankment looked down over the field giving the field a uniquely pastoral feeling, although it was in the middle of the city. Etched into the concrete facade above the main entrance was written, "Time Can Never Dim the Honor of Their Deeds," in honor of fighting men and women everywhere who have died for their country. ◆ The most famous fan was Wild Bill Hagy, the loud taxidriver who led the "Roar from 34," the cheers from section 34, and who also occasionally spelled out O-R-I-O-L-E-S by twisting

**M**emorial Stadium, Baltimore, Maryland. Way up at the top of the upper deck.

his body to spell the letters from atop the Oriole dugout, to the wild approval of the Baltimore faithful. ◆ The center field fence from June 1954 through 1957 was made of wire and stood in front of a row of 10-foot-high hedges. Previously, during April, May, and the beginning of June in 1954, the hedges themselves had formed the center field fence. Jim Diering leaped into these hedges to rob Mickey Mantle of a homer early in the 1954 season before the wire fence was created. A squirrel chewed through the wires in the outfield fence in 1969. ◆ Frank Robinson hit the only homer completely out of the park on May 8, 1966 on a fastball down and in from Luis Tiant, a towering 450-foot drive over the left field bleachers. At every home game, a flag reading "HERE" was flown at the spot where the ball left the park. ◆ Fans yelled "O" (for Orioles) in unison when the "Star Spangled Banner" reached "O say does that star spangled banner yet wave." ◆ Traditional Baltimore row houses were visible beyond the center field fence. ◆ Venable Stadium, a football stadium built in 1922 and converted for baseball use after the July 4, 1944 fire destroyed Oriole Park, was renovated to make way for Memorial Stadium. Home plate was moved from where it had been in the north to the south in 1950. ◆ The best crabcakes in baseball were served here.

# BIRMINGHAM, ALABAMA

# RICKWOOD FIELD

### OCCUPANTS
Negro National League Birmingham Black Barons, 1923–1925, 1927–1931; Negro Southern League Birmingham Black Barons, 1932; Negro American League Birmingham Black Barons, 1937–1938, 1940–1950

### CAPACITY
9,312

### DIMENSIONS
Left field: 405
Center field: 470
Right field: 334

### FENCES
Left field: 5
Left center: 35
Center field to right field: 15

### PHENOMENA
Patterned exactly after Pittsburgh's Forbes Field, this was the best Minor League park ever built. Opened on August 18, 1910, it was named after the owner of the 1910 Barons, Rick Woodward. ◆ This is where Willie Mays made his non–Negro League debut on July 4, 1948. ◆ A basketball goal with a net hung from a large Mellow Yellow sign in right center. A batter won $100 by hitting the sign, $500 for scoring a "basket." Although hitters hit the sign, no one ever made a basket. A large scoreboard stood in left center in the 1940s. ◆ This was the oldest Minor League park, followed by: Simmons Field, Kenosha, 1922; Bowman Field, Williamsport, 1923; McCormick Field, Asheville, 1924; War Memorial Stadium, Greensboro, 1927; Luther Williams Baseball Park, Macon, 1929; Silver Stadium, Rochester, 1929; and Engel Stadium, Chattanooga, 1930.

**R**ickwood Field, Birmingham, Alabama. Patterned after Pittsburgh's Forbes Field.

## BLOOMFIELD, NEW JERSEY

# SPRAGUE FIELD

**OCCUPANT**
Negro East-West League Newark Browns, 1932

**DIMENSIONS**
Left field: 330
Center field: 385
Right field: 325

**PHENOMENA**
There were several factories beyond center field.

## BOSTON, MASSACHUSETTS

# SOUTH END GROUNDS I

**A.K.A.**
Walpole Street Grounds; Union Base Ball Grounds; Boston Base Ball Grounds

**OCCUPANTS**
National Association Boston Red Stockings, May 16, 1871–October 30, 1875; National League Boston Red Caps, April 29, 1876–September 10, 1887

**PHENOMENA**
It was torn down in late September 1887.

# DARTMOUTH GROUNDS

**OCCUPANT**
Union Association Boston Unions, April 30–September 24, 1884

**PHENOMENA**
It was used by the National League Braves, then known as the Beaneaters, in 1894 while the South End Grounds II were being rebuilt after the May 15th fire.

# SOUTH END GROUNDS II

**S**outh End Grounds #2, Boston. Twin-spired roof of the Grand Pavillion, 1888–1894.

### OCCUPANT
National League Boston Beaneaters, May 25, 1888–May 15, 1894

### CAPACITY
6,800 (1888)

### PHENOMENA
The Grand Pavilion's most famous attraction was Sullivan's Tower, where fans could watch for free from just beyond the right field fence. Every time the Beaneaters management would raise the right field wall, Sullivan's Tower would get taller and taller, so that fans could still watch for free. This was Boston's only double-decked ballpark ever. The grandstand had 2,028 seats in the lower deck and 772 seats in the upper deck. There were about 2,000 seats in the left field bleachers and about 2,000 in the right field bleachers. The grandstand behind home plate, which was destroyed by fire during the bottom of the third of the Beaneaters-Orioles game on May 15, 1894, had six spires above it. The fire began in the right field bleachers.

# CONGRESS STREET GROUNDS

### OCCUPANTS
Players League Boston Reds, April 19–September 10, 1890; American Association Boston Reds, April 18–October 3, 1891; National League Boston Beaneaters, May 16–June 20, 1894

### DIMENSIONS
Left field: 250

# SOUTH END GROUNDS III

### OCCUPANT
National League Boston Beaneaters, July 20, 1894–August 11, 1914

### DIMENSIONS
Left field: 250
Left center: 445
Deepest left center: 450
Center field: 440
Right center: 440
Right field: 255

### FENCES
Center field: 6
Right field: 20

### PHENOMENA
The cigar factory behind right field is still standing. ◆ The park was completely rebuilt after the May 15, 1894 fire destroyed the Grand Pavilion structure built in 1888. Interestingly, this park was smaller than its predecessor, South End Grounds (II), and had only one deck because of insurance considerations. The destroyed ballpark had been severely underinsured. Not enough money resulted from the insurance claim to build a new park of equal size with two decks. ◆ There was an incline in right field. ◆ When the Braves left here on August 11, 1914, they existed in limbo over at Fenway, as guests of the Red Sox for more than a year, until they moved into Braves Field on August 18, 1915.

# HUNTINGTON AVENUE BASEBALL GROUNDS

### OCCUPANT
American League Boston Red Sox, May 8, 1901–October 7, 1911

### CAPACITY
9,000 (1901)

### DIMENSIONS
Left field: 350
Left center: 440
Center field: 530 (1901); 635 (1908)
Right field: 280 (1901); 320 (1908)
Backstop: 60

## FENCES

14

## PHENOMENA

The World Series Exhibit Room in Cabot Cage, on the current site, is devoted to numerous mementoes of the 1901–1911 Red Sox era. A plaque commemorating the location of where the right field foul pole used to be was unveiled in May 1956. Tufts Medical College is behind where third base used to be. There were large patches of sand in the outfield where grass would not grow. ◆ This was the scene of the first National League–American League World Series between the Boston Red Sox and the Pittsburgh Pirates in 1903. ◆ A toolshed in deep center was in play. ◆ The distance to center in 1908 has been approximated by Robert Bluthardt, working from a scale drawing, as 635 feet. ◆ Stuffy McInnis of the A's got an inside-the-park homer on June 27, 1911 off Ed Karger's warmup pitch when Red Sox center fielder Tris Speaker did not chase it. Umpire Ben Egan allowed the homer because American League President Ban Johnson had banned warmup pitches to speed up the game.

# BRAVES FIELD

## OCCUPANT

National League Boston Braves, August 18, 1915–September 21, 1952

## CAPACITY

40,000 (1915); 46,000 (1928); 41,700 (1937); 45,000 (1939); 37,746 (1941); 36,706 (1947); 37,106 (1948)

## LARGEST CROWD

Total—59,000 on September 1, 1933 vs. the Giants; Paid—51,331 on May 22, 1932 vs. the Phillies

## SMALLEST CROWD

95 on July 28, 1935 vs. the Dodgers

## DIMENSIONS

Left field: 402 (1915); 375 (1921); 404 (1922); 403 (1926); 320 (April 21, 1928); 353.5 (July 24, 1928); 340 (1930); 353.67 (1931); 359 (1933); 353.67 (1934); 368 (1936); 350 (1940); 337 (1941); 334 (1942); 340 (1943); 337 (1944)

Left center: 402.5 (1915); 396 (1916); 402.42 (1921); 404 (1922); 402.5 (1926); 330 (April 21, 1928); 359 (July 24, 1928); 365 (1942); 355 (1943)

Center field: 440 (1915); 387 (April 21, 1928); 417 (July 24, 1928); 387.17 (1929); 394.5 (1930); 387.25 (1931); 417 (1933); 426 (1936); 407 (1937); 408 (1939); 385 (1940); 401 (1941); 375 (1942); 370 (1943); 390 (1944); 380 (1945); 370 (1946)

Center field at the flagpole: 520

Deepest center field corner, just to the right of straightaway center: 550 (1915); 401 (1942); 390 (1943)

Right center: 402 (1915); 362 (1942); 355 (1943)

Right field: 402 (1915); 375 (1916); 365 (1921); 364 (1928); 297.75 (1929); 297.92 (1931); 364 (1933); 297 (1936); 376 (1937); 378 (1938); 350 (1940); 340 (April 1943); 320 (July 1943); 340 (April 1944); 320 (May 1944); 340 (April 1946); 320 (May 1946); 318 (1947); 320 (1948); 319 (1948)

Backstop: 75 (1915); 60 (1936)

## FENCES

Left field to right center: 10 (concrete, 1915); 8 (wood, 1928); 20 (wood, 1946); 25 (wood, 1953)

**B**raves Field, Boston. Right center field originally 550 feet from home plate.

Left field scoreboard: Sides 64 (1948); middle arch 68 (1929)
Left field: 1 (gravestones, July 24, 1928); 30 (canvas, 1929)
Right center exit gate: 8 (wire)
Right field: 10 (6 screen above 4 wood)

## PHENOMENA

Originally, there was a ground-level scoreboard in left. The infield grass was transplanted from the old South End Grounds (III) in 1915. The wind usually blew straight in from center, preventing many home runs. ◆ This was the home of the best fried clams served in all of baseball. ◆ On May 1, 1920 the Braves and the Brooklyn Robins tied 1–1 in 26 innings. The afternoon game was called a tie because of darkness. It remains the longest Major League game in terms of innings in history. ◆ In 1928, the plate was turned toward right, and inner fences were added. The left field bleachers installed before the 1928 home opener on April 21 were removed slowly in a process that took from mid-June to the end of the season. ◆ The scoreboard was moved from the top of the left center wall to the rear of right field in 1928. The same scoreboard was later moved to Kansas City's Municipal Stadium in 1955. The Jury Box was a small bleacher section behind the fence in right, with very vocal fans. In 1936, home plate was moved 15 feet closer to the backstop. ◆ From 1936 to April 29, 1941, the ballpark was officially called the Bee Hive, because during that period, the Braves were officially known as the Boston Bees. ◆ In 1937, a notch was cut in the right field bleachers, which can still be seen today in Boston University's Nickerson Field. ◆ The September 21, 1938 game was played in a hurricane vs. the Cardinals. The game was finally called off by umpire Beans Reardon, when what appeared to be a long high home run smash to deep center was finally caught foul behind the plate by catcher Al Lopez. ◆ In the 1940s, fir trees were planted beyond the fence in center, in an unsuccessful attempt to hide from the view of the fans

**B**raves Field, Boston. Left: As it looks now, looking into right field. Right: First baseline stands, now Boston University football stadium.

the huge clouds of railroad locomotive smoke belching from the Boston and Albany Railroad tracks in left and center. ◆ In 1946, the field was turned again slightly toward right. That same year, over 5,000 fans left the home opener with green paint on their clothing because the new paint on all the seats had not yet dried. The Braves paid over $6,000 to 5,000 of the over 18,000 irate fans who applied for claims. ◆ In June 1947, the field was lowered by 18 inches. Stories are told of home runs landing in moving railroad cars and travelling hundreds of miles. Braves Field contained only 16 posts, the least of any park built in the 1910s and 1920s. In 1948, a huge new 68-foot scoreboard was added in left. Three troubadours roamed the stands during the Braves pennant run in 1948. ◆ The right field foul line bleachers, extending from first base to the right field foul pole, still stand. The Gaffney Street first base entrance is still there. The concrete outer wall in right and center remains. Turned on its side, covered in cobwebs, in an inaccessible position under some concrete beneath the old right field foul line bleachers, an old ticket booth with a 1952 Boston Braves schedule remains. And in a Rhode Island softball stadium, fans sit on Braves Field (correction: Bee Hive) seats. No matter how hard the new tries to cover up the old, the past manages to live on. Although Boston University purchased the field in the 1950s and laid out a football carpet from the first base dugout to right center, Braves Field still is not dead. A plaque placed on the site in 1988 recounts the history of the park.

**B**raves Field, Boston. Ticket office, now Boston University Police Station.

# BROOKLYN, NEW YORK*

## UNION GROUNDS

### OCCUPANTS

National Association New York Mutuals, May 25, 1871–October 29, 1875; National Association Brooklyn Eckfords, May 9, 1871–October 22, 1872; National Association Brooklyn Atlantics, May 7, 1873–October 9, 1875; National League New York Mutuals, 1876; National League Hartfords of Brooklyn, April 30–September 21, 1877

### DIMENSIONS

Outfield—500; right field—350 to a one-story building, which was in play inside the right field fence

### FENCES

6

### PHENOMENA

The park opened on May 15, 1862. This was the first enclosed baseball field, invented and built by William Cammeyer. ◆ Located in the Williamsburg section, just across the East River from Manhattan.

## CAPITOLINE GROUNDS

### OCCUPANT

National Association Brooklyn Atlantics, May 6–October 9, 1872

### PHENOMENA

The park was built in 1864 by Reuben S. Decker and Hamilton A. Weed and opened on May 5, 1864. There was a round brick outhouse in right field. Anyone who hit a homer over the outhouse received a bottle of champagne. ◆ The park was flooded with 4 feet of water and turned into a skating rink on November 15 each winter. ◆ Union Grounds and Capitoline Grounds were indeed separate ballparks. There are interesting and confusing similarities: Both were on Marcy Avenue in Brooklyn; both were turned into skating rinks each winter; and both were opened in May in the early 1860s (Union Grounds on May 15, 1862; Capitoline Grounds on May 5, 1864). Most confusing of all is the fact that the Capitoline Grounds were sometimes incorrectly referred to as the Union and Capitoline Grounds. There is conclusive evidence, however, that they were separate ballparks, one in Williamsburg and one in Brownsville.

*See also Jersey City, New Jersey; Maspeth, New York; St. George, New York

# WASHINGTON PARK I

**OCCUPANT**

American Association Brooklyn Bridegrooms, May 5, 1884–May 4, 1889

**CAPACITY**

2,000

**PHENOMENA**

The park opened for Minor League play in the Interstate League on May 12, 1883. It was built in a hollow, with the field sunk about 25 feet below the surrounding land. Washington Park was named for General George Washington, whose Battle of Long Island headquarters during the Revolutionary War were located in Gowanus House, which still stands on the same block where the park was located. The ballpark was destroyed by fire on May 19, 1889.

# RIDGEWOOD PARK

**A.K.A.**

Wallace's Grounds; Horse Market; Meyerrose's Park

**NEUTRAL USES**

American Association Brooklyn Bridegrooms (Sundays), May 2, 1886–October 6, 1889

**OCCUPANT**

American Association Brooklyn Gladiators, April 17–June 8, 1890

**PHENOMENA**

Then in Queens, on the Brooklyn-Queens borderline, the location is now in Brooklyn, due to redistricting. The entrance was at Myrtle Avenue and Covert Street, now called Norman Street.

# WASHINGTON PARK II

**OCCUPANTS**

American Association Brooklyn Bridegrooms, May 30–October 5, 1889; National League Bridegrooms April 28–October 3, 1890

**CAPACITY**

3,000

# EASTERN PARK

**OCCUPANTS**

Players League Brooklyn Wonders, April 28–September 12, 1890; National League Brooklyn Bridegrooms, April 27, 1891–October 2, 1897

**PHENOMENA**

This is where the Trolley Dodgers name originated, with the fans having to dodge the dozens of trolleys to get to the park. It was the "Candlestick of the 1890s," with cool breezes blowing in from nearby Jamaica Bay.

# WASHINGTON PARK III

**OCCUPANTS**

National League Brooklyn Superbas, April 30, 1898–October 5, 1912; Federal League Brook-Feds, May 11, 1914–September 30, 1915

**CAPACITY**

18,800 (1914)

**DIMENSIONS**

Left field: 335 (1898); 375.95 (1908); 300 (1914)
Left center: 500 (1898); 443.5 (1908)
Center field: 445 (1898); 424.7 (1908); 400 (1914)
Right center: 300 (1898)
Right field: 215 (1898); 295 (1899); 301.84 (1908); 275 (1914)
Backstop: 90 (1898); 15 (1908)

**FENCES**

Left and center fields: 12
Right field: 42 (13 brick topped by 29 canvas)

**PHENOMENA**

Nearby factories and Gowanus Canal made the air putrid. Gowanus Canal was behind the railyards in left field. ◆ The Federal League Brook-Feds rebuilt the stands in 1914 with wood on a concrete base and put Native American Indian symbols on the outfield fence. ◆ The center field scoreboard rested on supporting legs, so that a fair ball could roll under it. The center fielders had to crawl underneath the scoreboard to retrieve the live ball. This resulted in some inside-the-park home runs, the most exciting play in baseball. Some current ballpark should install this kind of outfield feature to generate exciting action. ◆ The 220-foot flagpole was behind the scoreboard in center. The top was the mast of the America's Cup defender Reliance. Fans could watch the games from their living rooms (in apartments called the Ginney Flats), across the street from the right field wall. ◆ The right field distance shown as 215 in an 1898 news article diagram may be a misprint.

# EBBETS FIELD

### OCCUPANTS
National League Brooklyn Dodgers, April 9, 1913–September 24, 1957; Negro National League Brooklyn Eagles, 1935

### CAPACITY
18,000 (1913); 26,000 (1924); 28,000 (1926); 35,000 (1937); 32,000 (1938); 34,219 (1940); 34,000 (1941); 32,000 (1946); 31,902 (1952)

### LARGEST CROWD
41,209 on May 30, 1934 vs. the Giants

### DIMENSIONS
Left field: 419 (1913); 410 (1914); 418.75 (1921); 383.67 (1926); 382.83 (1930); 384 (1931); 353 (1932); 356.33 (1934); 365 (1938); 357 (1939); 365 (1940); 356 (1942); 357 (1947); 343 (1948); 348 (1953); 343 (1955); 348 (1957)
Left center: 365 (1932); 351 (1948)

**E**bbets Field, Brooklyn, New York. As opened in 1913.

Center field: 450 (1914); 466 (1930); 460.79 (April 1931); 447 (August 1931); 399.42 (1932); 399 (1936); 402 (1938); 400 (1939); 399 (1947); 384 (1948); 393 (1955)
Right center: 352
Right center scoreboard: left side, 344; right side, 318
Right field: 301 (1913); 300 (1914); 296.17 (1921); 292 (1922); 301 (1926); 296.08 (1930); 295.92 (1931); 296.5 (1934); 297 (1938)
Backstop: 64 (1942); 70.5 (1954); 72 (1957)

## FENCES

Left field to left center: 20 (wood, 1913); 3 (wood, 1920); 9.87 (concrete, 1931)
Center field: 20 (wood, 1913); from the 393 marker to the 376 marker (9.87 sloping upward to 15) (concrete, 1931)
Screen in center field: 20 (screen above sloping concrete, 1920s)
Right center: 9 (concrete, 1913), 15 to 19 to 13 (15 at the 376 point, sloping upward to 19, then back down to 13)
Right center to right field: 38 (top 19 screen, bottom 19 concave concrete wall, bent at the 9.5 midpoint, vertical on the top half, concave angled on the bottom half)
Right field before the screen: 9 (concrete, 1913)

## PHENOMENA

The scoreboard clock sits now on top of the outfield fence scoreboard at McCormick Field in Asheville, North Carolina. The Ebbets Rotunda, at the main entrance to the ballpark, was an incredible 80-foot circle enclosed in Italian marble, with a floor tiled with the stitches of a baseball, and a chandelier with 12 baseball bat arms holding 12 baseball-shaped globes. There were 12 turnstiles, and 12 gilded ticket windows. The domed ceiling was 27 feet high at its center. There was a large, beautiful bronze plaque on the Rotunda interior wall. ◆ "Howling" Hilda Chester, the cowbell-clanging chowder soup saleslady, and the most famous of all Dodger fans, sat in the center field bleachers with her cowbell. The Dodger Sym-Phony band played their version of music in section 8. ◆ In the first night game here on June 15, 1938, Johnny vander Meer of the Reds pitched his second consecutive no-hitter. It was a short walk from the BMT Prospect Park and the IRT Franklin Avenue subway stops. ◆ On May 30,

**E**bbets Field, Brooklyn, New York. Brooklyn's baseball palace in 1922.

**E**bbets Field, Brooklyn, New York. Right field scoreboard and slanted wall.

1946, a drive by Bama Rowell of the Braves broke the right center field scoreboard clock. This later inspired Roy Hobb's colossal clout in *The Natural* starring Glenn Close and Robert Redford. ◆ There is some confusion about distances, because the left field foul line and grandstand wall were the same near the corner between the 343 and 357 markers. ◆ Children watched the game through a gap under the metal gate in right center field. ◆ The scoreboard, built after 1930, jutted out 5 feet from the wall at a 45-degree angle. The overhang of the center field second deck hung out over the field. A Schaefer beer sign, erected after World War II, on the top of the right center scoreboard notified fans of the official scorer's decision. The "h" in Schaefer lit up for a hit, and the second "e" in Schaefer lit up for an error. The Abe Stark sign offered a free suit at 1514 Pitkin Avenue to any batter hitting the 3-foot by 30-foot sign. ◆ Joe Adcock hit the only home run over the roof. ◆ When Ebbets Field was opened on April 5, 1913 for an exhibition game vs. the Yankees, it was discovered that the flag, a press box, and the keys to the bleachers had been forgotten. The press box finally was added in 1929. On September 7, 1924, more than 500 fans gained admittance by battering down the left field exit gate with a telephone pole. In the winter of 1931 to 1932, the double-deck was extended from third base to the left field corner and across to center field. According to Roger Kahn, it was "a narrow cockpit of iron and concrete, along a steep cobblestone slope." In the winter of 1937 to 1938, box seats were added in center field. ◆ There were a DeSoto car dealership and a gas station behind the right field screen, across Bedford Avenue, where many customers rushed to retrieve home run balls. ◆ In the early 1940s, Lonnie Frey of the Reds hit a ball that fell off the screen onto the top of the wall in right between the scoreboard and the right field foul pole. It bounced up and down repeatedly and never came down, so he just kept running for an inside-the-park homer. Larry McPhail put up boards the next day to prevent similar homers. But on October 1, 1950, in the game that was to decide the National League pennant, Pee Wee Reese hit an exactly similar inside-the-park home run. ◆ In the winter of 1947 to 1948, more seats were added to left and center. Demolition began on February 23, 1960. The same wrecking ball was used four years later to demolish the Polo Grounds. After they were demolished, the eight light tower stanchions were moved to Downing Stadium on Randall's Island.

**E**bbets Field, Brooklyn, New York. Home of the Dodger Sym-Phony Band.

## BUFFALO, NEW YORK

# RIVERSIDE GROUNDS

**OCCUPANT**
National League Buffalo Bisons, May 1, 1879–September 8, 1883

**DIMENSIONS**
Foul lines: 210
Power alleys: 420
Center field: 410
Backstop: 37

**PHENOMENA**
The ballpark was located just across the street from Lizzie Bluett's cottage at 599 West Avenue. A home run broke Lizzie's collarbone on May 21, 1881. Her cottage still stands.

**R**iverside Grounds, Buffalo, New York. Grandstands here in 1879–1883 did not curve around the bases.

# OLYMPIC PARK I

**OCCUPANT**
National League Buffalo Bisons, May 21, 1884–October 7, 1885

**CAPACITY**
3,748

# OLYMPIC PARK II

# FEDERAL LEAGUE PARK

**OCCUPANT**

Players League Buffalo Bisons, April 19–October 4, 1890

**PHENOMENA**

The wooden bleachers and fences of Olympic Park I were moved to the new site, and used to build Olympic Park II in the winter of 1988–89.

**OCCUPANT**

Federal League Buf-Feds, May 11, 1914–September 29, 1915

**CAPACITY**

20,000

**DIMENSIONS**

Left field: 290
Center field: 400
Right field: 300

**F**ederal League Park, Buffalo, New York. Home of the Buf-Feds in 1914–1915.

# CANTON, OHIO

## MAHAFFEY PARK

### NEUTRAL USES
National League Pittsburgh Innocents, September 18, 1890; American League Cleveland Indians, June 15, 1902, May 10, June 21, 1903

### DIMENSIONS
Left field: 324
Center field: 385
Right field: 302

### PHENOMENA
At 1125 feet above sea level, Mahaffey Park is the scene of both the highest National League game ever, and the highest American League game ever. ◆ The turnstiles and ticket choppers from the St. Louis Exposition were installed after being acquired from a Chicago wrecking firm.

# CHARLOTTE, NEW YORK

## ONTARIO BEACH GROUNDS

### NEUTRAL USE
National League Cleveland Exiles, August 28, 1898

### PHENOMENA
The location then was just outside of Rochester, in what is now part of Rochester, on the Genesee River near Lake Ontario, one mile northwest of the Windsor beach ballpark in Irondequoit, New York.

# CHATTANOOGA, TENNESSEE

# ENGEL STADIUM

### NEUTRAL USES
Some Negro National League Nashville Elite Giants games in the 1930s

### CAPACITY
10,000 (1930); 8,000 (1988); 7,480 (1989)

### DIMENSIONS
Left field: 368
Center field: 471
Right field: 324 (marked), 318 (actual)

### FENCES
22 (all around); 42 (scoreboard in left)

### PHENOMENA
Engel was built in 1930, making it one of the oldest Minor League parks in use, but it may be the oldest because the prior ballpark, Andrews Field, was on the same site, and was built in 1909. Regardless of whether it is the oldest, it is definitely one of the best and most beautiful ballparks in the country. ◆ Joe Engel, owner of the Minor League Lookouts, provided a lot of fun during the Great Depression: free

**E**ngel Stadium, Chattanooga, Tennessee. Entrance for blacks in days of segregation.

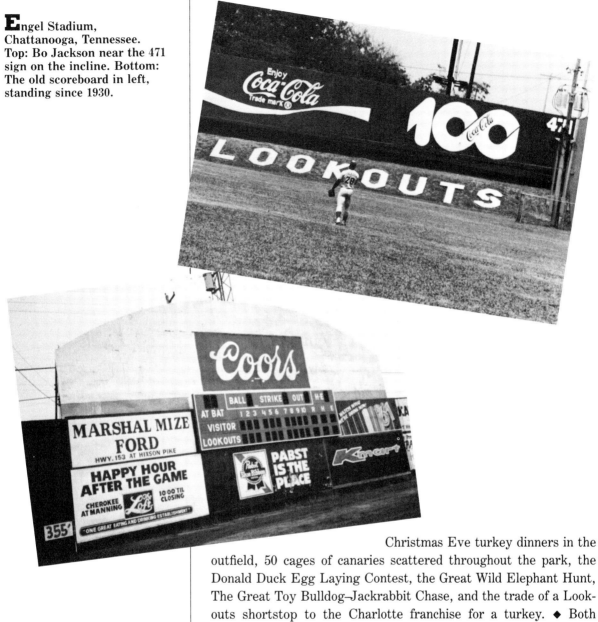

Engel Stadium, Chattanooga, Tennessee. Top: Bo Jackson near the 471 sign on the incline. Bottom: The old scoreboard in left, standing since 1930.

Christmas Eve turkey dinners in the outfield, 50 cages of canaries scattered throughout the park, the Donald Duck Egg Laying Contest, the Great Wild Elephant Hunt, The Great Toy Bulldog–Jackrabbit Chase, and the trade of a Lookouts shortstop to the Charlotte franchise for a turkey. ◆ Both Satchel Paige, at age 17, and Willie Mays, at age 15, played their first Major League games here, in the Negro Leagues. ◆ A 5-foot-high incline in center field is the only incline in ballpark history with sharp sides rather than gradual sloped sides. So a center fielder could be near the edge of the incline, drifting under a long fly, and fall 5 feet off the incline. ◆ The word Lookouts is written on the incline in huge concrete letters painted white. There used to be a rose bush garden up on the incline. The clock is in left center, and the scoreboard is in left.

## CHICAGO, ILLINOIS

# UNION BASE-BALL GROUNDS

**OCCUPANT**
National Association Chicago White Stockings, May 8–September 29, 1871

**CAPACITY**
7,000

**DIMENSIONS**
Foul lines: 375

**FENCES**
6

**PHENOMENA**
The ballpark burned down during the Great Chicago Fire on October 8–11, 1871, which was caused by Mrs. O'Leary's famous cow. In 1871, Lake Michigan came almost to the Illinois Central tracks. Now, much of the lake shore has been filled in.

# 23RD STREET GROUNDS

**OCCUPANTS**
National Association Chicago White Stockings, May 13, 1874–October 2, 1875; National League Chicago White Stockings, May 10, 1876–October 5, 1877

# LAKE FRONT PARK I

**OCCUPANT**
National League Chicago White Stockings, May 14, 1878–September 30, 1882

**PHENOMENA**
The infield was bumpy and uneven, and littered with stones, boulders, ashes, glass, and broken bottles. A large bridge, constructed so that fans could watch the games from outside the park, was completed on May 11, 1882.

# LAKE FRONT PARK II

## OCCUPANT

National League Chicago White Stockings, May 5, 1883–October 11, 1884

## CAPACITY

5,000

## DIMENSIONS

Left field: 186 (1883); 180 (1884)
Left center: 280
Center field: 300
Right center: 252
Right field: 196

## FENCES

Left field to right center 6; right field 37.5 (17.5 tarpaulin above 20 wood)

## PHENOMENA

Lake Front had the shortest outfield distances ever in a Major League ballpark: 180 feet to the left field foul pole and 196 feet to the right field foul pole. The left field fence was slightly shorter in 1884 than in 1883 because of a new row of private boxes built in front of the 1883 left field fence. In 1883 a ball hit over the left

**L**akefront Park #2, Chicago. Shortest outfield fences ever, left field was 180, right field was 196.

field fence was only a double, whereas in 1884 it was a home run. ◆ In 1883, the White Sox hit 13 homers, but in 1884 they hit 142. In 1883, the White Sox had 277 doubles, but many fewer in 1884 because they were homers instead of doubles when they flew over the left field fence. ◆ A pagoda, built for a bandstand and occupied by the First Cavalry Band, overlooked the main entrance. ◆ Forty-one people were employed for each game by the grounds: 7 ushers, 6 policemen, 4 ticket sellers, 4 gatekeepers, 3 field men, 3 cushion renters, 6 refreshment boys, and 8 musicians. ◆ The bleachers ran from left center to right center.

# SOUTH SIDE PARK I

**A.K.A.**
Chicago Cricket Club Grounds; Union Ball Park; 39th Street Grounds; Union Association Park; Union Grounds

**OCCUPANT**
Union Association Chicago Unions, May 2–August 1, 1884

**PHENOMENA**
It opened on June 18, 1883.

# WEST SIDE PARK

**OCCUPANT**
National League Chicago White Stockings, June 6, 1885–October 3, 1891 (1891 only on Mondays, Wednesdays, and Fridays)

**DIMENSIONS**
Foul lines: 216

**FENCES**
12

**PHENOMENA**
This park was long and narrow, bathtub-shaped like the Polo Grounds. A bicycle track surrounded the field. The Columbian Exposition in 1893 forced removal of the White Stockings from the park.

**W**est Side Park, Chicago. Cubs, then called Colts, won pennants here in 1885–1886, played here 1885–1891.

# SOUTH SIDE PARK II

### OCCUPANTS
Players League Chicago Pirates, April 30–October 4, 1890; National League Chicago White Stockings, May 5, 1891–September 27, 1893 (1891 only on Tuesdays, Thursdays, and Saturdays)

### FENCES
10

### PHENOMENA
Comiskey Park (I) stood on almost the same site. The two playing fields actually overlapped slightly, with the left field corner of South Side Park (II) corresponding to Comiskey Park (I)'s center field, and foul territory near third base in South Side Park (II) corresponding to Comiskey Park (I)'s right field.

# WEST SIDE GROUNDS

**W**est Side Grounds, Chicago. Fans standing in the outfield were commonplace a century ago. Cubs played here, 1894–1915.

**NEUTRAL USES**

National League Chicago Cubs May 14–September 17, 1893 (Sundays only)

**OCCUPANT**

National League Chicago Cubs, May 4, 1894–October 3, 1915

**CAPACITY**

16,000

**DIMENSIONS**

Left field: 340
Center field: 560
Right field: 316

**PHENOMENA**

A fire suspended the August 5, 1894 game in the 7th inning. It was caused by a lit cigar tossed into some rubbish. Using baseball bats, players Jimmy Ryan and Walt Wilmot were able to rescue 1,600 fans by hacking through a barbed wire fence, thus allowing the fans to escape onto the field.

# SOUTH SIDE PARK III

## OCCUPANTS
American League Chicago White Sox, April 24, 1901–June 27, 1910; Negro National League Chicago Giants, 1920; Negro National League Chicago American Giants, 1920–1931; Negro Southern League Chicago American Giants, 1932; Negro National League Chicago American Giants, 1933–1935; Negro American League Chicago American Giants, 1937–1940

## CAPACITY
15,000

## PHENOMENA
The fence cut back sharply around the J. F. Kidwell Greenhouse buildings in right center, making right center field relatively short compared to center field and right field. An overhanging roof was added in 1902. ◆ The park was used as a dog racing track during the summer of 1933, forcing the Negro National League American Giants to move all their home games from May 28 through the end of the 1933 season to Indianapolis.

# COMISKEY PARK I

## OCCUPANTS
American League Chicago White Sox, July 1, 1910–September 30, 1990; Negro American League Chicago American Giants, 1941–1950

## CAPACITY
28,800 (1910); 52,000 (1927); 50,000 (1938); 51,000 (1939); 50,000 (1940); 46,550 (1942); 46,500 (1947); 50,000 (1948); 46,550 (1953); 44,492 (1969); 43,931 (1989); 43,951 (1990)

## LARGEST CROWD
White Sox, 55,555 on May 20, 1973 for a Bat Day doubleheader vs. the Twins; Negro Leagues All Star Game, 51,723 in July 1943

## SMALLEST CROWD
511 on May 6, 1971 vs. the Red Sox

## SURFACE
Outfield: Bluegrass
Infield: Grass (1910); astroturf carpet, called Sox Sod (1969); bluegrass (1976)

## DIMENSIONS

Foul lines—363 (1910); 362 (1911); 365 (1927); 362 (1930); 342 (1934); 353 (1935); 340 (1936); 352 (1937); 332 (April 22, 1949); 352 (May 5, 1949); 335 (1969); 352 (marked 1971); 349 (actual 1971); 341 (1983); 347 (1986)

Power alleys: 382 (1910); 375 (1927); 370 (1934); 382 (1942); 362 (April 22, 1949); 375 (May 5, 1949); 382 (1954); 365 (1955); 375 (1956); 365 (1959); 375 (1968); 370 (1969); 375 (marked 1971); 382 (actual 1971); 374 (1983); 382 (1986)

Center field: 420 (1910); 450 (1926); 455 (1927); 450 (1930); 436 (1934); 422 (1936); 440 (1937); 420 (April 22, 1949); 415 (May 5, 1949); 410 (1951); 415 (1952); 400 (1969); 440 (1976); 445 (1977); 402 (marked 1981); 409 (actual 1981); 401 (1983); 409 (1986)

Backstop: 98 (1910); 71 (1933); 85 (1934); 86 (1955)

Foul territory: Large

## FENCES

Foul lines and power alleys: 12 (concrete, 1955); 9.83 (concrete, 1959); 5 (wire, 1969); 9.83 (concrete, 1971)

Center field: 15 (1927); 30 (1948); 17 (1976); 18 (1980)

Left center to right center inner fences: 5 (canvas, 1949); 6.5 (24-foot section in front of bullpens, 1969); 9 (1974); 7 (canvas, 1981); 7.5 (1982); 11 (1984); 7.5 (1986)

**C**omiskey Park #1, Chicago. Before the second deck was expanded in 1927.

South Side Base Ball Park, Chicago.

## PHENOMENA

Hall of Famer and Sox owner Bill Veeck painted a wild multicolor pattern in the left field upper deck seats in 1977, the year the Sox were labelled the South Side Hitmen. Despite numerous requests from fans and the media, he never explained why he did it. Not everything should be logical. ◆ Organist Nancy Faust played the Sox theme song during rallies, "Na-na-na-na, hey-hey-hey, Good-bye." ◆ There were showers in the bleachers in center. This was the scene of many masterful groundskeeping tricks by Roger, Gene, and Emil Bossard. In 1967 the name Camp Swampy referred to the area in front of the plate, which was dug up and soaked with water to make it soft when White Sox sinkerball pitchers were on the mound, but mixed with clay and gasoline and burned to provide hard soil when a sinkerballer was pitching for the visiting team. Opposing team bullpen mounds were lowered or raised from the standard 10-inch height to upset visiting pitchers' rhythm. Under Eddie Stanky's managerial tenure, the grass in front of the short-stop was cut long because the Sox shortstop had limited range, but at second the grass was cut short because the Sox second sacker had very good range. When the Sox had a lousy defensive outfield, the grass was cut long to turn triples into doubles, and when the Sox had good bunters, more paint was added to the foul line to tilt the ball back fair. ◆ One day, Sox shortstop Luke Appling heard his spikes hit metal. The game was delayed as a huge blue and white copper kettle was removed from the infield, and the resulting deep hole filled in. The site was formerly a city dump. ◆ This was the only place where the infield was made of astroturf (the

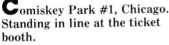

**C**omiskey Park #1, Chicago. Standing in line at the ticket booth.

Sox called it Sox Sod) and the outfield was grass from 1969 to 1975. ◆ For 81 consecutive years, Comiskey Park had the best foul lines in Major League baseball. They were old water hoses, painted bright white every year and flattened. ◆ In 1910, bleachers existed in left and right, but not in center. A section of the grandstand collapsed on May 17, 1913. The grandstand was originally double-decked from first to third base around behind home plate in 1910. During the winter of 1926 to 1927, the wooden bleachers were replaced with concrete and steel, and the single-deck pavilions from the bases out to center field were double-decked. The scoreboard was moved from right center field to two locations, on the left field and right field walls. The plate was moved 14 feet toward center field in the winter of 1933 to 1934 to give slugger Al Simmons a better chance at the seats, but it didn't help, so the plate was moved back to its original location in 1937. The center field bleachers were closed in 1947 to improve the batters' visibility. A special elevator, with inlaid tile flooring, for Lou Comiskey was in use from 1931 to 1982. ◆ All three homers in 1910 bounced through the iron gates near both foul poles. In 1949, Frank Lane constructed a low wire fence that reduced the fence distances down the lines from 352 to 332 but removed them in the middle of the night before the Yankees began a series in Chicago on May 5, because the opposing teams were hitting more homers into the 20-foot-wide strip between the 332 fence and the 352 fence. This caused the American League to pass a new rule that fences could not be moved more than once per season. In 1950, the bullpens were moved from foul territory down the lines to behind the center field fence. ◆ In 1960, Bill Veeck installed the first exploding scoreboard in the Majors, high above the bleachers in center, nicknamed the Monster. In 1982, when the Diamond Vision Board replaced the original, the pinwheels and fireworks for Sox home runs were retained. The green cornerstone laid on St. Patrick's Day in 1910 stayed green until 1960, when the exterior was painted white by Bill Veeck. ◆ A popcorn machine fire in the right field stands on June 4, 1974 caused a 70-minute delay. ◆ On July 12, 1979 the Tigers won the second game of a doubleheader by forfeit on Disco Demolition Night. ◆ The only seven batters to homer into the center field bleachers were Red Sox Jimmy Foxx off Ted Lyons on May 18, 1934; Tiger Hank Greenberg off Frank Gabler on May 27, 1938; Angel Alex Johnson off Billy Wynne on September 9, 1970; Dick Allen off Yankee Lindy McDaniel on August 23, 1972; Richie Zisk off Tiger Dave Rozema on May 22, 1977; Red Sox Tony Armas off Tom Seaver on April 28, 1984; and Blue Jay George Bell off Dave Wehrmeister on August

**C**omiskey Park #1, Chicago. Top: The scoreboard, built in 1960. Bottom: A tarp comes off after a rain delay.

23, 1985. ◆ There were nine speaker horns on the center field bleacher wall. There was a clock on the wall in center, to the left of the flagpole. There were picnic areas, including the Bullring in left and Bullpens I and II in right and right center, Bavarian and Mexican restaurants and beer halls under the stands behind the plate. Under Bill Veeck, this was a real ballpark, with everything happening at once and everyone having a good time. ◆ The foul poles bent back slightly to join the top of the roof. The 540 center field listing in the 1931 to 1933 Baseball Guides must be a misprint. There were open arches between first and second decks.

# CINCINNATI, OHIO*

## LINCOLN PARK GROUNDS

**A.K.A.**
Union Cricket Club Grounds; Union Grounds

**NEUTRAL USES**
National Association Washington Olympics, May 13, July 4, 1871; National Association Forest City of Cleveland, July 22, 1871

**PHENOMENA**
The ballpark opened on May 4, 1869, and was used by the professional Cincinnati Reds before the professional Major Leagues began in 1871.

## AVENUE GROUNDS

**OCCUPANT**
National League Cincinnati Reds, April 25, 1876–August 27, 1879

**PHENOMENA**
The first Major League Ladies Day was held here in 1876. The refreshment stand served hard-boiled eggs, ham sandwiches, and mineral water. Lemon peel-and-water drinks were 10 cents per glass.

## BANK STREET GROUNDS

**OCCUPANTS**
National League Cincinnati Reds, May 1–September 30, 1880; American Association Cincinnati Reds, May 21, 1882–September 29, 1883; Union Association Cincinnati Outlaw Reds, April 17–October 15, 1884

**PHENOMENA**
Location: Duck Street (W); Bank Street (S); Western Avenue (E); Cross Street (N). A levee on the west end kept out flood waters.
◆ When the Union Association team got the lease in November 1883, forcing the American Association team to move, the AA team decided to emply and scorched earth policy and dismantled everything, even removing the stone home plate from the ground.

*See also* Covington, Kentucky; Ludlow, Kentucky; Pendleton, Ohio

# LEAGUE PARK I

# LEAGUE PARK II

# PALACE OF THE FANS

**OCCUPANTS**

American Association Cincinnati Reds, May 1, 1884–October 15, 1889; National League Cincinnati Reds, April 19, 1890–September 29, 1893

**PHENOMENA**

On opening day, May 1, 1884, a section of the stands collapsed, injuring six people. ◆ A hit over the right field fence was only a double when the park first opened. ◆ During the first two weeks of May 1884, the park was enlarged by leasing additional land, moving the right fence back 50 feet.

**OCCUPANT**

National League Cincinnati Reds, April 20, 1894–October 2, 1901

**DIMENSIONS**

Left field: 253 (1894)

**PHENOMENA**

In 1895, the Reds were the first team to paint the center field wall black to help hitters see the pitch.

**OCCUPANT**

National League Cincinnati Reds, April 17, 1902–October 6, 1911

**DIMENSIONS**

Right field: 450

**P**alace of the Fans, Cincinnati. The police force passes in review, home of the Reds from 1902–1911.

# CROSLEY FIELD

## OCCUPANTS

National League Cincinnati Reds, April 11, 1912–June 24, 1970; Negro National League Cuban Stars, 1921; Negro American League Cincinnati Tigers, 1937; Negro American League Cincinnati Clowns, 1942–1945

## CAPACITY

25,000 (1912); 30,000 (1927); 33,000 (1938); 30,000 (1948); 29,980 (1952); 29,603 (1958); 30,328 (1960); 30,274 (1961); 29,603 (1964)

## LARGEST CROWD

Total—38,017 total, with 35,475 paid on August 29, 1943 vs. the Cardinals and 2,542 soldiers in uniform and blood donors admitted free; Paid—36,961 on April 27, 1947 vs. the Pirates

## DIMENSIONS

Left field: 360 (1912); 320 (1921); 352 (1926); 339 (1927); 328 (1938)
Scoreboard in left center: Left side—382 (1943–1956), 378 (1961–1970), right side—383 (1943–1956)
Left center: 380
Center field: 420 (1912); 417 (1926); 395 (1927); 393 (1930); 407 (1931); 393 (1933); 407 (1936); 387 (1938); 380 (1939); 387 (1940); 390 (1944); 387 (1955)
Right center: 383 (1955)
Right center deepest corner: 387 (1944)
Right field: 360 (1912); 384 (1921); 400 (1926); 383 (early 1927); 377 (late 1927); 366 (1938); 342 (1942); 366 (June 30, 1950); 342 (1953); 366 (1958)
Backstop: 38 (1912); 58 (1927); 66 (1943); 78 (1953)

## FENCES

Left field: 18 (1938); 12 (1957); 14 (1962); 18 (1963)
Clock on top of the scoreboard: 58 (1957); 55 (1967)
Left center scoreboard: 30 (1938); 37 (1943); 58 (1957); 50.17 (1958); 45 (1967)
Flagpole in left center: 82 in play
Exit gate left center 4 (before 1957)
Left center to right center 18 (1954); 14 (1962); 13.5 (1963); 23 (9.5 plywood over 13.5 concrete, 1965)
Center field: canvas shield above fence to protect against street light glare (1935–June 1940)
Right field: 7.5 (4.5 wire above 3 concrete, 1938); 7.5 (4.5 wire above 3 wood, 1942); 10 (7 wire above 3 wood, 1949); 12 (9 wire above 3

concrete, June 30, 1950); 10 (7 wire above 3 wood, 1953); 10 (7 wire above 3 concrete, 1958); 9 (6 wire above 3 concrete, 1959)

## PHENOMENA

Crosley Field's most famous fan was Harry Thobe, who entertained everyone in the 1940s. He danced a constant jig wearing a white suit, red stripes, one red shoe and one white shoe, a straw hat with a red band, and a red and white parasol, not to mention his 12 gold teeth. ◆ During the winter of 1926 to 1927, home plate was moved 20 feet toward center field, seats were added, and the field was turned slightly. A 40-foot net caught homers over the left field wall in the 1960s. ◆ This park was the scene on May 24, 1935 of the first night game in either the National League or the American League. President Franklin Delano Roosevelt turned on the 600 lights by pushing a button 500 miles away in the White House. ◆ In January 1937, the Mill Creek Flood covered the field with 21 feet of water. In the winter of 1937 to 1938, home plate was moved another 20 feet toward center. Thirteen loudspeaker horns were situated on top of the wooden left center scoreboard in the 1930s. ◆ In 1940, a canvas shield extended above the center field fence to protect batters' eyes from street light glare during night games. During day games it was taken down. It was accidentally left up

**C**rosley Field, Cincinnati. Inclined hill in left field.

21—Crosley Field, Cincinnati, Ohio, "Home of the Cincinnati Reds"

**C**rosley Field, Cincinnati. Left center scoreboard reconstructed in Blue Ash, Ohio.

for a day game
on June 7, 1940 and prevented Harry Craft of the
Reds from hitting a homer in the bottom of the 9th that would have
won the game. After the ensuing argument had raged for almost a
half-hour, the game resumed. The Reds' worst nightmare came
true, as the Dodgers won the game in the 11th. ◆ In 1957, a 58-
foot-high and 65-foot-wide scoreboard was installed. A ball could
roll under a low wooden fence in left center for a double, if it didn't
come out, or was in play if it rolled back out. ◆ There was a
Spiedler Suit sign on top of the Superior Towel and Linen Service
laundry building beyond the left field wall. By hitting the sign, 176
batters won free suits. ◆ Giles Gardens (also called Giles Chicken
Run and Giles Picnic Grounds) was an area behind the short right
field fence, when an inner 342-foot fence was in place to spur homer
production. ◆ There was a steep incline in front of the fence all
around the outfield, most noticeably in left and left center. ◆ The
park was named for Reds owner Powell Crosley, who built the
Crosley automobile. ◆ The center field wall was 13.5 feet high and
made of concrete. In 1963, in response to construction of an interstate highway behind the wall, 9.5 feet of plywood were added on
top of the concrete, making the wall 23 feet high altogether. But in
1963 and 1964, the plywood part was out of play. There was a home
run line painted where the concrete and plywood met, and the

umpires had to call a homer if the ball appeared or sounded as if it hit off the plywood. Then, because of all the controversies, the home run line was overpainted in 1965 and the entire 23-foot wall was in play. There was another home run line, this one in the right center corner where the center field concrete wall met the right center field fence. The vertical white line was painted on the concrete, with white letters adjacent to it reading: "Batted ball hitting concrete wall on fly to right of white line—home run." This is the only known ground rule ever painted on an outfield wall in Major League history. ◆ Ernie Lombardi's homer over the center field wall landed in a truck and travelled 30 miles. ◆ A three-story brick building in center, owned by the Regal Belting Company in the 1940s, and by Crowe Engineering Company in the 1950s, was the scene of a sign-stealing episode by Frank Hutchinson in 1960 against the Cubs. ◆ The first Crosley Field Old Timers Game was played at the newly reconstructed Crosley Field at Blue Ash Sports Center on August 13, 1989. ◆ The left center field scoreboard remains as it was on the last pitch back on June 24, 1970. There are 270 restored original Crosley Field seats. ◆ The right field bleachers had a sunburst painted on the rear wall with the words "Sun Deck" painted inside. It was called the Moon Deck for night games.

## CLEVELAND, OHIO*

# NATIONAL ASSOCIATION GROUNDS

### OCCUPANT
National Association Forest City of Cleveland, May 11, 1871–August 19, 1872

### LARGEST CROWD
3,000 on May 26, 1871 vs. the Fort Wayne Kekiongas

*See also Collinwood, Ohio; Geauga Lake, Ohio

# NATIONAL LEAGUE PARK I

**A.K.A.**
Kennard Street Park

**OCCUPANT**
National League Clevelands, May 1, 1879–October 11, 1884

**PHENOMENA**
There were trees in the outfield in 1879. ◆ The left field fence was so short in 1880 and 1881 that balls hit over the fence were only doubles.

# NATIONAL LEAGUE PARK II

**OCCUPANT**
American Association Cleveland Spiders, May 4, 1887–September 15, 1888; National League Cleveland Spiders, May 3, 1889–October 4, 1890

**DIMENSIONS**
Foul poles: 410
Center field: 420

**PHENOMENA**
A large fire in June 1890 was caused by lightning. ◆ The outfield fence was more than 400 feet all around.

# BROTHERHOOD PARK

**OCCUPANT**
Players League Cleveland Infants, 1890

**PHENOMENA**
Location: Kinsman Road (E); Diamond Park Street, now called Diamond Street (N); home plate: Willson Avenue, now East 55th Street (W); 1st base: New York, Chicago, and St. Louis railroad tracks, also called Nickel Plate Railroad, now called Cleveland RTA (S).

# LEAGUE PARK I

## OCCUPANTS
National League Cleveland Spiders, May 1, 1891–August 30, 1899; American League Cleveland Indians, April 29, 1901–September 6, 1909

## CAPACITY
9,000

## DIMENSIONS
Right field: 290

## FENCES
Right field: 20

## PHENOMENA
The park was struck by lightning during an 1892 game with the Chicago Colts, setting the park on fire and canceling the game.

# LEAGUE PARK II

## OCCUPANTS
American League Cleveland Indians, April 21, 1910–July 30, 1932; American League Cleveland Indians, April 17, 1934–September 21, 1946; Negro American League Cleveland Bears, 1939–1940; Negro American League Cleveland Buckeyes, 1943–1948, 1950

## CAPACITY
21,000 (1910); 22,500 (1939)

## LARGEST CROWD
Total—33,628 total, with 28,246 paid on June 15, 1930 vs. the Yankees; Paid—28,676 with 29,266 total on June 16, 1920 vs. the Yankees

## DIMENSIONS
Left field: 385 (1910); 376 (1920); 374 (1930); 373 (1934); 374 (1938); 375 (1942)
Left center: 415 (1942)
Deepest corner, just left of center field: 505 (1910); 450 (1920); 467 (1930); 465 (1938); 460 (1939)
Center field: 420
Right center: 400 (1942)
Right field: 290 (1921); 240 (when roped off for overflow crowds)
Backstop: 76 (1910); 60 (1942)

## FENCES

Left field: 5 (concrete)
Left center: 10 (7 screen above 3 concrete)
Center field scoreboard: 35
Right center clock: 20 (left and right sides); 22 (center of clock)
Right center field: Parts not covered by chicken wire screen, 45 (20 concrete topped by 25 steel chicken wire screen supports, 1920)
Right field: Parts covered by chicken wire screen, 45 (20 concrete topped by 25 chicken wire screen, 1920)

## PHENOMENA

The park was named Dunn Park from 1916 to 1927 after James Dunn, who owned it. Seats were added in left and center during August 1920, which considerably reduced the fence distances. Before then, the center field fence was as distant as center field at the Polo Grounds. ◆ Steel beams covered by concrete protruded from the wall in right, causing many balls to bounce at crazy angles. Only at League Park did left fielders field doubles to right field. ◆ A large chicken wire fence stood in right field. There were 24 vertical steel girders in right field, which were partially covered by chicken wire, from the right field foul line out into right center. The distance that was covered by chicken wire var-

**L**eague Park, Cleveland. Top: Outfield stands still exist, home of the Indians from 1910–1946. Bottom: Ticket booth is now a community center.

ied from season to season and from month to month. The supports that were not covered by chicken wire extended 25 feet above the concrete and were themselves in play. This created the situation in which a ball that went like a field goal between the supports, but over the concrete, was a home run, but a similarly hit ball that hit one of the supports was not a home run but remained in play and became probably a double or a triple. ◆ A large green scoreboard was in center field and a clock was just to the right of the scoreboard. The ball could roll under the scoreboard, and occasionally a center fielder would have to crawl under the scoreboard to recover a ball that was still in play. Nobody played center field here as well as Tris Speaker. ◆ The roof over the grandstand was 79 feet high above ground level. Megaphone speakers were on the left center wall. One of the two flagpoles rose from behind the bleacher seats in left center; the other one rose from the center field scoreboard. ◆ Teepees were erected in 1946. ◆ A historical marker notes that the Cleveland Buckeyes won the 1945 Negro World Series here.

# TATE PARK

**OCCUPANTS**

Negro National League Cleveland Tate Stars, 1922; Cleveland Tigers, 1923; Cleveland Browns, 1924; Cleveland Elites, 1926

# HOOPER FIELD

**OCCUPANT**

Negro National League Cleveland Hornets, 1927

# CUBS STADIUM

**OCCUPANTS**
Negro National League Cleveland Cubs, 1931; Negro East-West League Cleveland Cubs, 1932

**PHENOMENA**
A tiny park, it literally stood in the shadows of League Park II, home of the Indians, across the street.

# HARDWARE FIELD

**NEUTRAL USES**
Some Negro National League Cleveland Cubs games in 1931

**OCCUPANT**
Negro Southern League Cleveland Stars, 1932

**PHENOMENA**
It was located at East 79th Street and Kinsman Road.

# LUNA BOWL

**OCCUPANTS**
Negro National League Cleveland Giants, 1933; Cleveland Tigers, 1928; Cleveland Red Sox, 1934

**PHENOMENA**
Location: Ingersoll Road Southeast (N); Woodhill Road (W); Woodland Avenue Southeast (S); East 110th Street (E); currently part of an amusement park.

## COLLINWOOD, OHIO

# EUCLID BEACH PARK

**NEUTRAL USES**
National League Cleveland Exiles, June 12, 19, 1898

**PHENOMENA**
The park was 9 miles from Cleveland. Since then, Collinwood has been annexed into the city of Cleveland. The amusement park was built here in 1895, 3 years before the two Sunday Major League games came to the field. Sunday ball here ended with a bang when the Collinwood police arrested all the Cleveland players in the bottom of the 8th inning of the June 19, 1898 game, which was in violation of the Sunday blue laws. The Spiders had just pushed a run across the plate to take a 4–3 lead. The arrests assured Cleveland of the victory but ended Sunday baseball in Collinwood.

## COLUMBUS, OHIO

# RECREATION PARK I

**OCCUPANT**
American Association Columbus Senators, May 1, 1883–September 22, 1884

**PHENOMENA**
It was on a 450-foot square plot in 1884.

# RECREATION PARK II

**OCCUPANT**
American Association Columbus Solons, April 28, 1889–September 22, 1891

**DIMENSIONS**
Right field: 400

# NEIL PARK I

**NEUTRAL USES**

American League Cleveland Bronchos, August 3, 1902; Cleveland Naps, May 17, 1903

**DIMENSIONS**

Right field: 240

# NEIL PARK II

**NEUTRAL USES**

American League Detroit Tigers, July 23–24, 1905

**OCCUPANTS**

Negro National League Columbus Buckeyes, 1921; Negro Southern League Columbus Turfs, 1932

# RED BIRD STADIUM

**OCCUPANTS**

Negro National League Columbus Bluebirds, 1933; Negro National League Columbus Elite Giants, 1935

**CAPACITY**

17,500 (1938); 12,000 (1960); 15,000 (1978)

**DIMENSIONS**

Left field: 415 (1938); 336 (1960); 350 (1978); 355 (1984)
Center field: 450 (1938); 430 (1960); 400 (1978)
Right center: 337
Right field: 315 (1938); 345 (1960); 330 (1978)

**FENCES**

Left field: 6
Center field: 10
Right field: 8

**R**ed Bird Stadium, Columbus, Ohio.

## COVINGTON, KENTUCKY

# STAR BASEBALL PARK

**NEUTRAL USE**
National Association Philadelphia Pearls, September 21, 1875

**PHENOMENA**
Location: 17th Street (N); Madison Street (W); 18th Street (S); Scott Street (E); just across the river from Cincinnati.

## DAYTON, OHIO

# FAIRVIEW PARK

**NEUTRAL USE**
American League Cleveland Bronchos, June 8, 1902

**PHENOMENA**
Streetcars went up North Main Street, then across the north end of the park, and back to North Main Street.

# DUCKS PARK

**OCCUPANTS**
Negro National League Dayton Marcos, 1920; Negro National League Dayton Marcos, 1926

**CAPACITY**
5,000

**DIMENSIONS**
All around: 360

# DETROIT, MICHIGAN*

## RECREATION PARK

**OCCUPANT**
National League Detroit Wolverines, May 2, 1881–September 22, 1888

**FENCES**
9

## BENNETT PARK

**OCCUPANT**
American League Detroit Tigers, April 25, 1901–September 10, 1911

**CAPACITY**
5,000 (1896); 8,500 (1901); 14,000 (1910)

**FENCES**
10

## BURNS PARK

**A.K.A.**
West End Park

**OCCUPANT**
American League Detroit Tigers, April 28, 1901–September 7, 1902 (Sundays)

## MACK PARK

**OCCUPANT**
Negro National League Detroit Stars, 1920–1929

**PHENOMENA**
Located on the East Side of town, it was a ramshackle ballpark made of wood and tin sheeting. Fire halted a July 6, 1929 game vs. the Kansas City Monarchs, injuring 103 people.

*See also Hamtramck, Michigan

# DEQUINDRE PARK

### A.K.A.
Linton Field; Cubs Park

### OCCUPANT
Negro American League Detroit Stars, 1937

# DOVER, DELAWARE

# FAIRVIEW PARK FAIR GROUNDS

### NEUTRAL USE
National Association Philadelphia Athletics, June 24, 1875

### PHENOMENA
Used for Delaware's first state fair in 1878. Location: Ross Street (N); Delaware Railroad (W); William Street (S); Queen Street (E).

# EAST ORANGE, NEW JERSEY

# GROVE STREET OVAL

### OCCUPANTS
Negro National League New York Cubans, 1940–1948; Negro American League New York Cubans, 1949–1950

### DIMENSIONS
Left field: 240
Center field: 360 to the water fountain
Right field: 280

### FENCES
Left field: 25 (garage walls)
Center field: 4 (water fountain, but no fence)
Right field: 0 (trees and tennis courts in play, but no fence)

## PHENOMENA

The 4-foot-high water fountain was in play in the deepest part of center field. "Bujum" Jud Wilson hit the longest ball ever hit here, way over the water fountain in dead center. ◆ This ballpark was renamed Monte Irvin Field at a June 6, 1986 ceremony. ◆ There was no fence in center field, but there were some hedges. There were trees in right, as well as tennis courts beyond. The scoreboard was in left, as well as some poplar trees. The clubhouse down the right field line was in foul territory.

**G**rove Street Oval, East Orange, New Jersey. Top: As it appears today as Monte Irvin Field, water fountain was in play in center field. Bottom: Plaque designates the field as a historic site.

## ELMIRA, NEW YORK

# MAPLE AVENUE DRIVING PARK

**NEUTRAL USE**

National League Buffalo Bisons, October 10, 1885

**M**aple Avenue Driving Park, Elmira, New York. Horse carriages carried the fans to games in the 1880s.

## FORT WAYNE, INDIANA

# HAMILTON FIELD

**OCCUPANT**

National Association Fort Wayne Kekiongas, May 4–August 29, 1871

**PHENOMENA**

This was the scene of the very first Major League game on May 4, 1871. The Kekiongas beat Forest City of Cleveland 2–0 before 200 fans. News accounts referred to the "ever-present Menace of the St. Mary's River," to the north. Apparently there were a lot of floods.

# SWINNEY PARK

**NEUTRAL USE**

The ninth and decisive game of the 1882 post-season playoffs between the Chicago White Stockings and the Providence Grays on October 24, 1882

**LARGEST CROWD**

600 on October 24, 1882 between the White Stockings and the Grays

# JAILHOUSE FLATS

**A.K.A.**

League Park

**NEUTRAL USES**

American League Cleveland Bronchos, June 22, August 31, 1902

## GEAUGA LAKE, OHIO

# BEYERLE'S PARK

**NEUTRAL USES**

American Association Cleveland Blues, July 22, 29, August 26, September 2, 1888

**CURRENT USE**

Geauga Lake Amusement Park.

## GLOUCESTER CITY, NEW JERSEY

# GLOUCESTER POINT GROUNDS

**OCCUPANT**

American Association Philadelphia Athletics, August 5, 1888 to October 12, 1890 (Sundays)

## GRAND RAPIDS, MICHIGAN

# RAMONA PARK

### NEUTRAL USE
American League Detroit Tigers, May 24, 1903

### LARGEST CROWD
6000 on May 24, 1903 vs. Washington Senators.

## HAMTRAMCK, MICHIGAN

# HAMTRAMCK STADIUM

### OCCUPANTS
Negro National League Detroit Stars, 1930–1931; Negro East-West League Detroit Wolves, 1932; Negro National League Detroit Stars, 1933

### DIMENSIONS
Left field: 315
Right field: 407

### FENCES
12

### PHENOMENA
The first baseball game here followed the ballpark's dedication on May 11, 1930 as the Stars faced the New York Cubans. Ty Cobb threw out the first ball. ◆ Detroit's first Major League night game was held here on June 28, 1930 vs. the Kansas City Monarchs.

## HARRISBURG, PENNSYLVANIA

# WEST END GROUNDS

**OCCUPANT**
Eastern Colored League Harrisburg Giants, 1924–1927

# ISLAND STADIUM

**OCCUPANT**
Negro National League Harrisburg–St. Louis Stars, 1943

**PHENOMENA**
It was located on a city island in the Susquehanna River, also called Forsters Island.

## HARRISON, NEW JERSEY

# HARRISON PARK

**OCCUPANT**
Federal League Newark Peppers, April 16–October 3, 1915

**CAPACITY**
21,000 (1915)

**DIMENSIONS**
Foul lines: 375
Center field: 450

## HARTFORD, CONNECTICUT

# HARTFORD BALL CLUB GROUNDS

**NEUTRAL USES**

National Association Middletown Mansfields, 1872

**OCCUPANTS**

National Association Hartford Dark Blues, May 1, 1874–October 29, 1875; National League Hartford Dark Blues, May 1–September 30, 1876

## HOUSTON, TEXAS

# BUFF STADIUM

**OCCUPANT**

Negro American League Houston Eagles, 1949–1950

**CAPACITY**

14,000

**DIMENSIONS**

Left field: 344 (1928); 345 (1938)
Center field: 430 (1928); 440 (1938)
Right field: 344 (1928); 325 (1938)

**FENCES**

12

**PHENOMENA**

There were huge pictures of buffaloes on the adobe wall, high above the Spanish-style entrance's tile roof. ◆ Home plate's exact location is now marked by a plaque in the Houston Sports Hall of Fame, which is part of Fingers Furniture Store.

# COLT STADIUM

### OCCUPANT
National League Houston Colt .45's, April 10, 1962–September 27, 1964

### CAPACITY
32,601 (1962); 33,010 (1964)

### LARGEST CROWD
30,027 on June 10, 1962 vs. the Dodgers

### DIMENSIONS
Foul lines: 360
Power alleys: 395
Center field: 420
Deepest corners in center, just left and right of straightaway center: 427
Backstop: 60

### FENCES
Left and right: 8
Center field screen: 30

### PHENOMENA
The groundbreaking ceremony on January 3, 1962 used .45-caliber blanks rather than shovels. ◆ After the Astrodome was built right next door, this ballpark lay in decay until the early 1970s, when it was bought and moved to Torréon, Mexico's twin city, Gomez Palacio, by a Mexican League team called the Cotton Growers. There were scoreboards in center on both sides of the 30-foot-high batters' background. ◆ A stiff wind blew in from right toward the plate. Power alley measurements were not marked on the wall. ◆ It was the home of the largest and peskiest mosquitoes in Major League history, and the players referred to the park as Mosquito Heaven. The park was regularly sprayed with insect repellant by the ground crew between innings.

# INDIANAPOLIS, INDIANA

## SOUTH STREET PARK

**OCCUPANT**
National League Indianapolis Blues, May 1–September 14, 1878

**PHENOMENA**
It was converted from a cornfield in 1869. ◆ The ladies' entrance was on Alabama Street.

## SEVENTH STREET PARK I

**OCCUPANT**
American Association Indianapolis Blues, May 14–September 20, 1884

**PHENOMENA**
Location: North Mississippi Street, later Boulevard Street, later Senate Street (W); Seventh Street, later West 17th Street (S); North Tennessee Street, later Capitol Avenue (E); Eighth Street, later West 18th Street.

## BRUCE GROUNDS

**OCCUPANT**
American Association Indianapolis Blues, May 18–September 21, 1884 (Sundays)

**PHENOMENA**
Location: 21st Street (N); College Avenue (W); Bruce Street, later 25th Street (S); Wabash Railroad tracks (E). ◆ It was pretty small, on a plot 420 by 400 feet.

## SEVENTH STREET PARK II

**OCCUPANT**
National League Indianapolis Hoosiers, April 28–October 8, 1887

**DIMENSIONS**
Left field: 286
Right field: 261

# SEVENTH STREET PARK III

**OCCUPANT**

National League Indianapolis Hoosiers, April 20, 1888–October 5, 1889

**PHENOMENA**

Same location as Seventh Street Parks I and II, but turned around so that home plate was in the southwest rather than the southeast. ◆ A 10-foot net in left was added on June 24, 1889.

# INDIANAPO-LIS PARK

**NEUTRAL USES**

National League Cleveland Spiders, July 28–August 2, 1890

**LARGEST CROWD**

1,534 on July 31, 1890 vs. the Giants

# FEDERAL LEAGUE PARK

**OCCUPANT**

Federal League Indianapolis Hoosier-Feds, April 23–October 8, 1914

**CAPACITY**

20,000 (1914)

**DIMENSIONS**

Left field: 375
Center field: 400
Right field: 310

# ABC'S FIELD

**OCCUPANTS**

Negro National League Indianapolis ABC's, 1920–1926, 1931; Negro Southern League Indianapolis ABC's, 1932; Negro American League Indianapolis ABC's, 1937–1939; Negro American League Indianapolis Crawfords, 1940

# OWEN BUSH STADIUM

**O**wen Bush Stadium, Indianapolis, Indiana. A 1930s ballpark made to look even older for the movie *Eight Men Out,* the story of the 1919 Black Sox scandal.

**OCCUPANT**
Negro American League Indianapolis Clowns, 1944, 1946–1950

**CAPACITY**
15,000 (1938); 13,254 (1947); 12,934 (1985)

**°DIMENSIONS**
Foul lines: 350 (1938); 335 (1950)
Center field: 497 (1938); 500 (1947); 480 (1950); 395 (1985)

## IRONDEQUOIT, NEW YORK

# WINDSOR BEACH

**NEUTRAL USES**
American Association Rochesters, May 11–July 20, 1890 (Sundays)

## JACKSONVILLE, FLORIDA

# JACKSON-VILLE BASEBALL PARK

**OCCUPANT**
Negro American League Jacksonville Red Caps, 1938, 1941–1942

**CAPACITY**
4,564

**DIMENSIONS**
Left field: 350
Center field: 400
Right field: 309

## JERSEY CITY, NEW JERSEY

# OAKDALE PARK

**NEUTRAL USES**
National League New York Giants, April 24–25, 1889

**PHENOMENA**
Location: Oakland Avenue (NW); Hoboken Avenue (SW); Concord Street, then a wagon works, and a coal yard (SE); Fleet Street (NE).

# ROOSEVELT STADIUM

**NEUTRAL USES**
National League Brooklyn Dodgers for seven 1956 games and eight 1957 games from April 19, 1956 to September 3, 1957

**CAPACITY**
20,000 (1937); 26,000 (1938); 30,000 (1939); 25,000 (1947); 24,330 (1948); 24,330 (1952); 24,500 (1957)

**LARGEST CROWD**
Minor League—31,234 on April 23, 1937; Major League Dodgers—26,385 on August 15, 1956 vs. the Giants

**R**oosevelt Stadium, Jersey City, New Jersey. Left: The wrecking ball comes to center field. Right: The right center field scoreboard, 30 years after the Dodgers played here in 1956–57.

## DIMENSIONS

Foul lines: 330
Power alleys: 397
Center field: 411
Backstop: 60

## FENCES

Foul line corners: 11
Left field to center field: 4
Right center to right field: 7

## PHENOMENA

This was formerly a landfill for dirt excavated from the Holland Tunnel. The park was built as a Works Progress Administration (WPA) project in 1937 and named for President Franklin D. Roosevelt. ◆ Willie Mays hit the only ball ever knocked completely out of Roosevelt Stadium to beat the Dodgers 1–0 in 1956. ◆ A plaque now marks the spot where the ballpark used to stand. ◆ The Newark Bay mist brought mosquitoes and mist into the outfield. ◆ Thanksgiving Day morning football games between St. Peter's and Dickinson were always sold out in the 1940s.

# KANSAS CITY, MISSOURI

## ATHLETIC PARK

**OCCUPANT**
Union Association Kansas City Unions, June 7–October 19, 1884

**PHENOMENA**
Fly balls over the short right field fence were only doubles. ◆ Location: Summit Street, Southwest Boulevard.

## ASSOCIATION PARK

**OCCUPANTS**
National League Kansas City Cowboys, April 30–September 18, 1886; American Association Kansas City Cowboys, April 18–September 29, 1888

**PHENOMENA**
It was called The Hole because it was in a pit created when dirt was dug out to create a roadbed for Independence Avenue. On what had previously been the site of Ranson's Pond. The field was 25 feet below street level. ◆ An outfield sign read, "Please don't shoot the umpire. He is doing the best he can."

## EXPOSITION PARK

**OCCUPANT**
American Association Kansas City Cowboys, September 30, 1888–September 30, 1889

**PHENOMENA**
Exposition Park included a race track, an exhibition hall, and a ballpark. ◆ It was reopened on May 11, 1902, after having burned down.

## GORDON AND KOPPEL FIELD

**OCCUPANT**
Federal League Kansas City Packers, April 16, 1914–September 28, 1915

**CAPACITY**
12,000 (1914)

# MUNICIPAL STADIUM

**S**atchel Paige Memorial Stadium, Kansas City, Missouri. Dedicated August 9, 1984, the scene of the Kansas City Monarchs reunion.

## OCCUPANTS

Negro American League Kansas City Monarchs, 1923–1950; American League Kansas City Athletics, April 12, 1955–September 27, 1967; American League Kansas City Royals, April 8, 1969–October 4, 1972

## CAPACITY

17,476 (1923); 30,296 (1955); 30,611 (1956); 32,241 (1961); 32,561 (1964); 34,165 (1969); 35,057 (1970); 35,561 (1971)

## LARGEST CROWD

Royals—36,623 on August 3, 1971 vs. the Athletics; Athletics—35,147 on August 18, 1962 vs. the Yankees

## DIMENSIONS

Left field: 350 (1923); 312 (1955); 330 (1956); 370 (1961); 353 (1962); 331 (1963); 370 (1965); 369 (1967)

Left center: 408 (1923); 382 (1955); 375 (1957); 390 (1961); 364 (1963); 392 (1964); 409 (1965); 408 (1969)

Center field: 450 (1923); 432 (1950); 430 (1955); 421 (1956); 410 (1964); 421 (1965)

Right center: 382 (1955); 387 (1957); 364 (1962); 360 (1963); 392 (1964); 360 (1965); 382 (1969)

Right field: 350 (1923); 347 (1955); 352 (1956); 353 (1957); 338 (1963); 325 (1965); 338 (1966)

Backstop: 60 (1955); 70 (1963)

## FENCES

Left field: 24 (screen, 1955); 18.5 (concrete, 1958); 38.5 (20 screen over 18.5 concrete, 1959); 10 (1961); 13.5 (1962); 10 (1963); 22 (1967); 13 (1969)

Center field: 24 (1955); 12 (1958); 14 (1959); 12 (1961); 13.5 (1962); 10 (1963); 22 (screen, 1966); 40 (screen, 1969); 22 (screen, 1970)

Right field: 12 (1955); 14 (1959); 12 (1961); 13.5 (1962); 10 (1963); 4.5 (plywood, 1965); 40 (screen, 1966); 13 (1969); 12 (screen, 1970)

## PHENOMENA

This park was formerly a swimming hole, frog pond, and an ash heap. The right field embankment was a zoo: Sheep, Charlie O. the Mule, China golden pheasants, Capuchin monkeys, German checker rabbits, peafowl, and a German shorthaired pointer dog named Old Drum all lived out there. The animals were well fed with fresh food from the K. C. Farmers Market. One night, the Tigers players got the monkeys drunk with vodka-soaked oranges. Little Blowhard was a subterranean beast that blew compressed air through the middle of the plate so that the umpire didn't have to brush it off. Harvey the Mechanical Rabbit rose out of the ground to the right of the plate to give the plate umpire new baseballs from a basket between his ears. ◆ It opened on July 3, 1923 and was originally named for owner George Muehlebach. When the park was rebuilt in 1955, home plate was moved out 25 feet toward the outfield. During the spring of 1955, the right center field scoreboard was put into position. It had previously stood in Braves Field in Boston. The bottom of the left center light tower was in play; the warning track detoured around it, making for some very unusual bounces. The wind blew predominantly from the plate toward left field. ◆ Charlie O. Finley believed that one of the reasons that the Yankees won so many pennants was their Pennant Porch, a 296-foot short right field porch. In April 1965, he created his own 296-foot pennant porch in Municipal Stadium's right field. A 4.5-foot-high green plywood fence was installed and curved in from right center field to a spot 296 feet from home plate and 5 feet in fair territory from the foul line. The fence then curved back sharply to a new foul pole 325 feet from the plate. The fence had "K-C Pennant Porch" painted on it to the left of the 296 mark and "296 FT" painted on it to the right of the 296 mark. The 325-foot foul pole was not marked with a "325." After two home exhibition games,

**M**uehlebach Field, Kansas City, Missouri. Later known as Municipal Stadium, home of the Monarchs Negro League team, 1923–1950; Athletics, 1955–1967; Royals, 1969–1972.

**S**atchel Paige's All Stars, Kansas City, Missouri.

Commissioner Ford Frick, who never understood that the game is supposed to be entertainment for the fans, ordered the fence moved back so that it uniformly curved from right center to the 325-foot foul pole. Finley responded by building a flimsy roof extension on the top of the right field stands out to the 296-foot mark. At the home opener, the umpires ordered that this be removed also. Finley finally painted "K-C One-Half Pennant Porch" on the right field fence. ◆ One day Charles O. Finley was giving a pre-game tour of the park to a young fan who had come from Nebraska to see the game. Opening a gate in right center, he escorted the child into what he thought would be the right field embankment zoo behind the right field fence. Instead, he and the fan walked right into right center field near A's center fielder Jim Landis just as a pitch was being delivered. ◆ Sam's Baseball Parking sign can still be seen on the bridge over the nearby railroad tracks. Charlie Finley sometimes phoned the ballpark from Gary, Indiana, where he listened to the A's games on radio and directed hefty bonuses or free meals from Bryant's Bar-B-Q for the grounds crew or other employees. Finley doubled the grounds crew's daily salary whenever they got the tarp down in less than 45 seconds. ◆ When Charlie Finley brought Satchel Paige back for a few months to qualify for his pension, Smokey Olson, a member of the grounds crew from Florence, Montana, used Charley O. the Mule's blanket to keep Satch's legs warm as he rocked in a rocking chair in the bullpen.

## KEOKUK, IOWA

# PERRY PARK

### OCCUPANT
National Association Keokuk Westerns, May 4–June 14, 1875

### PHENOMENA
There were two lakes out in center field, into which some outfielders fell while chasing fly balls.

# LITTLE ROCK, ARKANSAS

## TRAVELLERS FIELD

**OCCUPANT**
Negro Southern League Little Rock Grays, 1932

**CAPACITY**
10,500 (1925); 7,000 (1938); 6,100 (1983)

**DIMENSIONS**
Left field: 325 (1925); 345 (1938); 320 (1983)
Center field: 405 (1925); 450 (1938); 390 (1983)
Right field: 300 (1925); 395 (1938); 340 (1983)

# LOS ANGELES, CALIFORNIA*

## LOS ANGELES MEMORIAL COLISEUM

**OCCUPANT**
National League Los Angeles Dodgers, April 18, 1958–September 20, 1961

**CAPACITY**
74,000 (1923); 75,000 (1928); 105,000 (1932); 103,000 (1941); 105,000 (1944); 103,500 (1947); 101,671 (1948); 105,000 (1952); 101,528 (1956); 93,000 (1958); 94,600 (1959); 70,000 (1965); 76,000 (1968); 78,000 (1972); 76,000 (1973); 92,000 (1974); 91,038 (1976); 71,432 (1977); 71,039 (1978); 73,999 (1979); 92,488 (1982); 92,498 (1983); 92,516 (1985); 92,488 (1988) The stadium was patterned after the Roman Colosseum, built in 82 A.D. in Rome, Italy, with a capacity of 50,000.

**LARGEST CROWD**
Exhibition—93,103 on May 7, 1959 for Roy Campanella Night vs. the Yankees; World Series—92,706 on October 6, 1959 vs. the White Sox; Regular season total—90,751, with 67,312 paid on August 8, 1959 vs. the Braves; Regular season paid—78,672 on April 18, 1958 vs. the Giants

**DIMENSIONS**
Left field: 250 (1958); 251.6 (1959)
Left center: 320 at end of screen rectangle
Left center where the fence met the wall: 425 (1958); 417 (1959)

*See also* Anaheim, California

Center field: 425 (1958); 420 (1959)

Right center: 440 (1958); 375 (1959); 394 (1960); 380 (1961)

Right field where the fence met the wall: 390 (1958); 333 (1959); 340 (1960)

Right field: 301 (1958); 300 (1959)

Backstop: 60 (1958); 66 (1959)

Foul territory: Tremendously large area on third baseline, but almost none on first baseline

### FENCES

Left field: 40 (screen, 1958); 42 (screen, 1959); 60 (2 support towers for screen, 1958)

Left center: 40 (fence, 1958); from foul pole 140 feet into left center, 42 sloping to ground at a 30-degree angle from 320 mark to 348 mark for a distance of 24 feet (1959 to 1960); 4 steps down from 42 to 8; first step left corner 42 sloping to 41, second step 31, third step 20, fourth step 12 (1961)

Right of screen in left center: 8 (wire)

Center field to right field corner: 6 (wire)

Right field corner: 4 (concrete)

**L**os Angeles Coliseum, Los Angeles. Not much foul territory down the first baseline.

## PHENOMENA

A 42-foot screen in left field was placed to prevent 251-foot popups from becoming homers. Commissioner Ford Frick attempted to order the Dodgers to construct a second screen in left, in the seats at 333 feet. A ball clearing both screens would be a home run, but a ball clearing just the shorter screen would be a double. The California Earthquake Law made construction of such a screen illegal. Imagine the arguments, had the second screen been built, over balls landing near the left center end of the second screen, and over whether it was a homer or a double. ◆ A girder over the left field screen caused the 1959 pennant race to be won by the Dodgers rather than the Braves. Joe Adcock's hit in the top of the 5th on September 15, 1959 cleared the screen but struck a girder behind the top of the screen and lodged in the overlapping mesh screens. The umpire ruled it a double but changed it to a homer when fans shook the screen and the ball landed in the seats behind the screen. Then he reversed again and called it a double. Adcock never scored. LA won in extra innings. LA and the Braves ended the season in a tie; LA won the playoff. If Adcock had scored, the Braves would have won the flag by two games. ◆ O'Malley considered using the Rose Bowl in Pasadena for the first years after the move from Brooklyn, before Dodger Stadium would be open. It would have been laid out much differently than the Coliseum. Ten rows would have been removed in right and left to deepen the foul lines to 300 feet, and center field would have been 460. The field would have been symmetrical, because home plate would have been in one endzone and center field in the other endzone. Box seats were to have been added behind the plate and between first and third. ◆ The first event here was a college football game on October 6, 1923. The Olympics have been held here twice, first in 1932, and then again in 1984. ◆ The wall in left center juts out twice, going from chest to thigh level, jutting out to ankle level, jutting out to thigh level, then back again to chest level. The concrete wall in the right field corner is the wall surrounding the football field. It slopes sharply away from home plate, making a Fenway-like shaped Belly and creating the situation in which a long drive near the right field foul line would be an out but a short fly right down the line would be a home run, just like at Fenway. ◆ Two huge stones are on exhibit under the peristylum atop the bleachers in right center at one end of the oval: The one on the left is from the Altis in Olympia, Greece, and the one on the right is from the Colosseum in Rome, Italy. It has a huge tunnel behind home plate. It was first used for baseball by the University of Southern California Trojans, who worked out here before the Dodgers opened the 1958 season. ◆ Two future Dodgers were the first to hit homers: Johnny Werhas over the left field screen and Ron Fairly over the deep right field fence. ◆ The park has 79 rows of seats. It is 700 feet from the plate to the furthest seats under the peristylum. The rim is 110 feet above ground level, the field is 33 feet below ground level. Cables, towers, and wires above the screen were in play. A small green light pole was in the field of play in right field. From 1921 to 1923, 74,000 seats were built; the park was expanded to 105,000 seats for the 1932 Olympic games. ◆ On June 3, 1958, after a successful Dodgers road trip, the citizens of Los Angeles voted 345,435 to 321,142 to give Chavez Ravine to the Dodgers for a new ballpark. If only 12,147 votes had gone the other way, or if the road trip had gone poorly, the Dodgers might still be in the Coliseum. With their winning ways, they might have drawn 5 million fans in a season. ◆ The Coliseum attracted the largest baseball crowd in American history when an exhibition crowd of 93,103 attended on May 7, 1959 vs. the Yankees, in a tribute honoring Dodgers catcher Roy Campanella, after he was paralyzed in an auto accident. The only baseball crowd bigger was at the 1936 Olympics in Berlin, Nazi Germany, when 120,000 filled the Reichsportfeld, the Olympic Stadium, for a night exhibition baseball game played under very poor lighting conditions between two American amateur teams. ◆ This ballpark was also the scene of the largest crowd for an official Major League game—92,706 vs. the White Sox in the 1959 World Series. The right center fence was shortened in 1959 after 182 homers were hit to left but only 3 to center and 8 to right. In 1959, 132 to left, 1 to center, 39 to right. In 1960, 155 to left, 3 to center, 28 to right. In 1961, 147 to left, 7 to center, 38 to right.

**L**os Angeles Coliseum, Los Angeles. Lots of foul territory down the third baseline.

# WRIGLEY FIELD

## OCCUPANT
American League Los Angeles Angels, April 27–October 1, 1961

## CAPACITY
22,000 (1925); 20,457 (1961)

## LARGEST CROWD
Minor League Angels—24,695 on September 6, 1933 vs. the Hollywood Stars; Major League Angels—19,930 on August 22, 1961 vs. the Yankees

## DIMENSIONS
Left field: 340
Power alleys: 345
Center field: 412
Right field: 338.5
Backstop: 56

Wrigley Field, Los Angeles. Top: Only 345 feet to the power alleys. Bottom: Minor League Angels played here for decades before Major League action in 1961.

### FENCES

Left field to center field: 14.5
Center field to right field: 9 (6 wire above 3 concrete)

### PHENOMENA

This park was designed to be like Wrigley Field in Chicago and was named for William Wrigley, who owned both the Cubs and the Angels. In its Minor League days, there were two walls here and a picnic area in right. A 12-story, 150-foot-tall office tower, the Memorial Tower, dedicated to baseball players who died in World War I, stood just to the first base side of home plate above the grandstand. ♦ The bottom of the light tower in left center was in play. The rear wall, out of play behind the inner fence at the foul pole, was marked 346.58 in 1961. In 1961, Wrigley Field set the current record for most homers in one league in one park in one season: 248. The reason was that the 345-foot power alleys were only 5 feet more distant than the foul pole in left, much shorter than normal. ♦ Television's "Home Run Derby" was filmed here as well as an episode of "The Munsters." ♦ An architect's 1957 drawing envisioned enclosing the field for use by the Dodgers, with double-decked stands in left and right, and center field bleachers, very much like the Polo Grounds. It was demolished in 1966.

## LOUISVILLE, KENTUCKY

# LOUISVILLE BASEBALL PARK

### OCCUPANT

National League Louisville Grays, April 25, 1876–September 29, 1877

### PHENOMENA

It was modeled after the Hartford Ball Club Grounds, and burned down in the late 1870s. ♦ Because of the Victorian homes which now occupy the spot, this is the only former ballpark site on the Register of National Historic Preservation Sites.

# ECLIPSE PARK I

### OCCUPANTS
American Association Louisville Colonels, May 5, 1882–September 27, 1891; National League Louisville Colonels, April 12, 1892–May 4, 1893

### DIMENSIONS
Left field: 360
Left center: 405
Center field: 495
Right center: 360
Right field: 320

### FENCES
8 (1882); 12 (1884)

# ECLIPSE PARK II

### OCCUPANT
National League Louisville Colonels, May 22, 1893–September 2, 1899

### PHENOMENA
Patterned after St. Louis's Sportsman's Park, it burned down on August 12, 1899. A temporary grandstand was built after the fire and used until 1920.

# PARKWAY FIELD

### OCCUPANTS
Negro National League Louisville White Sox, 1931; Negro Southern League Louisville Black Caps, 1932; Negro American League Louisville Buckeyes, 1949

### CAPACITY
13,198 (1938); 13,496 (1952)

### DIMENSIONS
Left field: 329
Deepest left center: 512
Center field: 467
Right field: 345

# LUDLOW, KENTUCKY

# LUDLOW BASEBALL PARK

### NEUTRAL USE
National Association Philadelphia Pearls, September 22, 1875

### PHENOMENA
The ballpark opened on May 28, 1875, with the Ludlows losing 25–5 to the Westerns of Keokuk, Iowa. ◆ The river bluffs high on the hill to the south of the park formed a natural amphitheatre for fans.

# MACON, GEORGIA

# LUTHER WILLIAMS FIELD

### NEUTRAL USES
Some Negro American League Birmingham Black Barons games in the 1940s

### CAPACITY
6,000 (1938); 5,000 (1960); 3,000 (1983)

### DIMENSIONS
Foul lines: 350 (1938); 330 (1983)
Center field: 450 (1938); 405 (1983)

**L**uther Williams Field, Macon, Georgia. Macon baseball since the 1920s.

## MASPETH, NEW YORK

# LONG ISLAND GROUNDS

**A.K.A.**
Maspeth Ball Grounds; Long Island Recreation Grounds

**NEUTRAL USES**
American Association Brooklyn Gladiators, July 27, August 3, 1890

## MEMPHIS, TENNESSEE

# MARTIN PARK

**CURRENT USE**
Truck terminal

**OCCUPANTS**
Negro National League Memphis Red Sox, 1923–1925, 1928–1931; Negro Southern League Memphis Red Sox, 1932; Negro American League Memphis Red Sox, 1937–1941, 1943–1950

## MIDDLETOWN, CONNECTICUT

# MANSFIELD CLUB GROUNDS

**OCCUPANT**
National Association Middletown Mansfields, May 2–July 4, 1872

**PHENOMENA**
Located along the Connecticut River, on site of present-day Connecticut Valley Hospital.

# MILWAUKEE, WISCONSIN

## MILWAUKEE BASE-BALL GROUNDS

**OCCUPANT**

National League Milwaukee Grays, May 14–September 14, 1878

**PHENOMENA**

It had a double row of shade trees down the 1st base line. ◆ Flies over the short right field fence were doubles.

## WRIGHT STREET GROUNDS

**OCCUPANT**

Union Association Milwaukee Unions, September 27–October 12, 1884

**PHENOMENA**

The park opened on May 1, 1884.

## BORCHERT FIELD

**OCCUPANTS**

American Association Milwaukee Brewers, September 10–October 4, 1891; Negro National League Milwaukee Bears, 1923

**CAPACITY**

10,000 (1891); 14,000 (1941)

**DIMENSIONS**

Foul lines: 266
Center field: 395

**B**orchert Field, Milwaukee. A goat mascot grazed in the outfield.

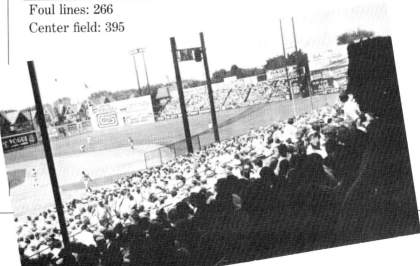

**B**orchert Field, Milwaukee.
Outside the wooden entrance.

When Bill Veeck bought the Minor League Brewers in 1941, he erected a 60-foot chicken wire fence in right because his team could not hit 266-foot homers. He didn't want the opposition to be able to, either. In 1942, as he describes in *Veeck as in Wreck*, he designed a system for sliding the wire fences back and forth along the top of the wall by means of a hydraulic motor. When the visiting team had more left-handed power, the fence would stay up. Otherwise, he would reel it back to the foul line. From there, it was only a short step to the ultimate refinement. In the best of all possible home parks, the fence would be up for the opposition and down for the home team. "We could do this," Veeck stated, "without any trouble at all—and we did do it—by reeling the fence in and out between innings. That is, we did it once. They passed a rule against it the next day." ◆ The park was opened on May 20, 1887. A goat, cared for by pitcher Ralph Cutting, grazed on the field between games. The park was used as an ice skating rink in the winter. The ice skaters' dressing room was converted into a chicken coop in 1919 by Otto Borchert, who in that year had purchased the Brewers Minor League team. ◆ A windstorm on June 15, 1944 ripped off the first base stands' roof during a game. ◆ There were two ways to see the games for free: through knotholes in the fence on Burleigh Street or from the second-story porches on Seventh Street. The ballpark was torn down in 1954. It was renamed Borchert Field in 1927 after Otto Borchert's death. In 1896, it was converted into a camp and stables for a Wisconsin National Guard cavalry troop. It was converted back to baseball use in 1902.

# LLOYD STREET GROUNDS

**OCCUPANT**
American League Milwaukee Brewers, May 3–September 12, 1901

**FENCES**
Left field: 20 (canvas screen)

Lloyd Street Grounds, Milwaukee. Brewers played here in 1901 before moving to St. Louis to become the Browns in 1902.

## MINNEAPOLIS, MINNESOTA

# ATHLETIC PARK

**NEUTRAL USE**
American Association Milwaukee Brewers, October 2, 1891

**DIMENSIONS**
Left field: 275
Right field: 250

# METROPOLITAN STADIUM

### OCCUPANT
American League Minnesota Twins, April 21, 1961–September 30, 1981

### CAPACITY
18,200 (1956); 21,000 (1957); 21,688 (1958); 30,637 (1961); 40,000 (1964); 45,921 (1973); 45,181 (1974); 45,919 (1975)

### LARGEST CROWD
50,596 on October 14, 1965 vs. the Dodgers

### SMALLEST CROWD
537 on September 20, 1965 vs. the Athletics

### DIMENSIONS
Left field: 329 (1961); 330 (1962); 344 (1965); 346 (1967); 330 (1975); 343 (1977)

Short left center: 365 (1961); 360 (1966); 373 (1972); 350 (1975); 346 (1976); 360 (1977)

Deep left center: 402 (1961); 435 (1965); 430 (1968); 410 (1975); 406 (1976)

**M**etropolitan Stadium, Minneapolis. After two decades, the Twins moved into a dome.

Deepest left center corner: 430 (1965); 406 (1975)
Center field: 412 (1961); 430 (1965); 425 (1968); 410 (1975); 402 (1977)
Deepest right center corner: 430 (1965)
Deep right center: 402 (1961); 435 (1965); 430 (1968); 410 (1977)
Short right center: 365 (1961); 373 (1968); 365 (1972); 370 (1977)
Right field: 329 (1961); 330 (1962)
Backstop: 60

### FENCES
Left field: 8 (wire, 1961); 12 (1964); 7 (1974); 12 (1977)
Center field: 8 (wire, 1961)
Right field: 8 (wire, 1961); 12 (1964); 8 (1970)
Right field corner by the foul pole: 5 (3 concrete base, then 2 steel)

### PHENOMENA
This was the second Major League park built in a cornfield. The first was Perry's Park in Walte's Pasture, home of the National Association Keokuk Westerns in Keokuk, Iowa in 1875. ◆ The 330-foot marker was curiously far away from the foul pole in right, raising the distinct possibility that the distance to right was significantly less than 330 feet. ◆ A bomb scare delayed the August 25, 1970 Twins–Red Sox game by 44 minutes, as 17,697 fans filed calmly into the outfield and the parking lots. ◆ It was by far the most poorly maintained ballpark in the Majors. In 1981, broken railings on the third deck overlooking the left field bleachers created a safety hazard. When the Hubert H. Humphrey Metrodome was finished, the Met became the first modern stadium to be abandoned.

# MONROE, LOUISIANA

# CASINO PARK

### OCCUPANT
Negro Southern League Monroe Monarchs, 1932

### DIMENSIONS
Left field: 360
Center field: 450
Right field: 330

## MONTGOMERY, ALABAMA

# CRAMTON BOWL

**OCCUPANT**
Negro Southern League Montgomery Grey Sox, 1932

**CAPACITY**
10,000

**DIMENSIONS**
Left field: 420
Center field: 600
Right field: 600

## MONTREAL, QUEBEC

# PARC JARRY

**OCCUPANT**
National League Expos de Montréal, April 14, 1969–September 26, 1976

**CAPACITY**
3,000 (1968); 28,456 (1969)

**LARGEST CROWD**
34,331 on September 15, 1973 vs. the Phillies

**DIMENSIONS**
Left field: 340
Left center: 368
Center field: 415 (1969); 417 (1971); 420 (1974)
Right center: 368
Right field: 340
Backstop: 62

**FENCES**
8 (1969); 5 (1970); 8 (1976)

**PHENOMENA**
On Opening Day, April 13, 1971, numerous fans stood on snow plowed high in mounds behind the 8½-foot wall that stood behind the 8-foot wire screen fence in right field and got a free view of the

Jarry Park, Montreal, Quebec. Top: Swimming pool beyond the right field fence. Bottom: "One year" temporary park hosted the Expos from 1969 to 1976.

game. ◆ The park was still under construction during April and May 1969 during the first two months of the Expos home games. ◆ Before the Expos decided to come here, it was a 3,000-seat amateur recreational ballpark. A jet stream wind helped drives to left center. Homers to right landed in a swimming pool.

## MOUNDS, ILLINOIS

# MOUNDS BALLFIELD

### OCCUPANT
Negro American League New Orleans–St. Louis Stars, August–September 1939

# NASHVILLE, TENNESSEE

# WILSON PARK

### OCCUPANTS
Negro National League Nashville Elite Giants, 1930–1931; Negro Southern League Nashville Elite Giants, 1932

### PHENOMENA
Named for Elite Giants owner Tom T. Wilson, it was located south of Meharry Medical College, which was at First Avenue and Chestnut Avenue.

# SULPHUR DELL

### OCCUPANT
Negro National League Nashville Elite Giants, 1933–1934

### CAPACITY
7,000 (1927); 8,500 (1938)

### DIMENSIONS
Left field: 334
Center field: 421
Right field: 262
Right field: 235 when fans sat behind the ropes on the bank

### FENCES
Left field and center field: 16 (1927)
Right field: 16 (1927); 38.5 to 46 (16 wood below 22.5 to 30 screen to a point 186 feet from the right field foul line, 1931)

### PHENOMENA
Sulphur Dell had the greatest and craziest right field in history. Right fielders were called mountain goats because they had to go up and down the irregular hills in right center and right. The incline in right rose 25 feet, beginning gradually behind first, then rising sharply at a 45-degree angle 224 feet from the plate, leveling off 235 feet from the plate at a 10-foot-wide shelf one-third of the way up the incline, and then continuing at a 45-degree angle to the fence. ◆ The park was often flooded by the Cumberland River, which was only one-quarter of a mile away. ◆ The park was nicknamed The Dump in honor of the exceptional fragrance that drifted

over from the nearby smoldering city dump and lent a unique character to Sulphur Dell hot dogs. ◆ Fielders used to play on the shelf, 235 feet from the plate. ◆ When overflow crowds were attracted to a game, a rope was extended in front of the shelf, and fans sat on the upper two-thirds of the incline, reducing right field to 235 rather than 262. The stands were exceptionally close to the pancake-shaped diamond. First base was only 42 feet from the seats, third base was only 26 feet from the seats. The embankments began in left at 301 and in right at 224. ◆ Casey Stengel once joked that he hit a bunt home run down the first baseline. Catcher Del Ballinger once dove into the dugout to catch a foul ball. The dugout was full of 4 feet of Cumberland River floodwater. Upon surfacing, he had the ball and an important out was recorded. Only later did he admit that he made the catch while swimming between the bat rack and the dugout steps 2 feet below the surface. ◆ The original diamond here was used just after the Civil War in the 1860s, but the original ballpark was not constructed until 1885. In the winter of 1926–27, the original ballpark was torn down, and the diamond was turned around, home plate moving from the northeast to the southwest. ◆ During the winter of 1930–31, a screen ranging in height from 22.5 to 30 feet was extended on top of the 16-foot wooden fence from the foul pole in right out 186 feet into right center. ◆ Until the park was torn down in the 1960s, the old basepaths remained visible in the outfield grass as a faint outline of the past. ◆ Fans now watching games at Hershel Greer Stadium, built in 1978, may have more conveniences, but they do not have nearly the exciting baseball atmosphere of Sulphur Dell.

# NEWARK, NEW JERSEY*

# WIEDEN-MEYER'S PARK

## NEUTRAL USE
American League New York Highlanders, July 17, 1904

*See also Bloomfield, New Jersey; Harrison, New Jersey; Waverly, New Jersey

# NEWARK SCHOOLS STADIUM

**OCCUPANT**
Eastern Colored League Newark Stars, 1926

**PHENOMENA**
It was built in 1925. ◆ Each foul line was so short that a hit over the fence down the lines was only a double.

# MEADOW-BROOK OVAL

**OCCUPANT**
Negro National League Newark Dodgers, 1934–1935

**DIMENSIONS**
Foul lines: 300
Center field: 380

**FENCES**
12

**PHENOMENA**
Location: South Orange Avenue, 12th Street.

# RUPPERT STADIUM

**OCCUPANT**
Negro National League Newark Eagles, 1936–1948

**CAPACITY**
19,000

**DIMENSIONS**
Foul lines: 305
Center field: 410

**PHENOMENA**
It was situated near a garbage dump. Some games had to be delayed because of the horrible smell and smoke from the dump. ◆ It was torn down in 1967.

## NEW HAVEN, CONNECTICUT

# HOWARD AVENUE GROUNDS

### OCCUPANT
National Association New Haven Elm Citys, April 21–October 28, 1875

## NEW ORLEANS, LOUISIANA

# PELICAN STADIUM

### OCCUPANT
Negro American League New Orleans–St. Louis Stars, 1941

### DIMENSIONS
Left field: 427
Center field: 405
Right field: 418

### PHENOMENA
It was opened on April 13, 1915, and torn down in October 1957, after a ban on African-American players and a black consumer boycott drove the Pelicans out of town.

# NEW YORK, NEW YORK*

# POLO GROUNDS I SOUTHEAST DIAMOND

**P**olo Grounds #1, New York. Originally used as a polo field, it was home of the Giants from 1883 to 1888.

### OCCUPANTS
National League New York Giants, May 1, 1883–October 13, 1888; American Association New York Mets, July 17, 1884–October 1, 1885

### LARGEST CROWD
20,709 on May 31, 1886 vs. the Detroit Wolverines

### SMALLEST CROWD
Mets–300 on October 25, 1884 vs. the Providence Grays in the World Series

### FENCES
None at first, later a 10-foot canvas barrier between the two outfields and a short fence in front of the right field bleachers

### PHENOMENA
This park used to be a polo field owned by James Gordon Bennett, publisher of the New York Herald and used by the Westchester and Manhattan Polo Associations. ◆ It opened for baseball on September 29, 1880. There were two diamonds

*See also Brooklyn, New York; East Orange, New Jersey; Jersey City, New Jersey; Maspeth, New York; Paterson, New Jersey; St. George, New York; Weehawken, New Jersey; West New York, New Jersey

in the southwest and southeast corners of a huge park. In 1883, the National League Giants, then called the Gothams, used the southeastern diamond, and the American Association Mets used the southwestern diamond. A ball rolling under the 10-foot canvas fence in center field into the other park's outfield was still in play. Sometimes there were bizarre scenes, with a National League center fielder crawling into the American Association outfield, recovering a ball, and then throwing it over the canvas fence back into his own park, and vice versa. ◆ This ballpark was the scene of the first American Association–National League World Series in 1884, with the Mets facing the National League Providence Grays. ◆ The first Major League game to attract a crowd of over 20,000 was played here. ◆ The National League Giants hosted the Detroit Wolverines for a Memorial Day morning/afternoon twin bill on May 31, 1886. To see the afternoon game, 20,709 fans paid to get in. The overflow crowd stood in the outfield and hits into the crowd standing in fair territory were singles. ◆ During 1884 and 1885 both the National League Giants and the American Association Mets were playing here, two-league doubleheaders took place here. The only other such dual-league doubleheader in Major League history took place on May 7, 1932 at Forbes Field in Pittsburgh. ◆ Just before the start of the 1889 season, the city took over the property in order to cut 111th Street through from 5th to 6th Avenues. This took the Giants by surprise and forced them to play in temporary quarters in Jersey City and St. George on Staten Island while Polo Grounds (III) was being built.

# POLO GROUNDS II SOUTHWEST DIAMOND

## OCCUPANT
American Association New York Mets, May 12–October 25, 1883

## FENCES
None at first; later a 10-foot canvas barrier between the two outfields and a short fence in front of the left field bleachers

# METROPOLITAN PARK

**OCCUPANT**

American Association New York Mets, May 13–August 23, 1884

**PHENOMENA**

High winds caused frequent homers at this small park, also called The Dump because the site had formerly been a city dump. It was so close to numerous factories across the East River that foul smoke made it dangerous for fans. ◆ Beginning July 17, the Mets moved over to the Polo Grounds Southeast Diamond. The only games played here after July 17 were when there was a schedule conflict with the Giants at the Polo Grounds Southeast Diamond.

# POLO GROUNDS III

**OCCUPANT**

National League New York Giants, July 8, 1889–September 13, 1890

**LARGEST CROWD**

14,364 on August 31, 1889 vs. the Beaneaters

**DIMENSIONS**

Center field: 360

**PHENOMENA**

There were stables for horses under the third base grandstand. ◆ Separated only by a steep dirt embankment and a canvas-covered wooden outfield fence in 1890, this park and Brotherhood Park, used in 1890 by the Players League Giants, often had games going on simultaneously. On May 12, 1890 a homer hit in the National League Polo Grounds (III), landed in the outfield during a Players League game at Brotherhood Park (Polo Grounds IV), and fans in both parks cheered the hitter, Mike Tiernan. ◆ This park had the steepest and largest embankment ever in the Majors, in center field and right field, dwarfing even the one at Holman Stadium in Vero Beach used by the Los Angeles Dodgers in spring training. ◆ The park was used until the 1930s as a cricket field by Haitian players. ◆ On September 14, 1889, Giants center fielder George Gore couldn't climb the muddy embankment, enabling Chicago's Cap Anson to stretch a double into an inside-the-park home run.

# POLO GROUNDS IV

**OCCUPANTS**

Players League New York Giants, April 19–September 18, 1890;
National League New York Giants, April 22, 1891–April 13, 1911

**CAPACITY**

16,000 (1891)

**LARGEST CROWD**

38,805 on June 11, 1904 vs. the Cubs

**DIMENSIONS**

Left field: 335 (April 19, 1890); 277 (July 1890)
Center field: 500 (1890); 433 (1909)
Right field: 335 (April 19, 1890); 258 (July 1890)

**FENCES**

Foul lines: 4
Bullpens: 25 sloping down to 15
Power alleys: 15 sloping down to 5
Center field: 3 (rope strung between posts)

**PHENOMENA**

Along with League Park II in Cleveland, this is the only place in Major League history where one ball could hit the stands for a home run, but another ball, hit higher and farther in the exact same direction, was in play. ◆ The left field stands curved into fair territory for about 10 feet but only the corner of the stands protruded into fair territory. Behind these seats were the bullpens, which were in play. There were two left field foul poles because of this unique situation. There was a sharp incline in the bullpens, as one reached the rear wall. ◆ James Mutrie's scheduled regular season Giants National League indoor games at Madison Square Garden and night games at the Polo Grounds in 1891 never materialized. ◆ The center field bleachers were named Burkeville, or the cigar boxes, for Irish immigrant fans who sat there. Fans could climb trees or just stand outside the park up on Coogan's Bluff and see the game from behind home plate. In 1890, there were several large buildings on stilts that loomed over the left field fence; from there, fans could see the games. During the 1890 season, the bleachers were extended to the power alleys, and two small bleacher sections were put in center. These were in front of, and to the left and right of, what would later be the clubhouse wall in center. In the winter of 1908 to 1909, the double deck was extended to the foul poles and

**P**olo Grounds #4, New York. View from right field in 1908, home of the Giants from 1891 to 1911.

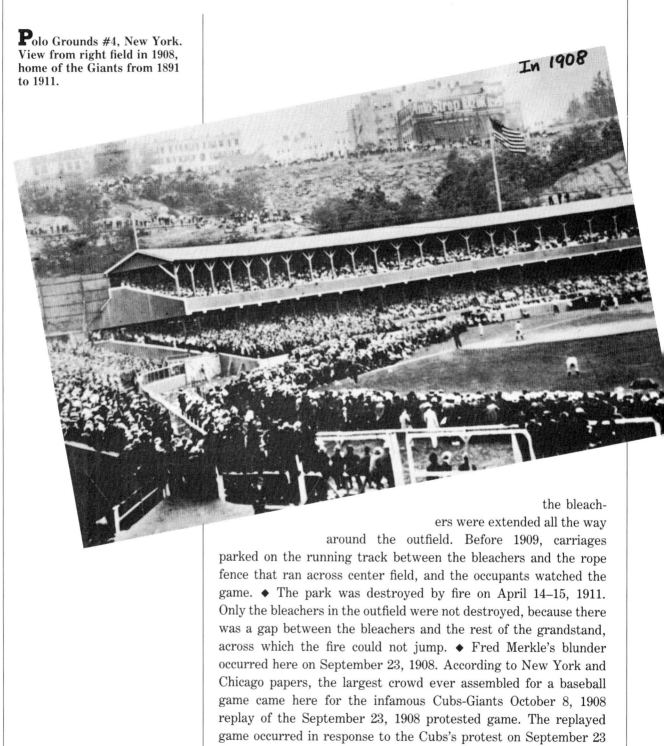

In 1908

the bleachers were extended all the way around the outfield. Before 1909, carriages parked on the running track between the bleachers and the rope fence that ran across center field, and the occupants watched the game. ◆ The park was destroyed by fire on April 14–15, 1911. Only the bleachers in the outfield were not destroyed, because there was a gap between the bleachers and the rest of the grandstand, across which the fire could not jump. ◆ Fred Merkle's blunder occurred here on September 23, 1908. According to New York and Chicago papers, the largest crowd ever assembled for a baseball game came here for the infamous Cubs-Giants October 8, 1908 replay of the September 23, 1908 protested game. The replayed game occurred in response to the Cubs's protest on September 23 that Harry McCormick should not have been allowed to score from third base because Fred Merkle, who was on first, had not touched second base on Al Bridwell's game-winning single to center. Umpire

Hank O'Day had witnessed Cubs infielder Johnny Evers recover the game ball and stand on second base to record a force-out. Late that night, O'Day upheld the Cubs' protest, and National League President Harry Pulliam upheld O'Day's ruling. In effect, the game was a National League pennant playoff game, because the teams were tied, and the season was over. According to the *Chicago Record-Herald*, the New York police officially estimated that approximately 250,000 people showed up, but of course only about a fifth that many could get in because of the limited number of seats. Seven fans who had reserved tickets but could not get in had to be carted away by the police after going "stark raving mad." The surging crowd outside tried to burn down the outfield fence, but the fire department put out the fire. The crowd also tried to storm the gates, and bent them, but could not break them down. With the stadium already overflowing, security personnel closed the gates at 1:30 P.M. for the 3:00 P.M. game, thus angering many in the crowd who had tickets but could not get in. The Giants had originally hoped to limit the crowd to what were called "National Commission Standards," which meant no overflow crowd in the outfield. But they were unable to prevent the crowd from surging onto the outfield, so at 1:45 P.M. ropes were extended to keep the crowd back in the outfield. As game time approached, the crowd managed to break down a portion of the outfield fence near the clubhouse, but police used clubs to push the fans back and managed to fix the fence to keep the fans out. In the 3rd inning, a few people got past the police and scaled the fence into the park in the northwest home plate area, but most were knocked down by high-pressure water aimed at them by firemen using fire hoses. A Brooklynite broke his leg falling out of the grandstand. Most of the people outside finally began to disperse, but about 40,000 remained throughout the game and watched from Coogan's Bluff, and from the tops of telephone poles, trees, and subway platforms. A fireman by the name of Henry T. MacBride fell from a pillar on the Elevated Train platform and was killed. Before the game, the Cubs could not practice because the fans were so hostile. After they had won the game 4–2, and the pennant with it, the Cubs had to fight their way to their clubhouse in center field; four Cubs were punched by irate New York fans; and the New York police had to draw their revolvers to keep the Giants fans from storming the visitors' clubhouse. ◆ The first base coaching box had "STOP" written in it in white letters in 1908.

# HILLTOP PARK

## OCCUPANTS

American League New York Highlanders, April 30, 1903–October 5, 1912; National League New York Giants, April 15–May 30, 1911

## CAPACITY

15,000

## LARGEST CROWD

28,584 on October 10, 1904 vs. the Bostons

## DIMENSIONS

Left field: 365
Center field: 542
Right field: 400
Backstop: 91.5

## PHENOMENA

Currently the former park site holds the Columbia Presbyterian Hospital. ◆ In 1911, the Highlanders were planning a new park, to be called Farrell Park, at 225th Street, but the plans never materialized. Then they thought of building a floating ballpark, which would float on the Harlem River. That plan never came to be either, although the Pittsburgh Pirates considered the idea also

**H**illtop Park, New York. Baltimore Orioles moved here in 1903 to become the Highlanders.

American League Base Ball Park, New York, N.Y.

American League Base Ball Park, New York.

**H**illtop Park, New York.
Highlanders action high above
the Hudson River.

in the late 1960s be-
fore deciding to build Three Rivers on dry
land. ◆ Hilltop Park had an excellent view of the Hudson River
and the New Jersey Palisades from the upper seats behind the
plate. There was a scoreboard in left. The clubhouse was in center
field, as at the Polo Grounds. There was a large exit gate in right
where fans left after the game, just as at Forbes Field. It had a
Bull Durham sign shaped like a bull in 1909 in right center, twice
the height of the rest of the fence. ◆ When the park opened on
April 30, 1903, there was a huge hollow in right field that had to be
roped off; a ball hit past the ropes was a double. When the Highlanders, later renamed the Yankees, began their second home stand
on June 1, 1903, a fence had been built in front of the hole, and
balls hit over the fence were homers.

# POLO GROUNDS V

**OCCUPANTS**

National League New York Giants, June 28, 1911–September 29,
1957; American League New York Yankees, April 17, 1913–October
8, 1922; National League New York Mets, April 13, 1962–September 18, 1963

**CAPACITY**

16,000 (June 28, 1911); 34,000 (World Series, 1911); 39,000 (1917);
38,000 (1919); 43,000 (1923); 55,000 (1926); 56,000 (1930); 51,856
(1937); 56,000 (1940); 54,500 (1947); 56,000 (1953)

## LARGEST CROWD

Giants: Total—64,417, with 57,900 paid on September 13, 1936 vs. the Cardinals; Paid—60,747, with 61,756 total on May 31, 1937 vs. the Dodgers; Mets—54,360 on May 30, 1962 vs. the Dodgers.

## DIMENSIONS

Left field: 277 (1911); 286.67 (1921); 279.67 (1923); 279 (1930); 280 (1943); 279 (1955)

Left field, second deck: 250

Left center, left of bullpen: 447

Left center, right of bullpen: 455

Front of the clubhouse steps: 460

Center field: 433 (1911); 483 (1923); 484.75 (1927); 505 (1930); 430 (1931); 480 (1934); 430 (1938); 505 (1940); 490 (1943); 505 (1944); 448 (1945); 490 (1946); 484 (1947); 505 (1949); 483 (1952); 480 (1953); 483 (1954); 480 (1955); 475 (1962); 483 (1963)

Bleacher corners: 425 when center field was 475

Right center, left of bullpen: 449

Right center, right of bullpen: 440

Right field: 256.25 (1921); 257.67 (1923); 257.5 (1931); 257.67 (1942); 259 (1943); 257.67 (1944)

Right field, second deck photographers' perch: 249

Backstop: 65 (1942); 70 (1943); 65 (1944); 70 (1946); 74 (1949); 65 (1954); 74 (1955); 65 (1962)

Foul territory: Very large.

## FENCES

1911–1922

Left field to center field: 10 (concrete)

Center field: 20 (tarp)

Right center: 10 (concrete)

Right field: 12, sloping to 11 at the foul pole (concrete)

1923–1963

Left field: 16.8 (concrete)

Left center: 18 (concrete)

Where left center wall ended at the bleachers: 12 (concrete)

Center field bleachers wall: 8.5 (4.25 wire on top of 4.25 concrete) on both sides of the clubhouse runway

Center field hitters' background: 16.5 on both sides of clubhouse runway

Center field clubhouse: 60 high and 60 wide; 50 high in 1963

Center field top of Longines clock: 80

Center field top of right side of scoreboard: 71

New York Daily News Photo

**P**olo Grounds, New York. Top: 279 feet to left field. Middle: No batted ball ever hit the center field clubhouse wall. Bottom: 258 feet to right field.

Center field top of left side of scoreboard: 68
Center field top of middle of scoreboard: 64
Center field top of five right scoreboard windows: 57
Center field top of four left scoreboard windows: 55
Center field bottom of five right scoreboard windows: 53
Center field bottom of four left scoreboard windows: 48
Center field bottom of clubhouse scoreboard: 31
Center field top of rear clubhouse wall: 28
Center field top of front clubhouse wall: 19
Center field top of 14 lower clubhouse windows: 16
Center field bottom of 14 lower clubhouse windows: 11
Center field clubhouse floor overhang: 8
Center field top of Eddie Grant Memorial: 5
Center field width of little office on the top of the lower clubhouse: 10
Right center: 12 (concrete)
Right field: 10.64 (concrete)

## PHENOMENA

There is much confusion here on distance measurements, especially in center field. There were several measurement changes over the years, and it is uncertain why. During the Giants' stay, it was perhaps 483 to the front of the clubhouse, and perhaps 505 to the rear clubhouse wall above the overhang. Another possibility is that it was 433 to the front of the bleachers, 475 to the beginning of the clubhouse overhang, 483 to the rear wall under the overhang, and 505 to the front of the high clubhouse wall. Why the 483 marker sometimes was changed to 480 or 475 is not known. It could have been remeasurements, or changes in the location of home plate, or any number of other factors. Or it could have been a measurement to the base of the Eddie Grant Memorial. In the Giants' time, reading from left field to right field, the markers read 315, 360, 414, 447, 455, 483, 455, 449, 395, 338, 294. In the Mets' time, they read 306, 405, 475, 405, 281. The foul line distances were never marked. ◆ The second deck in right had a 9-foot photographers' perch overhang, 60 feet from the foul pole out into right center. The bullpens were in fair territory, in left center and right center. There was no line on the 60-foot-high center field clubhouse above which a ball would be a home run. The outfield was slightly sunken. A manager, standing in his dugout, could see only the top half of his outfielders. At the wall, the field was 8 feet below the infield. The second deck overhang meant that a homer to left was easier than a homer to right, even though the wall in left was 279 and the wall in right was 258. The overhang was 21 feet, but it effectively shortened the distance required for a pop fly homer to the second deck in left to 250 feet. The hitters' background extended beyond the end of the bleacher wall, several feet into the clubhouse gap. The field sloped in a "turtle back" just beyond the infield dirt. It sloped down 1.5 feet to drains about 20 feet into the outfield, then back up again. The right center wall sloped gradually from 11 feet at the pole to 12 feet at the bleachers. The left center wall sloped from 16.8 feet at the pole up to 18 feet in left center, then abruptly fell to 16 feet, and then 14 feet, and sloped gradually to 12 feet at the bleachers. ◆ When advertising signs were removed in the 1940s, the abrupt changes in height in left center disappeared. After the all-wooden Polo Grounds (IV) burned down April 14, 1911, Polo Grounds (V) was built. With a concrete double deck from the left field corner, around the plate, and back out to right center field, this was the first concrete-era stadium in New York. ◆ On September 24, 1919, Babe Ruth hit the first homer over the right field roof. Willie Mays's most famous, but not necessarily his greatest, catch occurred here on September 29, 1954, in the World Series vs. Cleveland. ◆ Brush Stairway led down from Coogan's Bluff to the Speedway and the ticket booths

**P**olo Grounds #5, New York. Unique horseshoe-shaped stadium.

A Baseball Game at the Polo Grounds as seen from an airship, New York

behind home plate. The coats of arms of all the teams in the National League were on the top of the grandstand. They were removed in the 1920s. ◆ Dedicated on May 30, 1921 to a former Giant ballplayer, a member of the American Expeditionary Force, or A. E. F., killed in World War I, the Eddie Grant Memorial stood in center at the base of the clubhouse wall. It was 5 feet high. The memorial read:

In Memory of
Capt. Edward Leslie Grant
307th Infantry–77th Division
A. E. F.
Soldier–Scholar–Athlete
Killed in Action
Argonne Forest
October 5, 1918
Philadelphia Nationals
1907–1908–1909–1910
Cincinnati Reds
1911–1912–1913
New York Giants
1913–1914–1915
Erected by friends in Baseball,
Journalism, and the Service.

Harry Danning once hit a drive that bounced behind the Eddie Grant Memorial. Center fielder Vince DiMaggio had trouble finding the handle, and the slow-footed Danning got an inside-the-park homer. ◆ In the winter of 1922 to 1923, the concrete double decks were extended all the way to either side of the new concrete bleachers in center, housing the clubhouse. Unfortunately, the Roman Colosseum facade frescoes were removed during that winter also. The bleachers in center were remodeled in 1923. In 1929, the first attempt was made to wire the umpires for sound and connect them into the Public Address (PA) system. It didn't work too well. A speaker was added above the Eddie Grant Memorial in 1931. ◆ The first home run into the center field bleachers, over the screen, was hit by Luke Easter in a Negro League game in 1948. The second was struck by Joe Adcock of the Braves on April 29, 1953 off Jim Hearn. Only two others later managed this feat: Lou Brock on June 17, 1962 and Henry Aaron one day later, on June 18. ◆ No batter ever hit the clubhouse wall, much less hit one over it. In 1962 and 1963, the Howard Clothes sign on the outfield wall promised a boat to any player who hit the sign. Bobby Thomson's

**P**olo Grounds #5, New York. Bullpens were in play in the power alleys.

"Shot Heard Round the World" homer occurred here at 4:11 P.M. on October 3, 1951 vs. the Dodgers and ended the "Greatest Game Ever Played." ◆ A 1939 rhubarb about a "foul" homer resulted in the first foul pole net to help umpires decide whether balls were foul or fair. Left vague to this day though is the logic as to why a ball that hits the foul pole is fair. Demolition began on April 10, 1964 with the same wrecking ball that had earlier demolished Ebbets Field.

# DYCKMAN OVAL

### OCCUPANTS
Negro National League New York Cuban Stars, 1922; Eastern Colored League New York Cuban Stars East, 1923–1928; Negro American League New York Cuban Stars East, 1929; Negro National League Cuban House of David, 1931; Negro East-West League New York Cuban Stars, 1932

### PHENOMENA
The first Major League ballpark lights in New York were installed here in 1930 by Cuban Stars owner Alex Pompez. ◆ Located near the Harlem Ship Canal, it was bounded by Nagle Avenue on the northwest at third base, Academy Street on the southwest at first base, Tenth Avenue on the southeast in right field, and West 204th Street on the northeast in left field. This places it four blocks north of Dyckman Street.

# DEXTER PARK

**OCCUPANT**

Eastern Colored League Brooklyn Royal Giants, 1923–1927

**PHENOMENA**

This park probably had the most creative outfield wall billboard ever. An optician's advertisement read "Don't Kill the Umpire— Maybe It's Your Eyes?" ◆ Owners Max and Milt Rosner also operated the semi-pro Brooklyn Bushwicks. ◆ There was a huge incline in right field, caused by a horse buried beneath the grass. Right field was commonly referred to as Horse Heaven.

# CATHOLIC PROTECTORY OVAL

**OCCUPANTS**

Eastern Colored League New York Lincoln Giants, 1923–1926; Negro National League New York Cubans, 1935–1936

**PHENOMENA**

The Protectory was a Catholic home and school for impoverished boys, whose 50-piece brass marching band was much in demand. There was no grass in the infield. The park was levelled in 1939, so that the Parkchester Apartments could be built.

# CAPITAL TEXTURE

**OCCUPANTS**

Eastern Colored League New York Lincoln Giants, 1928; Negro American League New York Lincoln Giants, 1929

**PHENOMENA**

The Riverton Apartments stand here now. The ballpark ran from East 138th to East 135th between Fifth Avenue and Madison Avenue.

# TRIBOROUGH STADIUM

**OCCUPANT**

Negro National League New York Black Yankees, 1938

**CAPACITY**

21,441 (1936); 25,000 (1939); 21,400 (1947); 21,441 (1948); 20,690 (1952)

**PHENOMENA**

This is a U-shaped stadium, out on Randall's Island, open at the southwest end. Eight Ebbets Field light tower stanchions were moved here in 1960. It was used for WFL Stars football games in 1974 and NASL Cosmos soccer games in 1975. It is located near the Triborough Bridge on Sunken Meadow, between the East River and the Harlem River, near Little Hell Gate.

# 59TH STREET BRIDGE

**OCCUPANT**

Negro National League New York Cubans, 1939

**PHENOMENA**

This was the first Major League covered ballpark. The Astrodome was the second. The infield was covered with cinders and ashes. It was located between East 59th and East 60th, between First Avenue and the East River, under the Queensboro Bridge.

# PATERSON, NEW JERSEY

# HINCHLIFFE STADIUM

**OCCUPANT**

Negro National League New York Black Yankees, 1936–1937, 1939–1945

**PHENOMENA**

It opened in 1932.

## PENDLETON, OHIO

# PENDLETON PARK

**OCCUPANT**
American Association Cincinnati Kelly's Killers, April 25–August 13, 1891

**DIMENSIONS**
Right field: 400

**PHENOMENA**
Both the Louisville and Cincinnati teams were arrested following the April 26th, 1891 game, for playing on Sunday. The same thing happened with the Athletics on May 24, and with Washington on June 7.

## PHILADELPHIA, PENNSYLVANIA*

# JEFFERSON STREET GROUNDS

**OCCUPANTS**
National Association Philadelphia Athletics, May 15, 1871–October 28, 1875; National Association Philadelphia Quakers, May 1, 1873–October 25, 1875; National League Philadelphia Athletics, April 22–September 16, 1876; American Association Philadelphia Athletics, May 10, 1883–October 11, 1890

**DIMENSIONS**
Center field: 500

**PHENOMENA**
This was the scene of the first National League game on April 22, 1876 between the A's and the Boston Red Caps. It had very short fences at the foul line and a swimming pool behind the right field fence.

# CENTENNIAL PARK

**OCCUPANT**
National Association Philadelphia Centennials, April 21–May 24, 1875

*See also Gloucester City, New Jersey; Yeadon, Pennsylvania

# OAKDALE PARK

**OCCUPANT**
American Association Philadelphia Athletics, May 2–September 21, 1882

**PHENOMENA**
It replaced a former park that the A's had used at 15th and Columbia Avenue.

# RECREATION PARK

**OCCUPANT**
National League Philadelphia Phillies, May 1, 1883–October 9, 1886

**PHENOMENA**
It opened on April 8, 1882, but Major League games were not played here until 1883.

# KEYSTONE PARK

**OCCUPANT**
Union Association Philadelphia Keystones, April 17–August 7, 1884

**PHENOMENA**
It later became a semi-pro park for many years.

# PHILADELPHIA BASEBALL GROUNDS

**OCCUPANT**
National League Philadelphia Phillies, April 30, 1887–August 6, 1894; August 18–September 6, 1894

**CAPACITY**
15,000

**LARGEST CROWD**
20,000 on April 30, 1887 vs. the Giants

**DIMENSIONS**
Left field: 500
Right field: 310

**FENCES**
25

# FOREPAUGH PARK

**PHENOMENA**

The pavilion was flanked by five turrets: One at 15th and Hunting-don was 122 feet high, and the other four were 75 feet high. The infield was full of ruts, the worst in the league in 1888. A 15-foot-wide bicycle track rimmed the field, causing an incline in front of the outfield fences. ◆ The park burned down on August 6, 1894 in a fire started by a plumber's stove and was replaced by Baker Bowl. A temporary set of bleachers was used from August 18 to September 6, 1894.

**OCCUPANTS**

Players League Philadelphia Quakers, April 30–September 17, 1890; American Association Philadelphia Athletics, April 8–October 5, 1891

**LARGEST CROWD**

17,182 on April 30, 1890 vs. the Boston Reds

**DIMENSIONS**

Left field: 345
Center field: 450
Right field: 380

# UNIVERSITY OF PENN. ATHLETIC FIELD

**NEUTRAL USES**

National League Philadelphia Phillies, August 11, 14–17, 1894

**PHENOMENA**

It was used temporarily during the rebuilding of the Philadelphia Baseball Grounds after the August 6, 1894 fire.

# BAKER BOWL

National League Philadelphia Phillies, May 2, 1895–August 8, 1903; April 14, 1904–May 14, 1927; June 24, 1927–June 30, 1938

**CAPACITY**
18,000 (1895); 20,000 (1929); 18,800 (1930)

**LARGEST CROWD**
23,377 on August 8, 1908 vs. the Pirates

**DIMENSIONS**
Left field: 335 (1921); 341.5 (1926); 341 (1930); 341.5 (1931)
Center field: 408
Right center: 300
Right field: 272 (1921); 279.5 (1924); 280.5 (1925)

**FENCES**
Left field: 4 (1895); 12 (July 1929)
Center field clubhouse to right center: 35 (1895); 47 (with 12 screen on top, 1915)
Right field: 40 (tin over brick, 1895); 60 (40 tin over brick, topped by 20 screen, 1915)

**B**aker Bowl, Philadelphia. Railroad tunnel ran under center field.

**B**aker Bowl, Philadelphia.
After being rebuilt in 1894.

The park was named after Phillies owner William F. Baker. Lightning split the flagpole in half in 1935. The park was called The Hump because it was on an elevated piece of ground, allowing a huge railroad tunnel to run underneath center field. ◆ It housed a circus in the early 1900s. From a high-level platform, a horse dove into a huge hole, filled with water near third base. There was a swimming pool in the basement of the center field clubhouse, prior to World War I. Coca Cola and Lifebuoy Health Soap Stops B. O. signs were on the high right field wall. Three sheep and a ram grazed on the outfield grass between games. Over the years, it housed various events such as donkey baseball, midget auto racing, crusades, police and fire department parades, roller skating, and ice skating. ◆ The second game of a twin bill with Boston on August 8, 1903 was cancelled when, during the game, the third base stands collapsed into 15th Street, killing 12 people and injuring several hundred. ◆ Extra seats were added in front of the fence in center for the 1915 World Series, which led directly to the Phillies losing the Series' last game. ◆ On May 14, 1927, 10 rows of the right field stands collapsed. ◆ The clubhouse was used for the Alpine Musical Bar in the 1940s. During Prohibition, the outfield wall liquor ads were boarded over with blank boards. ◆ Home plate was moved back a foot in 1925, making the right field foul pole 280.5 rather than 279.5. ◆ In the 1920s, policemen sat on milk cartons every 5 or 10 yards, all around the outfield. ◆ No ball was ever

# COLUMBIA PARK

**C**olumbia Park, Philadelphia. Home of the Athletics from 1901 to 1908.

hit over the center field clubhouse wall, but Rogers Hornsby hit one through a clubhouse window in 1929. ◆ The most famous fan here was "Ball Hawk" George, who stood behind the plate at 15th and Huntingdon to catch foul balls and was featured on the Fox Movietone newsreels. ◆ The park was torn down in 1950.

### OCCUPANTS
American League Philadelphia Athletics, April 26, 1901–October 3, 1908; National League Philadelphia Phillies, August 20–September 10, 1903

### CAPACITY
9,500 (1901); 13,600 (1905)

### LARGEST CROWD
25,187 on September 30, 1905 vs. the White Sox

### PHENOMENA
In the Brewerytown section, the ballpark smelled heavily of hops, yeast, and beer. ◆ There were no dugouts. The players sat on benches, placed at the sidelines of the field. Most of the seats were along the foul lines in bleacher sections, and they only cost a quarter.

# SHIBE PARK

## OCCUPANTS

American League Philadelphia Athletics, April 12, 1909–September 19, 1954; National League Philadelphia Phillies, May 16–28, 1927; July 4, 1938–October 1, 1970

## CAPACITY

20,000 (1909); 33,500 (1925); 27,500 (1926); 30,000 (1929); 33,000 (1930); 32,750 (1947); 32,500 (1948); 33,300 (1952); 33,166 (1953); 33,359 (1960); 33,608 (1961); 5,100 (1991)

## LARGEST CROWD

Phillies—41,660 total, with 40,720 paid on May 11, 1947 vs. the Dodgers; Athletics—38,800 on July 13, 1931 vs. the Senators

## SMALLEST CROWD

Athletics—18, with 23 total, on September 8, 1916 vs. the Yankees

## DIMENSIONS

Left field: 360 (1909); 378 (late 1909); 380 (1921); 334 (1922); 312 (1926); 334 (1930)
Left center: 393 (1909); 387 (1922); 405 (1925); 387 (1969)
Center field: 515 (1909); 502 (late 1909); 468 (1922); 448 (1950); 440 (1951); 460 (1953); 468 (1954); 447 (1956); 410 (1969)
Right center, just left of scoreboard: 400 (1942)
Right center: 393 (1909); 390 (1969)

**S**hibe Park, Philadelphia. Second deck ended at third base in 1909, home of the A's from 1909 to 1954, home of the Phillies from 1938 to 1970.

Interior Shibe Park Ball Grounds, Philadelphia, Pa.

Shibe Park, Athletic Base Ball Club, American League, 21st Street and Lehigh Avenue, Philadelphia. The Largest and Best Appointed Base Ball Park in the World.

**S**hibe Park, Philadelphia. Home plate entrance looked like a church.

Right field: 360 (early 1909); 340 (late 1909); 380 (1921); 307 (1926); 331 (1930); 331 (to lower concrete wall, 1934); 329 (to upper iron fence, 1934)
Backstop: 90 (1942); 86 (1943); 78 (1956); 64 (1960)

### FENCES

Left field to left center: 12 (4 screen above 8 concrete, 1949)
Center field, just a small section: 20 (1955); 8 (wood, 1956); 3 (canvas, 1969)
Right center scoreboard: 50 (top of black scoreboard, 1956); 60 (top of Ballantine Beer sign, 1956)
Right field: 12 (concrete, 1909); 34 (22 corrugated iron above 12 concrete, 1935); 30 (1943); 50 (1949); 40 (1953); 30 (1954); 40 (1955); 32 (1956)

### PHENOMENA

Currently the Deliverance Evangelistic Church seating 5,100 wor-shippers, it is 108 feet tall at the tip of its cross, is made of red brick and concrete, and includes a gymnasium, day care center, chapel, and huge sanctuary. The main entrance is on the first base side. ◆ This was a vacant lot from 1976 to 1990. ◆ Several hundred seats now reside in Duncan Park, home of the Sally League Phillies in Spartanburg, South Carolina, and in War Memorial Sta-dium, Greensboro, North Carolina. ◆ The park was named for Ben

Shibe, an A's stockholder and baseball manufacturer. ◆ Ted Williams went 6 for 8 here on the last day of the 1941 season to raise his average from .39955 to .406. Many urged Ted to sit out the last day of the season to ensure winning the .400 average, but he never gave it a thought. ◆ A 1948 plan to add 18,000 seats in right field and reduce the foul line to 315 feet never materialized. ◆ In 1910, manager Connie Mack had Danny Murphy use opera glasses to steal signs from a building in right center and use a weather vane to signal A's hitters. ◆ Shibe had a beautiful French Renaissance church-like dome on the exterior roof behind the plate, which housed Connie Mack's office. ◆ The sod was transplanted here from Columbia Park. ◆ The park had the highest pitcher's mound, 20 inches high, in the Major Leagues. The batting cage sat in play in center field when the measurement was 468 and behind the short fence in center when the measurement was only 447. ◆ There was a corrugated iron fence in right. Balls bounced at crazy angles off it, just like at Cleveland's League Park. ◆ The conduit on the right field wall was in play. There were slopes in front of the outfield fences in the early years. A ladder went all the way to the top of the left field scoreboard in 1909. It was double-decked in 1925. Also in that year, the left field stands were added. The mezzanine was added in 1929. ◆ Bull and Eddie Kessler have the distinction of being the loudest fans of the 1930s. ◆ The right field wall reinforcement in 1934 reduced the distance to the front of the frame from 331 to 329, but the sign wasn't changed until

**S**hibe Park, Philadelphia. Site now occupied by Deliverance Evangelistic Church.

1956. ◆ Before 1935, 20th Street residents could sit in their front second story bedroom, or on the roof, and see the game for free over the 12-foot right field fence. Fans could see the lines of laundry on the roof of the 20th Street houses. Connie Mack lost a suit to prevent this, so he built the high right field fence. ◆ A practice wartime blackout caused a 65-minute delay in a 1943 A's–Red Sox game. ◆ In 1956, the old Yankee Stadium scoreboard was installed in front of the right center wall; later a clock was added. Balls that hit the 75-foot-high clock were homers. The top of the Ballantine Beer sign was 60 feet high.

# CHESSLINE PARK

**OCCUPANT**

Eastern Colored League Philadelphia Tigers, 1928

# PASSON FIELD

**OCCUPANTS**

Negro National League Philadelphia Stars, 1934–1935; Negro National League Philadelphia Bacharach Giants, 1934

# PENMAR PARK

**OCCUPANTS**

Negro National League Philadelphia Stars, 1936–1948; Negro American League Philadelphia Stars, 1949–1950

**DIMENSIONS**

Left field: 330
Center field: 410
Right field: 310

**PHENOMENA**

The ballpark was built by the Pennsylvania Railroad in the mid-1920s for use by the company's YMCA. Dense coal smoke from the locomotives moving in or out of the Pennsy roundhouse behind first base often made fielders lose fly balls and delayed games for 10 or 15 minutes, frequently three or four times in one game. All the stands on the first base side were by railroad tracks. Most people went to the games on the #15 Trolley, getting off at the stop for the Stephen Smith Home for Aged and Infirm Colored Persons. ◆ The lighting system was installed by Eddie Gottlieb in 1933 for his All-Phillies semipro team. Cut infrequently, the grass was usually very tall. ◆ Satchel Paige pitched a perfect game here in 1947 through eight innings. He intentionally walked three batters to start the 9th, then signalled for all of his seven fielders to sit down, and struck out the side on nine pitches to end the game. ◆ The hot dog stand behind the plate was run by Miss Hattie Williams. Her hot dogs were boiled in a washtub over a wood fire. Amazingly, the wooden stands never fell down, even though Hattie obtained firewood by chopping away at the grandstand supports with her hatchet.

# PITTSBURGH, PENNSYLVANIA

# UNION PARK

**NEUTRAL USES**
National League Providence Grays, August 22–24, 1878

**CAPACITY**
2,500

# EXPOSITION PARK I— LOWER FIELD

**OCCUPANTS**
American Association Pittsburgh Alleghenies, May 9–September 23, 1882; June 12–September 6, 1883; Union Association Pittsburgh Unions, August 25–30, 1884

**CURRENT USE**
Three Rivers Stadium stands on this exact site today

# EXPOSITION PARK II— UPPER FIELD

**OCCUPANT**

American Association Pittsburgh Alleghenies, May 1–June 9, 1883

**PHENOMENA**

The opening games of the 1883 season were switched from Exposition Park's Lower Field to this hastily constructed upper field due to flooding at the normal field. The upper and lower fields overlapped, but because of the slope of the land, the upper field was not flooded.

# RECREATION PARK

**OCCUPANTS**

American Association Pittsburgh Alleghenies, May 1, 1884–October 12, 1886; National League Pittsburgh Alleghenies, April 30, 1887–September 30, 1890

**CAPACITY**

17,000 (1884)

**PHENOMENA**

In 1887, the Alleghenies catcher Fred Carroll had a pet monkey which accompanied him everywhere. When the pet died, he was buried with honors during a pre-game ceremony, directly beneath home plate.

# EXPOSITION PARK III

**OCCUPANTS**

Players League Pittsburgh Burghers, April 19–October 4, 1890; National League Pittsburgh Pirates, April 22, 1891–June 29, 1909; Federal League Pittsburgh Rebels, April 14, 1914–October 2, 1915

**CAPACITY**

16,000 (1914)

**DIMENSIONS**

Foul lines: 400
Center field: 450

# FORBES FIELD

## PHENOMENA

There were twin spires behind home plate on the roof of the grandstand. On July 4, 1902, with the Allegheny River at flood tide, and more than a foot of water in large parts of the outfield, the Pirates swept a doubleheader from Brooklyn with special ground rules: All outfield hits into the water were singles.

## OCCUPANTS

National League Pittsburgh Pirates, June 30, 1909–June 28, 1970; Negro National League Homestead Grays, 1939–1948

## CAPACITY

23,000 (1909); 25,000 (1915); 41,000 (1925); 40,000 (1938); 33,537 (1939); 33,467 (1942); 33,730 (1947); 33,730 (1948); 34,249 (1953); 35,000 (1960)

## LARGEST CROWD

44,932 on September 23, 1956 vs. the Dodgers

## SMALLEST CROWD

200 on June 10, 1938 vs. the Phillies

## DIMENSIONS

Left field: 360 (1909); 356.5 (1921); 356 (1922); 360 (1926); 365 (1930); 335 (1947); 365 (1954)
Left center: 406 (1942); 355 (1947); 406 (1954)
Deepest corner, just left of straightaway center, at the flagpole: 462 (1909); 457 (1930)
Center field: 422 (1926); 435 (1930)
Right center, right side of the exit gate: 416 (1955)
Right center: 408 (1942)
Bend at left end of screen: 375
Right field: 376 (1909); 376.5 (1921); 376 (1922); 300 (1925)
Backstop: 110 (1909); 84 (1938); 80 (1947); 84 (1954); 75 (1959)

## FENCES

Left field wall: 12 (wood, 1909); 12 (brick and ivy, 1946)
Left field scoreboard: 25.42 (steel left and right sides); 27 (middle)

Wooden U. S. Marine sergeant at parade rest to right of scoreboard: 32 (June 26, 1943 to the end of the season)

Left field front fence for Greenberg Gardens: 8 (5 screen above 3 wood, 1947); 12 (9 screen on top of 3 wood, 1949); 14 (screen, 1950)

Side wall from Greenberg Gardens, angling back to meet brick wall in left center: 12 (wood, when front fence was up)

Cages around light tower just right of scoreboard and in power alleys: 16.5

Center field: 12 (wood, 1909); 12 (brick and ivy, 1946)

Right center: 9.5 (concrete, 1925)

Right field: 9.5 (concrete, 1925)

Right field screen, left side at 375 mark: 24 (14.5 wire above 9.5 concrete, 1932)

Right field screen, right side at foul pole: 27.67 (18.17 wire above 9.5 concrete, 1932)

### PHENOMENA

The park was named for General John Forbes, a British general in the French and Indian War, who captured Fort Duquesne from the French Army and renamed it Fort Pitt in 1758. Thick ivy covered the brick wall in left and left center. ◆ The 14-foot Longines clock and the speaker horns on top of the left field scoreboard were out of play. A drive hitting the clock or the speakers was a home run. ◆ There were 12 seats where fans in the upper left corner of the left field bleachers could not see the plate because of the third base grandstand which stood between them and the plate. ◆ The right field roof was 86 feet high. Only 16 home run balls were ever hit onto or over it. The first one was the last home run ever hit by

**F**orbes Field, Pittsburgh. Roberto Clemente, #21, in right field, home of the Pirates from 1909 to 1970.

Babe Ruth. It came on May 25, 1935 as the Babe closed out his career with the Boston Braves with a monstrous homer off Pirates pitcher Guy Bush. The last of these 16 blasts came off Braves pitcher Ron Reed by Pirates slugger Willie Stargell. ◆ First base was near a misspelled street (Boquet Street) named for General Henry Bouquet, a Swiss soldier who fought for the British in the French and Indian War's decisive battle at Fort Duquesne in Pittsburgh. ◆ The street dead-ending into Sennott Street by third base was variously called Pennant Place and Forbes Field Avenue. Many fans walked down this street from the trolley stop on Forbes Avenue, including the author. ◆ No no-hitter was ever pitched here. Given the fact that the Pirates, Grays, and Craws played here for 62 years, that is an incredible statistic. ◆ Home plate remains in almost its exact original location; only now, it is encased in glass on the first floor walkway of the University of Pittsburgh's Forbes Quadrangle near the exact original location, which is now in a ladies bathroom. ◆ The bottoms of the light tower cages in left center, center, and right center were in play, as was the bottom of the center field flagpole. ◆ Back in the 1910s, there was a small scoreboard on the center field wall. ◆ In the 1920s, cars and trucks were repaired and sold beneath the bleachers down the left field line. ◆ Just to the left of the flagpole in deep left center, stood the batting cage, also in play. Before being placed in left center sometime in the 1920s, it stood in play behind home plate, up against the backstop. The right field stands were built in 1925, reducing the distance to the right field foul pole by 76.5 feet. ◆ "Screech Owl" McAllister was the most famous fan in the 1930s. ◆ A right field screen was added in 1932. ◆ One of the greatest joys at old Forbes Field was to sit in the right field seats behind that screen on Knot Hole Gang Day (Saturdays when kids got in for free) and watch the Great One, Roberto Clemente (known in our Smoky City as Arriba) play defense off that screen as if it were a violin. ◆ The right field screen was taken down for a short period once, then put back up almost immediately. Despite much research, I have been unable to determine when the screen was down for a short period of time. Perhaps one of you readers can help us figure out this mystery. ◆ A rare dual-league doubleheader occurred here on May 7, 1932. The first game had the National League Pirates playing the Philadelphia Phillies, and the second game featured the Negro East-West League local Homestead Grays against the Philadelphia Hilldales. ◆ The Barney Dreyfuss Monument was just to the left of the exit gate in right center, where fans exited the ballpark into Schenley Park after a game. It was installed on June 30, 1934, on the park's 25th anniversary and was made of granite with a bronze tablet. ◆ In 1938, with the Bucs on their way to the World Series, the team built a third deck of seats behind the plate called the Crow's Nest, which had the Major League's first elevator. By way of a slight detour, caused by player/manager Gabby Hartnett's Homer in the Gloamin' in the darkness of Wrigley Field, the Bucs finally made it to the Series 22 years later. ◆ The first night games here were played in 1940. ◆ During World War II, from June 26 through the end of the 1943 season, a huge wooden U. S. Marine sergeant stood against the left field wall, in play just to the right of the scoreboard. Standing at parade rest, the marine sergeant was 32 feet high, and 15 feet wide across his feet. ◆ During World War II, the right field screen could not be replaced due to the priority given to the war effort. The wooden walls installed in left and center in 1909 were replaced with brick and ivy in 1946. ◆ When the Greenberg Gardens were in place, a Western Union clock stood on top of the scoreboard, to the right of the familiar Gruen Clock. Greenberg Gardens (1947), also called Kiner's Korner (1948–1953) referred to the area between the left field scoreboard and a short fence in left of chicken coop wire put there to increase home run production. ◆ Another Forbes Field first in the Major Leagues was the green foam rubber crash pads that were placed on the concrete wall in right and right center in the 1950s. ◆ Erected in 1955, the Honus Wagner statue stood in Schenley Park, behind the left field brick wall. It was 18 feet high and was a popular meeting place for fans before and after a game. The statue (all 1,800 pounds of it) was moved to Three Rivers with the Bucs in 1970. ◆ The park had a very hard infield surface; ask veteran broadcaster and former Yankees shortstop Tony Kubek. Without the bad hop that knocked Kubek out in the fateful seventh and deciding game of the 1960 World Series, the Yankees might have won instead of the Bucs. ◆ A plaque, placed in the cement sidewalk, today marks the spot where Billy Mazeroski's World Series winning homer left the park in 1960 and flew into the trees above Yogi Berra's head. ◆ Broadcasters Bob Prince and Jim Woods led fans waving Green Weenies and Polish babushkas in the 1960s.

**F**orbes Field, Pittsburgh. Fans standing behind a rope in right field.

# AMMON FIELD

**OCCUPANT**
Negro National League Pittsburgh Keystones, 1922

# GRAYS FIELD

**OCCUPANT**
Negro American League Homestead Grays, 1929

# GUS GREENLEE FIELD

**OCCUPANTS**
Negro East-West League Homestead Grays, 1932; Negro East-West League Pittsburgh Crawfords, 1932; Negro National League Homestead Grays, 1933, 1935–1938; Negro National League Pittsburgh Crawfords, 1933–1938

**PHENOMENA**
The ballpark opened on April 29, 1932. The left field foul line was longer than at Forbes Field, where it was 365. ◆ Gus Greenlee was a very wealthy black man, who had a great deal of influence over Negro League baseball in Pittsburgh, which involved both the Grays and the Crawfords. He is rumored to have made his money running the numbers rackets in Pittsburgh. Greenlee was infuriated that a Pennsylvania Blue Law prevented him from scheduling Sunday night games because all sports events in Pennsylvania had to conclude immediately at 6:59 P.M. on Sundays. So he held one game between the Craws and the Grays that began at 12:01 A.M. on a Monday morning to get around the law. There was a sellout crowd, but unfortunately, as is the case with all other Negro League games, there is no record of the ending time. ◆ There was a tin fence in the outfield. The structure was torn down on December 10, 1938.

**T**op: Gus Greenlee Field, Pittsburgh.
Pittsburgh Crawfords' team bus. Bottom:
Hilldale Park, Philadelphia. Scrip Lee at
Hilldale Park at Yeadon, near Philadelphia.

## PROVIDENCE, RHODE ISLAND*

# ADELAIDE AVENUE GROUNDS

# MESSER STREET GROUNDS

**NEUTRAL USES**

National Association New Haven Elm Citys, June 12, 1875; National Association Boston Red Stockings, June 22, 1875

**PHENOMENA**

The park was built in the spring of 1875.

**OCCUPANT**

National League Providence Grays, May 1, 1878–September 9, 1885

**PHENOMENA**

It was the first Major League park to have a screen behind home plate to protect the fans from foul balls.

## RICHMOND, VIRGINIA

# VIRGINIA STATE AGRICULTURAL SOCIETY FAIR- GROUNDS

**CURRENT USE**

Science Museum of Richmond, formerly the Union Railroad Station.

**NEUTRAL USES**

National Association Washington Nationals, April 29, May 1, 1875

**FENCES**

None.

*See also* Warwick, Rhode Island

# VIRGINIA BASE-BALL PARK

### OCCUPANT
American Association Richmond Virginians, August 5–October 15, 1884

## ROCHESTER, NEW YORK*

# CULVER FIELD I

### OCCUPANT
American Association Rochesters, April 28–October 6, 1890

### LARGEST CROWD
4156 on September 1, 1890, for the afternoon game vs. the Louisville Colonels.

### PHENOMENA
It burned down in 1892.

# CULVER FIELD II

### NEUTRAL USES
National League Cleveland Exiles, August 27–29, 1898

### PHENOMENA
Location: Same as Culver Field I: University Avenue, now Atlantic Avenue (N); Jersey Street, now Russell Street (NW); Culver Park, now 1000 University Avenue (SW); Culver Road (E).

*See also Charlotte, New York; Irondequoit, New York

## ROCKFORD, ILLINOIS

# AGRICULTURAL SOCIETY FAIR GROUNDS

**OCCUPANT**

National Association Forest Citys of Rockford, May 5–September 26, 1871

**PHENOMENA**

This park is definitely the most interesting and the strangest ballpark in Major League history. There were numerous trees just behind the catcher, and along the foul lines, reducing foul territory to just several feet all around the field. Third base was up on a hill, and home plate was down in a deep depression. When tagging up from third on a sacrifice fly, one ran downhill all the way! At the edge of the outfield, there was the first warning track in the Major Leagues: a deep gutter providing drainage from the adjacent quarter-mile horse racing track.

## ST. GEORGE, NEW YORK

# ST. GEORGE CRICKET GROUNDS

**OCCUPANTS**

American Association New York Mets, April 22, 1886–October 7, 1887; National League New York Giants, April 29–June 14, 1889

**PHENOMENA**

From July 12, 1886 through the end of the 1886 season, Mets fans could stand on the top row of the grandstand, look back to the north, and watch the Statue of Liberty being riveted together. The last rivet was driven, and President Grover Cleveland dedicated the monument on October 28, 1886, after the season was concluded. ◆ A ticket for admission to the ball game also bought a free ferryboat ride to and from the game and Manhattan. The new owner of the Mets in 1886, Erastus Wiman, owned the ferryboat as well as the Staten Island Amusement Park. ◆ The Giants used this field for 25 home games in 1889. During that time, the field was bare and stony from second base to center field because the 1888 stage production of *Nero, The Fall of Rome* by the Kiraltys had been staged there. The play scaffolding remained in place, surrounding the outfield. In addition, the swampy flooded outfield was covered with inclined boards, forcing outfielders to wear rubber-soled shoes. Buffalo Bill's *Wild West Show* was staged here often. ◆ This was considered by far the prettiest park in the league in 1887. The diamond was in the center of the field in 1886 but was moved to the west end of the grandstand in 1887 because a large structure was built in right field to be used in the play *The Fall of Babylon*. A hit into Babylon counted only as a single. One day, two actors dressed as warriors held their polished shields so as to reflect the sun into the eyes of Baltimore batters. One day some elephants and camels, on their way to the zoo, paraded through the outfield while the Athletics were taking fielding practice. ◆ The field sloped sharply downward back of third base in fair and foul territory all the way down the left field line. The grounds also included tennis courts, an ice cream saloon, and a picnic area adjacent to the field, as well as lacrosse fields, a restaurant, and the 7th Regiment Band, complemented by water fireworks and illuminated geysers.

# ST. LOUIS, MISSOURI*

# RED STOCKING BASE-BALL PARK

### OCCUPANT
National Association St. Louis Red Stockings, May 4–July 4, 1875

### PHENOMENA
The ballpark was built in 1874, renamed Compton Park in 1885, and torn down in 1898.

*See also* Mounds, Illinois

# GRAND AVENUE PARK

**OCCUPANTS**

National Association St. Louis Brown Stockings, May 6–October 8, 1875; National League St. Louis Brown Stockings, May 5, 1876–October 6, 1877

**CAPACITY**

9,000 (1875)

# SPORTSMAN'S PARK I

**OCCUPANTS**

American Association St. Louis Browns, May 2, 1882–October 4, 1891; National League St. Louis Browns, April 12–October 13, 1892

**CAPACITY**

6,000 (1882); 12,000 (1886)

**DIMENSIONS**

Left field: 350
Left center: 400
Center field: 460
Right center: 330
Right field: 285
Backstop: 70

**PHENOMENA**

In 1881, in preparation for the 1882 season, Browns owner Chris Von der Ahe converted Augustus Solari's two-story house in the right field corner into a beer garden, complete with lawn bowling and handball courts. This beer garden was in play, in accordance with the rules of the pre-1888 World Series era, and the right fielder

**S**portsman's Park #1, St. Louis. Home of the American Association Browns from 1882 to 1891.

could go into the seats to retrieve the ball and relay it to the pitcher's box, after which the ball was eligible to be used to put out a runner. This rule was changed immediately prior to the 1888 World Series. Then, balls hit into the outfield seats fair were automatic home runs. Imagine, a beer garden with people eating and drinking at their picnic tables, in the field of play in a Major League ballpark. Fans stood behind ropes only a dozen feet behind the outfielders. There was a clubhouse in the right field corner, behind the beer garden. ◆ A Japanese fireworks cannon, made of bamboo and wrapped with steel wire, was on display during the 1882 American Association season.

# UNION GROUNDS

**OCCUPANTS**
Union Association St. Louis Maroons, April 20–October 19, 1884; National League St. Louis Maroons, April 30, 1885–September 23, 1886

**CAPACITY**
10,000 (1884)

**DIMENSIONS**
Foul lines: 285
Backstop: 25

# ROBISON FIELD

**OCCUPANT**
National League St. Louis Cardinals, April 27, 1893–June 6, 1920

**CAPACITY**
14,500 (1893); 15,200 (1899); 21,000 (1909)

**DIMENSIONS**
Left field: 470 (1893); 380 (1909)
Shoot the chutes at the left field foul pole and in right center: 625 (1896)
Deepest left center: 520 (1893); 400 (1909)
Center field: 500 (1893); 435 (1909)
Right center: 330 (1893); 320 (1909)
Right field: 290 (1893)
Backstop: 120 (1893)
Foul territory: Huge

**R**obison Field, St. Louis. The May 4, 1901 fire during the game, home of the Cardinals from 1893 to 1920.

# SPORTSMAN'S PARK II

### OCCUPANT
American League St. Louis Browns, April 23, 1902–October 6, 1908

### CAPACITY
18,000 (1907)

### FENCES
Left field: 15

# SPORTSMAN'S PARK III

### OCCUPANTS
American League St. Louis Browns, April 14, 1909–September 27, 1953; National League St. Louis Cardinals, July 1, 1920–May 8, 1966

### CAPACITY
17,600 (April 14, 1909); 24,040 (June 1909); 25,000 (1912); 34,000 (1921); 33,699 (1925); 34,023 (1926); 34,000 (1929); 33,500 (1939); 33,343 (1940); 33,699 (1941); 34,500 (1946); 31,250 (1947); 34,000 (1948); 34,450 (1952); 30,500 (1954)

## LARGEST CROWD

Cardinals—45,770 on July 12, 1931 vs. the Cubs; Browns—37,815 total, 35,518 paid on October 1, 1944 vs. the Yankees; Negro Leagues—21,000 total, with 17,906 paid on July 4, 1941 between the Kansas City Monarchs and the Chicago American Giants

## SMALLEST CROWD

Browns—66 on October 7, 1911 vs. the Tigers

## DIMENSIONS

Left field: 368 (April 1909); 350 (May 1909); 340 (1921); 355 (1926); 360 (1930); 351.1 (1931)
Left center: 379
Center field: 430 (1926); 450 (published, 1930); 430 (actual, 1930); 445 (published, 1931); 430 (actual, 1931); 420 (1938); 422 (published, 1939); 420 (actual, 1939); 420 (1940)
Deepest corner just left of dead center: 426 (1938)
Deepest corner just right of dead center: 422 (1938)
Right center: 354 (1942)
Right field: 335 (April 1909); 325 (May 1909); 315 (1921); 320 (published, 1926); 315 (actual, 1926); 310 (1931); 332 (published, 1938); 310 (actual, 1938); 309.5 (1939)
Backstop: 75 (1942); 67 (1953)

## FENCES

Left field to center field: 11.5 (concrete)
Right center from the 354 mark to right field: 11.5 (1909); 33 (11.5 concrete below 21.5 wire, July 5, 1929); 11.5 (1955); 36.67 (11.5 concrete below 25.17 wire, 1956)

## PHENOMENA

Sportsman's most famous fan was Screechin' Screamin' Mary Ott, who used to drive visiting players crazy from her seat behind the first base dugout. ◆ A plaque commemorating this ballpark was dedicated in the foyer of the lobby of the Herbert Hoover Boys' Club on April 27, 1991 before 60 people, including 20 former Major League ballplayers. ◆ Beyond the center field wall, at the corner of Sullivan and North Grand, there was a bar called the Club Boulevard that was actually a part of the ballpark, just like the bowling alley that is structurally a part of Fenway Park. ◆ Amazingly, there had never been a regular-season tie for the league championship in Major League baseball during its first three-quarters of a century from 1871 to 1946. On October 1, 1946, the first-

**S**portsman's Park #3, St. Louis. Left field upper deck ended on the foul line, home of the Cardinals from 1920 to 1966, home of the Browns from 1909 to 1953.

ever League Playoff game was held here between the Cardinals and the Dodgers. There have only been seven regular-season first-place ties during the almost half-century since, resulting in 13 playoff games. Incredibly, the Red Sox have been involved in both American League playoff games, and the Dodgers have been involved in all 11 National League playoff games. ◆ Since the League Championship Series began in 1969, the rules in both leagues have provided for a one-game division playoff. That has happened only twice, in 1978 and in 1980 in the National League West. Prior to 1969, in the American League, the league rule provided for one-game playoffs whereas in the National League, the league rule provided for best-two-out-of-three-games playoffs. In the American League, the Indians defeated the Red Sox in 1948 for the American League pennant, and the Yankees defeated the Red Sox in 1978 for the American League East flag, with both games played in Fenway Park. In 1946, the Cardinals swept the Dodgers: the first game played here in Sportsman's Park, the second in Ebbets Field. In 1951, the Dodgers beat the Giants in Ebbets Field, before the Giants swept two games in the Polo Grounds. In 1959, the Dodgers swept the Braves, the first game played in Milwaukee County Stadium and the second in the Los Angeles Coliseum. In 1962, the Giants beat the Dodgers in Candlestick Park. Then the Dodgers beat the Giants in Dodger Stadium. Finally, the Giants won the pennant by beating the Dodgers in Dodger Stadium. And lastly, in 1980, the Astros beat the Dodgers in Dodger Stadium for the National League West flag. ◆ Interestingly, of the 13 playoff games (11 League Playoff games and 2 Division Playoff games), only 5 have been sellouts. This can perhaps be attributed to the lack of advance notice, since the tie occurs on the last day of the season, and the fact that most playoff games are played on weekday afternoons. ◆ The 1902 to 1908 curved grandstand behind home plate became the left field pavilion in this park from 1909 until 1912, when it was replaced by a rectangular, single-decked pavilion. A similar single-decked pavilion was also built in 1912 behind the right field wall. The second deck was expanded to the foul poles during the winter of 1925 to 1926. The bleachers were then expanded in the outfield in 1926, and a roof was built over the right field section, creating the pavilion. Black fans were restricted to the right field pavilion seats during the era of segregation. ◆ The wire screen, installed on July 5, 1929, in front of the right field pavilion was removed for the entire 1955 season because Manager Eddie Stanky and General Manager Dick Meyer thought that the Cards would benefit with their predominantly left-handed batting lineup. After the season, the new general manager, Frank Lane, decided to put the screen back up because he thought the fans liked it. ◆ During the 1930s, a goat grazed in the outfield. ◆ The first night games here, for both the Browns and the Cardinals, were played in 1940. ◆ The local St. Louis newspaper, the *Globe-Democrat*, had an ad on the right center wall which showed the star of the previous game in the 1940s. Just to the right of this ad, the league standings for both leagues were listed. On August 19, 1951, Bill Veeck pulled his great stunt: "Now pinch-hitting for the Browns is Eddie Gaedel, 3 feet 7 inches tall, Number 1/8, weighing 65 lbs." ◆ When he bought the stadium from the Browns in 1953, Cardinals owner Gussie Busch wanted to name the park Budweiser Stadium, but he changed the name to Busch Stadium because of league pressure not to name a ballpark after a brand of beer. ◆ There was a flagpole in fair territory in center field, until it was moved beyond the outfield fence during the winter of 1953 to 1954. At the same time, the center field bleachers were permanently closed, and the outfield warning track was installed. ◆ Beginning in 1954, the Busch Eagle would flap its wings after each Cardinal home run. It sat on top of the left center scoreboard. During World War II, there was a War Chest sign there. ◆ The Cards office was at 3623 Dodier; the Browns office was at 2911 North Grand. Bill Veeck's family lived in an apartment under the stands during the 1950s. ◆ After the Cards' last home game here, a 10–5 loss to the Giants on May 8, 1966, groundskeeper Bill Stocksick pulled home plate out of the ground and put it aboard a helicopter for delivery to the new Busch Memorial Stadium, as a band played "Auld Lang Syne."

# FEDERAL LEAGUE PARK

**OCCUPANT**
Federal League St. Louis Terriers, April 16, 1914–October 3, 1915

**CAPACITY**
12,000 (1914); 15,000 (1915)

**DIMENSIONS**
Left field: 325
Center field: 375
Right field: 300
Backstop: 90

# GIANTS PARK

**OCCUPANTS**
Negro National League St. Louis Giants, May 9, 1920–August 30, 1921; Negro National League St. Louis Stars, May 30–June 15, 1922

**PHENOMENA**
Kuebler's Park was a block away, north of Clarence Avenue, east of Prescott Avenue, and south of Pope Avenue, and was apparently abandoned after 1917. After the Giants folded, the Tigers, a Negro Minor League team in the Southern League, took over Giants Park in 1922 and renamed it Tigers Park.

# STARS PARK

**OCCUPANT**
Negro National League St. Louis Stars, July 9, 1922–August 11, 1931

**CAPACITY**
10,000 (1922)

**DIMENSIONS**
Left field: 250
Left center: 425

# METROPOLITAN PARK

**OCCUPANT**
Negro American League St. Louis Stars, 1937

**PHENOMENA**
Location was the same as Giants Park.

# SOUTH END PARK

**A.K.A.**
National Nite Baseball Park

**CURRENT USE**
American Can Company Plant

**OCCUPANT**
Negro American League St. Louis Stars, April–August 1939

## SAN FRANCISCO, CALIFORNIA

# SEALS STADIUM

**OCCUPANT**
National League San Francisco Giants, April 15, 1958–September 20, 1959

**CAPACITY**
16,000 (1931); 18,600 (1932); 20,700 (1933); 25,000 (1938); 23,601 (1939); 22,900 (1940); 20,700 (1941); 22,500 (1947); 22,180 (1953); 22,900 (1958)

**LARGEST CROWD**
23,192 on April 15, 1958 vs. the Dodgers

**DIMENSIONS**
Left field: 340 (1931); 365 (1958); 361 (1959)
Left center: 375 (1958); 364 (1959)
Just left of dead center in the corner: 404 (1958)
Center field: 400 (1931); 410 (1958); 400 (1959)
Just right of dead center in the corner: 415 (1958)
Just right of the 415 mark where the seats jutted out: 397 (1958)

**S**eals Stadium, San Francisco. Top: Giants and Dodgers open the 1958 season. Bottom: Bleachers were added in left field for the Giants 1958–1959.

Right field: 385 (1931); 365 (1940); 355 (1958); 350 (1959)
Backstop: 55.42

### FENCES
Left field: 15 (5 concrete below 10 wire)
Center field scoreboard: 30.5
Right field: 16 (5 concrete below 11 wire)

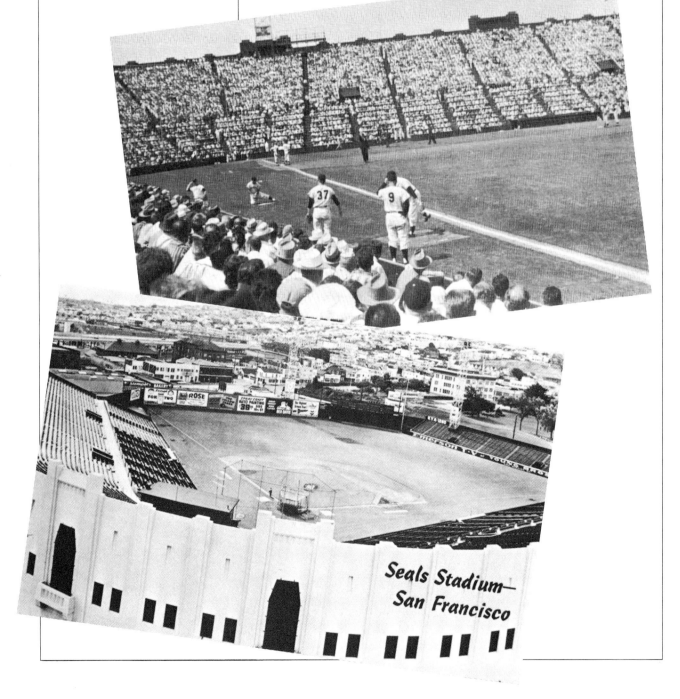

# SEATTLE, WASHINGTON

## SICK'S STADIUM

**OCCUPANT**

American League Seattle Pilots, April 11–October 2, 1969

**CAPACITY**

15,000 (1913); 11,000 (1938); 18,000 (April 11, 1969); 25,420 (June 1969)

**LARGEST CROWD**

23,657 on August 3, 1969 vs. the Yankees

**DIMENSIONS**

Left field: 325 (1938); 305 (1969)
Power alleys: 345 (1969)
Corners just right and left of center: 405 (1969)
Center field: 400 (1938); 402 (1969)
Right field: 325 (1938); 320 (1969)
Backstop: 54
Foul territory: Very small

**FENCES**

Left field: 8 (3 concrete below 5 wire)
Center field: 12.55 (3 concrete below 9.55 wire)
Right field: 8 (3 concrete below 5 wire)

**S**ick's Stadium, Seattle. 1969 Pilots played here, then moved to Milwaukee.

## SPRINGFIELD, MASSACHUSETTS

# HAMPDEN PARK RACE TRACK

**NEUTRAL USES**
National Association Troy Haymakers, July 23, 1872; National Association Boston Red Stockings, July 16, 1873; National Association Boston Red Stockings, May 14, 1875

**PHENOMENA**
The ballpark was located at the southern end of a mile-long oval bicycle track, which ran along a northwest-southeast axis.

## SYRACUSE, NEW YORK*

# STAR PARK I

**OCCUPANT**
National League Syracuse Stars, May 28–September 10, 1879

**PHENOMENA**
The neutral site game between the Grays and the Bisons in 1885 was rained out.

# STAR PARK II

**OCCUPANT**
American Association Syracuse Stars, April 28–October 6, 1890

**PHENOMENA**
It was built in 1886.

*See also Three Rivers, New York

# IRON PIER

**NEUTRAL USE**
American Association Syracuse Stars, August 3, 1890

**PHENOMENA**
After the police banned Sunday ball at Three Rivers Park, 12 miles north of Syracuse in Three Rivers, the Stars scheduled their August 3, 1890 game here. Because the police had announced they would stop any Sunday games, Louisville did not show up. But the umpires and the Syracuse players did. So Syracuse was awarded a forfeit victory, which did count in the standings, in the only Major League game ever "played" at Iron Pier. Iron Pier was an amusement park resort.

# THREE RIVERS, NEW YORK

# THREE RIVERS PARK

**NEUTRAL USES**
American Association Syracuse Stars, May 18–July 20, 1890 (Sundays)

**PHENOMENA**
The ballpark was located adjacent to Phoenix, New York, twelve miles north of Syracuse, where the Oswego River is formed by the confluence of the Seneca and Oneida Rivers at Three Rivers Point, on the Rome, Ogdersburg, and Watertown Railroad.

# TOLEDO, OHIO

# LEAGUE PARK

**OCCUPANT**
American Association Toledo Blue Stockings, May 14–September 23, 1884

**LARGEST CROWD**
4,000 for the afternoon game on July 4, 1884 vs. the Washingtons.

# TRI-STATE FAIR GROUNDS

**NEUTRAL USE**
American Association Toledo Blue Stockings, September 13, 1884

**PHENOMENA**
Location: Frazier Street, later Oakwood Avenue (N); Woodstock Avenue, later Addington Street (W); Door Street (S); Ravensburg Avenue, later Upton Avenue (E).

# SPERANZA PARK

**FORMER USE**
Armory

**OCCUPANT**
American Association Toledo Black Pirates, May 1–October 2, 1890

**LARGEST CROWD**
5,500 on May 11, 1890 vs. the St. Louis Browns

# ARMORY PARK

**NEUTRAL USES**
American League Detroit Tigers, June 28, August 16, 1903

**PHENOMENA**
Location: Left field: Armory, then Orange Street (N); 3rd base: Speilbusch Avenue (W); 1st base: Gas Company Shop, then the County Jail and Jackson Street (S); Right field: Ontario Street (E).

# SWAYNE FIELD

**OCCUPANTS**
Negro National League Toledo Tigers, April–July 15, 1923; Negro American League Toledo Crawfords, July–September 1939

**CAPACITY**
10,000 (1923); 12,500 (1938)

**DIMENSIONS**
Left field: 472
Center field: 482 (1923); 448 (1938)
Right field: 327
Backstop: 72

## TORONTO, ONTARIO

# EXHIBITION STADIUM

**OCCUPANT**
American League Toronto Blue Jays, April 7, 1977–May 28, 1989

**CAPACITY**
25,303 (1959); 38,522 (1977); 43,737 (1978)

**LARGEST CROWD**
47,828 on July 1, 1987 vs. the Yankees

**DIMENSIONS**
Foul lines: 330
Power alleys: 375
Center field: 400
Backstop: 60

**FENCES**
12 (8 canvas below 4 wire)

**PHENOMENA**
The first game played here was on April 7, 1977 vs. the Chicago White Sox. It was the only Major League game ever played with snow covering the entire field. The teams played the entire game, with snow covering the outfield carpet, and the first three innings with both the infield and outfield carpets covered with snow, despite the fact that the infield had been repeatedly cleared of snow by the Zamboni machine borrowed from Toronto's Maple Leaf Gardens. The weather during the game brought light continuous snow, winds southeast at 33 km/hr, and −10 degrees Fahrenheit windchill through the 3rd inning. After that, the snow stopped falling, and the sun came out and melted most of the snow.

# TROY, NEW YORK *

## HAYMAKERS' GROUNDS

**OCCUPANTS**

National Association Troy Haymakers, May 9, 1871–June 6, 1872; National League Troy Trojans, May 18, 1880–September 30, 1881

**H**aymakers Grounds, Troy, New York. In 1871, the Chicago White Stockings, now called the Cubs, on the left, the Troy Haymakers on the right.

## PUTNAM GROUNDS

**OCCUPANT**

National League Troy Trojans, May 28–September 20, 1879

**PHENOMENA**

Location: People's Avenue (N); 15th Street (W).

*See also* Albany, New York; Watervliet, New York

## WARWICK, RHODE ISLAND

# ROCKY POINT PARK

**NEUTRAL USE**
National League Boston Pilgrims, September 6, 1903

**PHENOMENA**
The only park in Major League history where the entire outfield was surrounded by the ocean so that all home runs went into the water. ◆ It was used for Sunday games by the International League Providence Grays until 1914.

## WASHINGTON, D.C.

# OLYMPIC GROUNDS

**OCCUPANTS**
National Association Washington Olympics, May 4, 1871–May 24, 1872; National Association Washingtons, April 15–October 23, 1873; National Association Washingtons, April 26–June 8, 1875

**CAPACITY**
500

# NATIONALS GROUNDS

**OCCUPANT**
National Association Washington Nationals, April 20–May 25, 1872

**PHENOMENA**
It was located at 16th Street and R Street.

# ATHLETIC PARK

**OCCUPANT**

American Association Washingtons, May 1–August 5, 1884

**PHENOMENA**

It was situated on a plot 450 by 490 feet. Location: Center field: S Street, NW (S); Third base: Ninth Street, NW (E); Home plate: T Street, NW (N); First base: Tenth Street, NW (W). Westminster Street now runs parallel to, and between S and T Streets.

# CAPITOL GROUNDS

**OCCUPANT**

Union Association National Unions, April 18–September 25, 1884

**CAPACITY**

6,000

**PHENOMENA**

The right field was very short, the left field very roomy. ◆ It was situated opposite the grounds of the Capitol Building, currently the United States Senate underground parking garage and R.A. Taft Memorial.

# SWAMPOODLE GROUNDS

**OCCUPANT**

National League Washington Statesmen, April 29, 1886–September 21, 1889

**CAPACITY**

6,000

**PHENOMENA**

The right field and the infield are now the western section of the Union Station National Visitors Center, and left field is now the City Post Office.

# BOUNDARY FIELD

**OCCUPANTS**

American Association Washington Nationals, April 13–October 5, 1891; National League Washington Senators, April 16, 1892–October 14, 1899

**CAPACITY**

6,500

# AMERICAN LEAGUE PARK I

# AMERICAN LEAGUE PARK II

**PHENOMENA**

The park was built in the spring of 1891 by felling 125 oak trees and filling in the stump holes to make the infield. In 1891, some trees hung over the outfield fences. Some apparent homers hit the trees and bounced back in play. These same trees interfered with the outfielders' attempts to catch fly balls.

**OCCUPANT**

American League Washington Senators, April 29, 1901–September 29, 1903

**PHENOMENA**

Baseball's first public address announcer, Mr. E. Lawrence Phillips, gave the lineups here by megaphone for the first time in 1902. ◆ The stands were transferred to Seventh and Florida for the 1904 season as American League Park II.

**OCCUPANT**

American League Washington Senators, April 14, 1904–October 6, 1910

**PHENOMENA**

The grounds crew had a Dog House in the outfield near the flagpole where they stored the flag between games. One day, the grounds-keeper forgot to close the Dog House door in the morning when taking out the folded flag to run it up the nearby flagpole. It just so happened that a Senators batter hit a line drive that afternoon over the head of Philadelphia Athletics center fielder Socks Seybold, and the ball rolled inside the Dog House. Seybold stuck his head and shoulders inside to get the ball and promptly got stuck in the Dog House. Three minutes later, A's teammates got Socks out, but the batter had long since crossed home plate with the only inside-the-dog-house homer in Major League history. ◆ A fire caused by a plumber's blow lamp burned down the field during spring training on March 17, 1911.

# GRIFFITH STADIUM

OCCUPANTS

American League Washington Senators, April 12, 1911–October 2, 1960; Eastern Colored League Washington Potomacs, 1924; Negro East-West League Washington Pilots, 1932; Negro National League Washington Elite Giants, 1936–1937; Negro National League Washington-Homestead Grays, 1937–1948; Negro National League Washington Black Senators, 1938; American League Washington Senators, April 10–September 21, 1961

**CAPACITY**

32,000 (1921); 30,171 (1936); 31,500 (1939); 29,473 (1940); 29,613 (1941); 29,000 (1947); 25,048 (1948); 35,000 (1952); 28,587 (1956); 28,669 (1960); 27,550 (1961)

**LARGEST CROWD**

38,701 on October 11, 1925 vs. the Pirates

**SMALLEST CROWD**

460 on September 7, 1954 vs. the Athletics

**G**riffith Stadium, Washington, D.C. Josh Gibson rounding third base.

## DIMENSIONS

Left field: 407 (1911); 424 (1921); 358 (1926); 407 (1931); 402 (1936); 405 (1942); 375 (opening day, 1947); 405 (remainder of 1947); 402 (1948); 386 (1950); 408 (1951); 405 (1952); 388 (1954); 386 (1956); 350 (1957); 388 (1961)

Left of left center at corner: 383 (1931); 366 (1954); 360 (1956)

Right of left center at bend in bleachers: 409 (1942); 398 (1954); 383 (1955); 380 (1956)

Left center: 391 (1911); 372 (1950)

Center field: 421

Center field corner to left of building-protection wall: 423 (1926); 441 (1930); 422 (1931); 426 (1936); 420 (1942); 426 (1948); 420 (1950); 394 (1951); 420 (1952); 421 (1953); 426 (1954); 421 (1955); 426 (1961)

Inner tip of building-protection wall: 409 (1943); 408 (1953)

Deepest corner at right end of building-protection wall: 457 (1953); 438 (1955); 401 (1956)

Right center: 378 (1954); 372 (1955); 373 (1956)

Right field: 328 (1909); 326 (1921); 328 (marked, 1926); 320 (actual, 1926); 320 (1955)

Backstop: 61

## FENCES

Left field: 11.23 (foul pole to 408 mark concrete, 1953); 12 (from 410 corner near left field foul pole to 408 mark just right of dead center, 1954); 8 to 10 (wood in the corner in front of the bullpen at the foul pole, 1955); 6.5 (wire and plywood in front of bullpen, 1956)

Center field: 30 (concrete 408 mark to 457 mark, 1953); 31 (concrete 408 mark to 457 mark, 1954); 6 (wire and plywood, 1956)

Right center, to the left of the scoreboard in front of the bullpen: 4 (wood from 457 mark to 435 mark, 1953); 10 (wood, 1955); 4 (wood, 1959)

Right center scoreboard: 41 (1946)

National Bohemian beer bottle: 56 (1946)

Right field: 30 (concrete, 1953); 31 (concrete, 1954)

## PHENOMENA

The center field wall detoured around five houses and a huge tree in center, jutting into the field of play. ♦ The first night games here were played in 1941. The lights went out in a Senators-Tigers game with the pitcher in his windup with a 2 and 2 count on batter George Kell of the Tigers. When the lights came on again, all the infielders and outfielders, the umpires, the batter, and the catcher were all lying flat on the ground. Only the pitcher remained standing because only he knew that the ball had not been pitched. ◆ The right field foul line was the grandstand wall for the last 15 or so feet in front of the foul pole, so that there was no way to catch a foul ball there. A similar condition exists today at Wrigley Field in Chicago. ◆ Legend has it that it was downhill, and only 89 feet, from the plate to first base, supposedly to help save a step for slow Washington batters. ◆ The right field clock was out of play. A ball rolling between the top of the scoreboard and the bottom of the clock was in play. If it didn't come out, it was a homer; if it did, the outfielder could throw it back into play. ◆ U.S. presidents traditionally opened each season here by throwing out the first ball. ◆ The only men to clear the back left field bleacher wall were Josh Gibson (twice) and Mickey Mantle (once). Yankees Public Relations Director Red Patterson promptly measured Mantle's ball as having rolled to a stop 565 feet from the plate in Mr. Perry L. Cool's backyard at 434 Oakdale Street: 391 feet to the outfield bleacher wall, 69 feet to the rear bleacher wall, plus 105 feet across Fifth Street to the Cool backyard. Mantle's ball nicked the beer sign as it left the park, 60 feet above the playing surface. ◆ There was a loudspeaker horn high on the wall in center. ◆ Memorials honoring Walter Johnson and Clark Griffith stood outside the main entrance to the first base grandstand. The Walter Johnson Memorial now stands at Walter Johnson High School in Bethesda, Maryland.

**G**riffith Stadium, Washington, D.C. Left: Flag-raising ceremony at opening day in 1952. Right: Flag-raising ceremony at All Star Game in 1956.

# ROBERT F. KENNEDY MEMORIAL STADIUM

The Clark Griffith Memorial, dedicated by Vice President Nixon on August 8, 1956, now stands at Robert F. Kennedy Stadium. ◆ The height of the National Bohemian Beer Bottle, in play above the right center field scoreboard, was 56 feet. ◆ The park was rebuilt after the March 17, 1911 fire and completed on July 24, 1911. The park was double-decked in 1920, from the bases down to the foul poles. The new roof was higher than the original second-deck roof behind the plate. ◆ Seventeen rows of temporary seats were placed in front of the left field bleachers for the 1924 World Series. A small section of temporary bleachers was also inserted into the right center field corner. ◆ The Senators were leading the Red Sox 6–3 on August 15, 1941 but lost by forfeit when the grounds crew failed to cover the field quickly enough during a rainstorm. ◆ Ten Senator players had to sleep in the dressing room in April and May 1946 due to a post-war housing shortage. ◆ In 1954, the visitors' bullpen was enclosed behind a screen fence in the left field corner in fair territory. In 1956, all the distances to the outfield fences were re-measured, and it was discovered that the right field had lost 8 feet over the years. Ten rows of temporary seats were added in 1956 in front of the left field bleacher section. ◆ The park was demolished in 1965.

**OCCUPANT**

American League Washington Senators, April 9, 1962–September 30, 1971

**CAPACITY**

43,500 (1962); 45,016 (1971); 45,010 (1991)

**LARGEST CROWD**

48,147 on August 1, 1962 vs. the Yankees

**DIMENSIONS**

Left field: 335 (1962); 260 (1982); 335 (1991)
Left center: 385 (1962); 381 (1963); 295 (1982); 385 (1991)
Center field: 410
Right center: 385 (1962); 378 (1963); 385 (1991)
Right field: 335
Backstop: 60

**R**FK Stadium, Washington, D.C. Old Timers Game, with short left field fence.

Left field: 7 (wire screen, 1962); 24 (wood, 1987);
7 (wire screen, 1991)
Rest of the outfield: 7 (wire screen)

## PHENOMENA

The park looks like a wet straw hat, or a waffle whose center stuck to the griddle, because of its curved, dipping roof. This is a great football stadium: Its ugly modern lines seem designed by Stalin, and they work very well to hold in the cacophony of sound that football generates. Its formal, pretentious, martial, classically antiseptic, and cold style suit football just fine. But for baseball, there is too little intimacy with the game, and the fans are too far away from the action. ◆ During the 1962 season, sections of left and left center sank 6 feet due to leveling after the recent stadium construction. ◆ The main entrance on the west side is flanked on the left (or north) by the Clark Calvin Griffith Monument, and on the right (or south) by the George Preston Marshall Monument. There is a huge scoreboard (375 feet by 35 feet) in right center. Many of the center field seats have been painted to designate the landing sites of some of Frank Howard's longest homers. ◆ Hall of Famer Luke "Old Aches and Pains" Appling homered to left here off Hall of Famer Warren Spahn in an Old Timers Game in 1982. Even though the fence in left was only 260 feet away, nobody cared: The 73-year old Appling received a standing ovation. During his career, Appling had 2,749 hits, only 45 of which had been home runs. ◆ A 24-foot Blue Monster wooden fence in left field was added for the Mets-Phillies exhibition on April 5, 1987, as the football configuration made the left field line only 260 feet.

## WATERVLIET, NEW YORK

# TROY BALL CLUB GROUNDS

**OCCUPANT**
National League Troy Trojans, May 20–August 26, 1882

**LARGEST CROWD**
3,000 on May 30, 1882 for the afternoon game vs. the Chicago White Stockings

## WAVERLY, NEW JERSEY

# WAVERLY FAIR-GROUNDS

**A.K.A.**
Domestic Field, Waverly Park, Weequahic Park, B'nai Jeshuron Cemetery

**OCCUPANT**
National Association Elizabeth Resolutes, April 28–July 23, 1873

## WEEHAWKEN, NEW JERSEY

# MONITOR PARK

**NEUTRAL USE**
American Association New York Mets, September 11, 1887

**PHENOMENA**
Miller Stadium in Hudson County, N.J., is now only three blocks away from where Monitor Park used to be.

## WEST NEW YORK, NEW JERSEY

# WEST NEW YORK FIELD CLUB GROUNDS

**NEUTRAL USES**

National League Brooklyn Bridegrooms, September 11, 18, October 2, 1898; National League New York Giants, June 4, July 16, August 13, September 17, 1899

**PHENOMENA**

Location: Bergenline Avenue (W); Sixteenth Street, now 60th Street (S); Twelfth Street, now Monroe Place (E); Niles Avenue, now 61st Street (N).

## WHEELING, WEST VIRGINIA

# ISLAND GROUNDS

**NEUTRAL USE**

National League Pittsburgh Pirates, September 22, 1890

**PHENOMENA**

Situated on Wheeling Island in the Ohio River, between Wheeling, W.V., and Bridgeport, Ohio. ◆ The grass was so long on September 22, 1890, that a hit by Mike Tiernan was lost in the outfield grass for an inside-the-park homer.

## WILMINGTON, DELAWARE

# UNION STREET PARK

**OCCUPANT**

Union Association Wilmington Quicksteps, September 2–15, 1884

**PHENOMENA**

The home game of September 15, 1884 vs. the Kansas City Unions attracted exactly 0 fans. Faced with the prospect of a game with no fans at all, between his last-place team, the 2–15 Quicksteps, and the next-to-last place team, 16–63 Kansas City, Wilmington manager Joe Simmons called his Quicksteps off the field and forfeited the game.

# WORCESTER, MASSACHUSETTS

# AGRICULTURAL COUNTY FAIR GROUNDS

### OCCUPANT
National League Worcester Brown Stockings, May 1, 1880–September 29, 1882

### PHENOMENA
The site of the first two-games-for-one-admission doubleheader in Major League history on September 25, 1882 vs. the Providence Grays. All prior events that may have been referred to as doubleheaders were actually two separate admissions events, one in the morning and one in the afternoon. ♦ The Brown Stockings drew less than 100 fans on three occasions in 1882, all in games against the Troy Trojans: 18 on September 29, 25 on September 28, and 54 on May 15.

# YEADON, PENNSYLVANIA

# HILLDALE PARK

### OCCUPANTS
Eastern Colored League Philadelphia Hilldales, 1923–1927; Negro American League Philadelphia Hilldales, 1929; Negro East-West League Philadelphia Hilldales, 1932

### DIMENSIONS
Left field: 315
Right center: 400
Right field: 370

# BIBLIOGRAPHY

**BOOKS**

Allen, Lee. "Locations of Major League Parks," *1961 Baseball Dope Book*, pp. 110–114. St. Louis: Sporting News, 1961. (article)

Amadee and Lowell Reidenbaugh. *Take Me Out to the Ball Park*. St. Louis: Sporting News, 1983.

Benswanger, William. *Forbes Field: 60th Birthday*. Pittsburgh: Pittsburgh Pirates, 1969.

Bess, Philip. *City Baseball Magic*. Minneapolis: Minneapolis Review of Baseball, 1989.

Bready, James. "Eight Leagues, Eight Parks," *The Home Team*. Baltimore: Hawke, 1979. (article)

Charleton, James H. *Recreation in the United States, National Historic Landmark Theme Study*, pp. 1–64. Washington: Department of the Interior, 1986.

Cook, Dan, and Toman, Jim. *Cleveland Municipal Stadium*. Cleveland: Cleveland Landmarks Press, 1981.

Durso, Joseph. *Yankee Stadium: Fifty Years of Drama*. Boston: Houghton Mifflin, 1974.

Higgins, George. "Ballpark: Fenway, with Tears," *Ultimate Baseball Book*. Boston: Houghton Mifflin, 1981. (article)

James, Bill. *The Bill James Historical Abstract*. New York: Villard Books, 1986.

James, Bill, "Raising the Roof," *The Bill James Baseball Abstract*, p. 82. New York: Ballantine Books, 1984. (article)

Jaspersohn, William, *The Ballpark*. Boston: Little, Brown and Company, 1980.

Jennison, Christopher. "The Ball Parks," Chapter 9, *Wait 'Til Next Year*. New York: W.W. Norton and Company, 1974. (article)

Kalinsky, George, and Bill Shannon, *The Ballparks*. New York: Hawthorne Books, 1975.

Mack, Gene. *Hall of Fame Cartoons of Major League Ball Parks.* Boston: Sporting News, 1947.

Mona, Dave. *Hubert H. Humphrey Metrodome Souvenir Book.* Minneapolis: MSP Publications, 1982.

Moss, Richard J. *Tiger Stadium.* Lansing: Michigan Department of State, 1976.

Riess, Steven. "Politics, Ball Parks, and the Neighborhood," Chapter 4, *Touching Base: Professional Baseball and American Culture in the Progressive Era.* Westport, Connecticut: Greenwood Press, 1975.

Rohrk, Mark, *Crosley Field, 1912–1970.* Blue Ash, Ohio: Crosley Field Fund-Raising Committee, 1986.

Schlossberg, Dan. "Ballparks," Chapter 6, *Baseball Catalog.* Middle Village, New York: Jonathan David Publishers, 1980. (article)

Serby, Myron W. *The Stadium.* New York: American Institute of Steel Construction, 1930.

Shaver, Leslie. *Aud Arena Stadium—International Guide and Directory.* Nashville: Billboard Publications, 1983.

Sullivan, George. "Fenway," Chapter 1, *The Picture History of the Boston Red Sox.* New York: Bobbs-Merrill Company, 1979. (article)

Wood, Bob. *Dodger Dogs to Fenway Franks.* New York: McGraw-Hill, 1988.

Woodbury, William N. *Grandstand and Stadium Design.* New York: American Institute of Steel Construction, 1947.

Wray, J. E. *How to Lay Out a League Diamond.* New York: American Sports Publishing Co., 1921.

### LETTERS

Over 3500 letters were received in response to my requests for information to every Major League team, ballpark, mayor, league, hall of fame, newspaper, historical society, and public library associated with a franchised city in this book, as well as many other sportswriters, researchers, authors, groundskeepers, ballplayers, umpires, and baseball executives.

### PH.D. DISSERTATIONS

Goldstein, Warren. "Playing for Keeps: A History of American Baseball, 1857–1876." Yale University: New Haven, 1983.

Kammer, David. "Take Me Out to the Ballgame: American Cultural Values as Reflected in the Architectural Evolution and Criticism of the Modern Baseball Stadium." University of New Mexico: Albuquerque, 1981.

Rogosin, Donn. "Black Baseball: The Life in the Negro Leagues." University of Texas: Austin, 1981.

Ruck, Robert. "Sandlot Season: Sport in Black Pittsburgh." University of Pittsburgh: Pittsburgh, 1983.

## MASTER'S THESIS

Heaphy, Leslie. "The Growth and Decline of the Negro Leagues." University of Toledo: Toledo, 1989.

## GRADUATE SCHOOL PAPER

Bluthardt, Robert. "Fenway Park and the Golden Age of the Baseball Park, 1909–1915." George Washington University: Washington, 1980

## CALENDARS

Dudrear, Kent. "The American Ballpark 15-Month Calendar." Scottsville, New York: Scottsville Sports, 1983, 1984, etc.

Wolff, Miles. "Great Minor League Baseball Parks Calendar." Durham, North Carolina: Baseball America, 1983, 1984, etc.

## BASEBALL GUIDES

*Baseball Almanacs*

*Blue Books*

*Dewitt Guides*

*Dope Books*

*Reach Guides*

*Spalding Guides*

*Spink Guides*

*Sporting News Guides*

*Sporting News Record Books*

## JOURNAL ARTICLES

Bess, Philip H. "From Elysian Fields to Domed Stadiums." *Threshold 2*, University of Illinois at Chicago, School of Architecture, Autumn 1983, pp. 116–128

Hilton, George. "Comiskey Park," *Baseball Research Journal*, 1974, pp. 3–10.

Davids, Robert. "A Major League Game in Grand Rapids?" *Baseball Research Journal*, 1976, pp. 120–122.

Doherty, Paul, and Bill Price. "Braves Field," *Baseball Research Journal*, 1978, pp. 1–6.

Doyle, Dutch, et al. "The History of Baker Bowl," *Baseball Research Journal*, 1981, pp. 1–12.

Gold, Eddie. "Wrigley Field," *Baseball Research Journal*, 1979, pp. 120–125.

Kush, Raymond. "The Building of Wrigley Field," *Baseball Research Journal*, 1981, pp. 10–15.

Lancaster, Donald. "Forbes Field," *Baseball Research Journal*, 1986, pp. 26–29.

Oriard, Michael V. "Sports & Space," *Landscape*, Autumn 1976, pp. 32–40.

Overfield, Joseph. "Offermann Stadium in Buffalo," *Baseball Research Journal*, 1979, pp. 43–46.

Pastier, John. "The Business of Baseball," *Inland Architect*, January/February 1989, pp. 56–62.

Riess, Steven. "Power Without Authority: Los Angeles' Elites and the Construction of the Coliseum," *Journal of Sport History*, North American Society for Sport History, Spring 1981, pp. 50–65.

## NEWSPAPER ARTICLES

Boswell, Tom. "A Passion for Parks." *Washington Post*, 17 May 1978; "Fenway to Chavez." *Washington Post*, 9 June 1973; "The Diamond Palaces." *Washington Post*, 9 August 1984.

Falls, Joe. "Take Me Out to a Great Old Ballpark," and others. *Detroit News* and *Sporting News*.

Gammons, Peter. "Fenway: Beauty or Beast." *Boston Globe*, 4 April 1986, pp. 73–82.

James, Bill. "Those Distorted Stadia." *Sporting News*, 10 August 1987, pp. 10–11.

Logan, Bob. "Baseball's Heirlooms." *Chicago Tribune*, 26–30 June, 1985.

Martney, Larry. "Park Tampering Is Old Custom." *Detroit News*, 7 April 1959.

Miher, Michael. "What Will Become of Wrigley Field," and "16 Ways to Save Wrigley Field," *Chicago Reader*, 12 April 1985 and 12 July 1985, pp. 10–11+ and pp. 10–11+.

Nightingale, Dave. Playing the Field, So to Speak." *Sporting News*, 4 April 1983, p. 23.

Ryan, Bob, "The Old Ballparks—A Dying Breed." *Boston Globe*, 4–6 August 1985.

Seaver, Tom. "Artificial Turfs Put Accent on Speed." *Boston Herald-American*, 22 September 1981.

## MAGAZINE ARTICLES

"Chicago Baseball Grounds," *Harper's Weekly*, 12 May 1883, p. 299.

Daley, Arthur. "Like Pitchin' in a Phone Booth." *New York Times Magazine*, 1 September 1957, pp. 13–16

"Daymares in the Dome." *Time*, 16 April 1965, pp. 97–98.

Durslag, Melvin. "Hectic Home of the Dodgers." *Saturday Evening Post*, 18 April 1959, pp. 28–29.

"Evolution of the Baseball Grandstand." *Baseball Magazine*, April 1912, pp. 1–3.

Furillo, Carl. "How I Play the Outfield Wall." *Sport*, November 1956.

Garrity, John. "The Newest Look Is Old." *Sports Illustrated*, October 12, 1987.

Garrity, John. "Nitty, Gritty Dirt Man—Groundskeeper George Toma. *Sports Illustrated*, 17 May 1982, pp. 42–44+.

Heyes, Sam. "Diamonds Aren't Forever—The Final Days of Rickwood Field." *Atlanta Weekly*, 2 August 1987, pp. 5–7+.

Hinden, Rick. "Take Me Back to the Ball Park." *Historic Preservation*, July–August 1979, pp. 42–50.

James, Bill. "Rating the Ballparks." *Sport*, May 1983, pp. 52–57.

McCarthy, Joe. "Yankee Stadium." *Holiday*, October 1956, pp. 55, 113–121.

Meany, Tom. "Craziest Wall in Baseball." *Collier's*, August 6, 1954, pp. 56–57.

Montville, Leigh, "The Old Ballparks Remain the Best Parks." *Sporting News*, 21 January, 1985.

Pastier, John. "The Business of Baseball." *Inland Architect*, January/February 1989, pp. 56–62.

Paxton, Harry. "What a Difference a Ballpark Makes." *Saturday Evening Post*, 5 September 1959, pp. 20–21+.

Riley, Gavin. "Stadium Postcards," *Baseball Hobby News*, numerous articles, May, 1979 through 1985.

Robinson, Matthew, "Requiem for Black Baseball," *Philadelphia Magazine*, May 1967, pp. 130–133.

Schuessler, Raymond. "The 32-Mile Home Run." *Modern Maturity*, April–May 1978, pp. 7–10.

Smith, Curt. "Rating the Ballparks." *Baseball Magazine*, August 1980, pp. 29–32.

"Stadium Profiles." *Sport*, September 1952–November 1953.

"Swardsmanship." *Newsweek*, 6 June 1966, p. 86.

Terrell, Roy. "Every Sixth Hit a Homer!" *Sports Illustrated*, 5 May 1958, p. 11+.

Veeck, Bill. "How I'd Build the Perfect Ball Park." *Popular Science*, March 1964, pp. 94–95+.

"Yankees' New Home, Baseball's Largest and Most Costly Stadium," *Baseball Magazine*, May 1923, pp. 552–555+.

## BASEBALL MODELS

Bauer, Greg & Lois & Mark & Rod & Steve. "Ebbets Field." "Yankee Stadium." "Polo Grounds." "Fenway Park." Burdett, Kansas: Bauer Diamonds, 1984, 1985, 1986.

Carlson, Thomas. "Ebbets Field." Fruitport, Michigan: Anderson Enterprises, 1986.

BULLETIN MDK. "Yankee Stadium." Chapel Hill, North Carolina: MDK, 1986.

Medeiros, Ray. "The Ballparks Bulletin." Wauna, Washington. Published 6 times per year, first issue March 1986.

# CREDITS

Photographs are from the collections of the following people:

p. 12 (Top), Phil Lowry; p. 12 (Middle), Harvey Schoewe; p. 12 (Bottom), Phil Lowry; p. 15 (Top), Harvey Schoewe; p. 15 (Bottom), Phil Lowry; p. 17 (Top), Phil Lowry; p. 17 (Bottom), Hugh Moore, Jr.; p. 19, Harvey Schoewe; p. 21, Phil Lowry; p. 23, Hugh Moore, Jr.; pp. 24–25, Phil Lowry; p. 29, Phil Lowry; p. 30, Gordon Tindall; p. 31, Gordon Tindall; p. 33, Philip Bess; p. 34, Phil Lowry; p. 35, Phil Lowry; p. 36, Phil Lowry; p. 38, Hugh Moore, Jr.; p. 39, Hugh Moore, Jr.; p. 42, Phil Lowry; p. 43, Phil Lowry; p. 46, Harvey Schoewe; p. 48, Phil Lowry; p. 50, Richard Ockomon; p. 51, Phil Lowry; p. 56, Phil Lowry; p. 57, Phil Lowry; p. 59, Phil Lowry; p. 60, Paul Soyka; p. 62 (Top), Phil Lowry; p. 62 (Middle), Phil Lowry; p. 62 (Bottom), Phil Lowry; p. 64, Phil Lowry; p. 65, Phil Lowry; p. 67, Vic Pallos/Jacobson Collection; p. 68, Brad Merila; p. 70 (Left), Phil Lowry; pp. 70–71, Phil Lowry; p. 71, Harvey Schoewe; p. 72, Hugh Moore, Jr.; p. 73, Phil Lowry; p. 74, Hugh Moore, Jr.; p. 75, Phil Lowry; p. 77, Harvey Schoewe; p. 81, Harvey Schoewe; p. 84 Hugh Moore, Jr.; p. 86, Phil Lowry; p. 88, Phil Lowry; p. 91, Phil Lowry; p. 92 (Top), Phil Lowry; p. 92 (Middle), Vic Pallos/Richard Beveridge; p. 92 (Bottom), Phil Lowry; p. 94, Hugh Moore, Jr.; p. 95 (Top), Hugh Moore, Jr.; p. 95 (Bottom), Hugh Moore, Jr.; p. 96, Phil Lowry; p. 98, University of Texas; p. 103, Phil Lowry; p. 105, Hugh Moore, Jr.; p. 106, Hugh Moore, Jr.; p. 108, Gordon Tindall; p. 111, Phil Lowry; p. 112 (Left), Hugh Moore, Jr.; p. 112 (Right), Hugh Moore, Jr.; p. 113, Hugh Moore, Jr.; p. 117, Phil Lowry; p. 118, Vic Pallos and Brian Merlis; p. 119, Phil Lowry; p. 120, Phil Lowry; p. 121, Joseph Overfield; p. 122, Joseph Overfield; p. 124, Hugh Moore, Jr.; p. 125 (Top), Hugh Moore, Jr.; p. 125 (Bottom), Hugh Moore, Jr.; p. 127, Gordon Tindall; p. 129, Gordon Tindall; p. 130, Phil Lowry; p. 161, Harvey Schoewe; p. 163 (Left), Phil Lowry; p. 163 (Right) Phil Lowry; p. 165, Larry Lester; p. 166, Vic Pallos/Jacobson Collection; p. 167, Larry Lester; p. 169, Phil Lowry; p. 171, Phil Lowry; p. 172, Vic Pallos and Dick Dobbins;

p. 175, Hugh Moore, Jr.; p. 177, Vic Pallos and Richard Beveridge; p. 178, Gordon Tindall; p. 179, Gordon Tindall; p. 180, Vic Pallos and Fred Gregurus; p. 183 (Top), Phil Lowry; p. 183 (Bottom), Phil Lowry; p. 188, Phil Lowry; p. 192, Phil Lowry; p. 194, Phil Lowry; p. 195, Phil Lowry; p. 197 (Top), Phil Lowry; p. 197 (Middle), Vic Pallos/Jacobson Collection; p. 197 (Bottom), Phil Lowry; p. 199, Phil Lowry; p. 201, Phil Lowry; p. 207, Phil Lowry; p. 208, Bill Price; p. 209, Phil Lowry; p. 210, Phil Lowry; p. 211, Phil Lowry; p. 212, Phil Lowry; p. 217, Phil Lowry; p. 219, Phil Lowry; p. 221 (Top), Larry Lester and Jimmie Critchfield; p. 221 (Bottom), Larry Lester; p. 228, Gordon Tindall; p. 230, Phil Lowry; p. 234 (Top), Phil Lowry; p. 234 (Bottom), Vic Pallos and Gordon Tindall; p. 235, Phil Lowry; p. 240, Transcendental Graphics; p. 244, Larry Lester/Hall of Fame; p. 246 (Left), Oscar Eddleton; p. 246 (Right), Oscar Eddleton; p. 248, Hugh Moore, Jr.

# INDEX